MENTAL HEALTH IN COUNSELLING AND PSYCHOTHERAPY

Other books in this series

Counselling and Psychotherapy in Organisational
Settings by Judy Moore and Ruth Roberts   ISBN 978 1 84445 614 7

Creating the Therapeutic Relationship in
Counselling and Psychotherapy by Judith Green   ISBN 978 1 84445 463 1

Effective Counselling with Young People
by Hazel Reid and Jane Westergaard   ISBN 978 0 85725 295 1

Reflective Practice in Counselling and
Psychotherapy by Sofie Bager-Charleson   ISBN 978 1 84445 360 3

Understanding Assessment in Counselling and
Psychotherapy
by Sofie Bager-Charleson and Biljana van Rijn   ISBN 978 0 85725 473 3

What is Counselling & Psychotherapy?
by Norman Claringbull   ISBN 978 1 84445 361 0

Books in the Mental Health Practice series

Child and Adolescent Mental Health: A Guide
for Practice by Steven Walker   ISBN 978 0 85725 057 5

Cognitive Behavioural Interventions for Mental
Health Practitioners by Alec Grant   ISBN 978 1 84445 210 1

Mental Health Law in England and Wales
by Paul Barber, Robert Brown and Debbie Martin   ISBN 978 1 84445 195 1

To order, please contact our distributor: BEBC Distribution, Albion Close,
Parkstone, Poole, BH12 3LL. Telephone 0845 230 9000,
email: **learningmatters@bebc.co.uk**. You can also find more
information on each of these titles and our other learning resources at
www.learningmatters.co.uk

Want to write for the Counselling and Psychotherapy Practice series? Contact the
Commissioning Editor, Luke Block (Luke@learningmatters.co.uk), with your ideas
and proposals.

MENTAL HEALTH IN COUNSELLING AND PSYCHOTHERAPY

NORMAN CLARINGBULL

Series editor: Norman Claringbull

LearningMatters

First published in 2011 by Learning Matters Ltd

British Library Cataloguing in Publication Data
A CIP record for this book is available from the British Library.

ISBN: 978 0 85725 377 4

This book is also available in the following ebook formats:

Adobe ebook   ISBN: 978 0 85725 379 8
EPUB ebook   ISBN: 978 0 85725 378 1
Kindle   ISBN: 978 0 85725 380 4

Cover design by Code 5 Design Associates
Project management by Diana Chambers
Typeset by Kelly Winter
Printed and bound by CPI Group (UK) Ltd, Croydon, CR0 4YY

Learning Matters Ltd
20 Cathedral Yard
Exeter EX1 1HB
Tel: 01392 215560
info@learningmatters.co.uk
www.learningmatters.co.uk

FSC
www.fsc.org
MIX
Paper from
responsible sources
FSC® C014540

Contents

Acknowledgements

With thanks to Luke Block, Lauren Simpson, Di Page and all the team at Learning Matters.

About the author

Norman Claringbull is the former Head of Counselling and Psychotherapy Studies at Southampton University. He currently combines his commercial consultancy work and private practice with ongoing research and various academic appointments at a number of UK universities. Norman is also series editor for the Counselling and Psychotherapy Practice series by Learning Matters. His website is www.normanclaringbull.com.

Preface

The British Association for Counselling and Psychotherapy believes that people choose to go and see counsellors and psychotherapists because 'they are experiencing difficulties and distress in their lives' (O'Driscoll, 2010, p1). That may well be true, but it does not mean that counselling and psychotherapy are necessarily the best way, or even always a particularly effective way, of helping such clients. Help is available from the other caring professions too, and this includes, of course, help from the medical world's various disciplines. It should be noted that in this book, the terms 'counsellor' and 'psychotherapist' will be used interchangeably.

Traditionally, many counsellors and psychotherapists have seen themselves as being ideologically separate from those championing a 'medicalised' approach to mental distress. Have a look at most of the major counselling and psychotherapy handbooks. You will not find much information about the medical 'take' on mental health. Nevertheless, it can be argued (see reviews by Pilgrim, 2009; Hales, Yudofsky and Gabbard, 2010; Geddes, Price and McKnight, 2011) that medical practitioners can often be excellent sources of help for a good many people who have mental health worries. Clearly, counsellors cannot afford to ignore what the medics have on offer.

In this book we will investigate the boundaries (and the gaps) between the medical and the psychotherapeutic approaches to mental health. We will also explore the common ground between these two disciplines. After all, they are not really rival callings; each complements the other. Helping counsellors and psychotherapists learn how to work productively with the various sorts of medical professionals is a key aim of this book.

In most medical settings it is commonly believed that a comprehensive approach to mental health is the best way forward. That is why the National Health Service (NHS) provides a wide range of services and treatments for the mentally distressed. Not all those provisions involve the talking therapies. Nevertheless, the NHS clearly values counselling and psychotherapy. That is why in June 2010, the UK Department of Health confirmed that 'psychological therapies will continue to be rolled out across the National Health Service' (www.dh.gov.uk). In other words, counsellors and psychotherapists will increasingly be important members of the NHS's mental healthcare services at all levels. Therefore counsellors and psychotherapists need to know as much as they can about what their various NHS colleagues are doing.

Of course, a lot of counselling and psychotherapy takes place in non-medical settings (private practice, voluntary sector, etc.). However, even there therapists often find that their clients have received, or are receiving, medical help with their mental health concerns. This is another reason why counsellors and psychotherapists need to be up to speed on the medical approaches to mental health. Doctors' professional efforts impact on the work of talking therapists, and talking therapists' efforts impact on doctors' treatment plans. This book will help you to find out more about what doctors do and how they do it.

So it seems that the talking therapies are already established as integral elements in the national mental health care 'package'. However, they are clearly only part of that package; there are other players in the team. This means that counsellors and psychotherapists cannot exist in a disciplinary vacuum; they cannot separate themselves from the other caring professions. It is therefore essential that psychotherapeutic practitioners are aware of what their colleagues in the other caring professions, especially the medics, are doing.

Dr Norman Claringbull
Series editor

CHAPTER 1

Core concepts in mental health

> **CORE KNOWLEDGE**
>
> - 'Mental health' is a generic term that usually refers to the quality of a person's general psychological functioning.
> - In the UK at any given time, about 1 in 6 people are experiencing some sort of a mental health worry.
> - It can be argued that in the appropriate circumstances, directly applied 'treatments' (medical and psychological) can have a useful place in the talking therapies.
> - The mentally troubled do not necessarily have to choose 'pills' *or* 'talk'. 'Pills' *and* 'talk' can often be a very productive way forward.
> - Psychopathology is the systematic study of abnormal experience, cognition and behaviour – often seen as the study of the mental disorders.

FIRST THINGS FIRST: WHAT IS A MENTAL HEALTH ISSUE?

Confused about mental health? Do not worry; you are not alone. After all, a lot of mental health's professional practitioners are just as confused too. That is why many of them find it difficult to agree about precisely what a mental health issue is. Indeed, some theorists do not even accept that there is such a human quality as 'mental health'. For those thinkers, the mental condition that some call 'madness' cannot possibly exist (Vaknin, 2009; Barker and Buchanan-Barker, 2010).

A number of counsellors and psychotherapists also do not find the very idea of mental health (especially when it has a medical flavour) to be particularly helpful. It does not seem to sit right with a lot of their core beliefs around respect for individuals. Neither does it gel with their ideas about personally directed routes to emotional fulfilment. For example, one counselling trainer wrote:

> *When I first heard the term 'personality disorder' I found it offensive: it seemed to imply that the totality of an individual was deficient in some way.*
> (Churchill, 2011, p155)

Despite all these doubts, many talking therapists – just like the public generally – often use the term 'mental health' as a convenient sort of short-hand to say something about the quality of someone's mental functioning. Once we start talking about this functioning in terms of mental health, we inevitably go on to talk about 'good' mental health (sanity) and 'bad' mental health (insanity). 'Health' is, of course, a medical term; for those who have a medicalised world view, therefore, it seems obvious that mental ill health is probably caused by mental illness – it must be a disease.

Not everyone agrees. Some well-known psychiatrists such as Thomas Szasz and Ronald Laing have argued that the whole concept of 'madness' is only a convenient myth (see review by Double, 2006). Nobody is really crazy, they say; it is just that sane people sometimes find themselves in insane situations. In other words, so-called 'abnormal' behaviour might actually be a perfectly normal reaction to a very abnormal situation. So by this argument, a soldier showing signs of mental disturbance due to combat stress is not 'mad'. He is reacting perfectly rationally to the lunacy of battle. It is, of course, also true that some apparently mentally disturbed people are not suffering from mental ill health at all. Malfunctioning thyroid glands, blood sugar level imbalances or any one of a wide range of physical medical conditions can make sane people act in some bizarre ways.

There are a number of difficulties that arise when we use the term 'mental ill health'. For example, if we think that mental distress is caused by mental 'illness', then we probably assume – or at least hope – that doctors will be able to cure it. Regrettably, all too often that aspiration cannot be met. Another problem arises, as the Royal College of Psychiatrists (RCPsych) tells us, from the sad fact that there is often a huge stigma attached to those who are deemed to be mentally unwell (RCPsych, 2009a; Boardman et al., 2010). Such unfortunates are often commonly, but incorrectly, seen as being dangerous 'crazies', unpredictable and best avoided. This view leads to the false belief that the mentally ill all need to be locked away and quarantined.

MENTAL HEALTH ISSUES: WHO HAS THEM – WHAT ARE THEY?

So, who are the psychologically troubled? Who is mentally ill and who is not? The fact of the matter is that there is still considerable debate about what 'mental health', 'mental ill health', 'sanity', 'insanity' and so on actually are. Just what do these terms really mean? Are the supposedly mentally ill truly so frighteningly different from the rest of us?

The simple fact is that contrary to popular myth, the overwhelming majority of people with mental health issues are not out-of-control 'freaks' (Freidman, 2006). Actually, they are mostly just like you and me. In fact, they *are* just you and me: ordinary, everyday people who sometimes find that their lives are getting a bit too much for them. All of us – you, me, the man next door, the woman up the road – occasionally get a bit depressed, a bit anxious, a bit stressed. Sometimes these unpleasant feelings distort our lives and sometimes they do not.

However, most of us, most of the time, seem to be able get past these difficulties in one way or another. We somehow struggle across the bad bits and get through to the good bits. Unfortunately, some of us might occasionally need a bit of extra help to get there – to get by. The fact is that in the UK, at any given time, something like 1 in 6 of all adults are experiencing some sort of a mental health worry (McManus et al., 2007). This is where counsellors and psychotherapists enter the picture. They provide some of the ways in which people troubled by mental (psychological) health difficulties can be helped.

A WORKING DEFINITION OF MENTAL HEALTH

As interesting as these sorts of debates might be, we really do need to put all the academic discussions aside – at least for now – because, as real-world practitioners, we have to have a workaday definition of mental health. The problem is that finding one that we can all generally agree on, is far from easy.

As you might be starting to see, just what we mean by the term 'mental health issue' seems to vary according to circumstances. Indeed, some of the more all-encompassing definitions seem to suggest that we are all mentally incapacitated, or potentially so, in some way or another all of the time (see review by Pilgrim, 2009). Just to begin with, we will use the term 'mental disturbance' to describe psychological and emotional distress. One way of looking at mental disturbance (mental health level) is to think of it as lying along an intensity continuum. Just where any particular individual is on that continuum will vary from time to time during that person's life. The levels of help or treatment that such a person may or may not need will vary too, as can be seen in Figure 1.1.

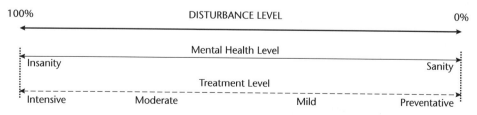

Figure 1.1: Mental health continuum

CE FOR THE TALKING THERAPIES?

So, what does all this mean to those of us who regularly practise in the talking therapies? What is our place in all this? How might it affect our therapeutic practices? First of all, the notion that our clients might need treatment brings any medical responses to their psychological needs firmly into the counselling and psychotherapeutic equation. Whether or not therapists ought to include such a directive approach in their professional toolboxes is likely to remain an ongoing debate. Ultimately, of course, it is a matter of professional choice and you must make up your own mind.

Some counsellors and psychotherapists might take the purist view that the psychotherapeutic explorations of our emotional or psychological concerns have nothing to do with medical models of humanity. They might argue that all mental events and experiences (good and bad) are merely part of the everyday human condition. Yet others might take the view that there is some sort of a level of mental disturbance (or distress) present in any of our clients (Claringbull, 2010). Whether this disturbance requires treatment (medical or non-medical) is a matter for even more debate. Indeed, some practitioners might argue that counselling and psychotherapy are not treatments as such but simply mutually beneficial emotional and/or psychological collaborations between therapists and their clients. Again, you must make up your own mind.

One way of exploring the 'medical/non-medical' (drugs/psychotherapy) question is to suggest that all of our clients/patients are experiencing some form of psychological discomfort. After all, that is why they come to see us in the first place. Whether this discomfort is an 'illness' or just part of being human, might be further investigated by considering just how much our clients' supposed mental conditions affect – or even disrupt – their own lives or the lives of the people around them. It might be convenient (in this chapter anyway) to continue to view the available professional responses to emotional or mental disturbance as usually lying along a sort of psychotherapeutic/psychiatric continuum. This might suggest that as mental disturbances vary in their intensity so too should their treatment styles. See Figure 1.2.

Obviously, for some counsellors and psychotherapists the idea of 'mental illness' and its treatment is not a very useful concept. Their own views of the positive and negative aspects of human emotional and psychological make-up are very different. Medical science simply does not come into it. However, in this book we are going to explore the therapist's tasks mainly from, or at least including, the medicalised aspect of mental health. Whether or not such a therapeutic attitude is likely to prove helpful for any particular client, or indeed for any particular practitioner, is of course a matter of individual judgement. As always, you must make up your own mind.

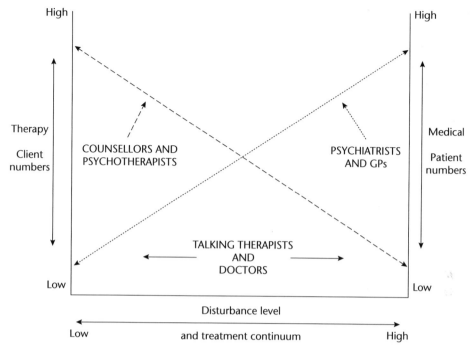

Figure 1.2: Disturbance level and medical/non-medical
treatment continuum

HOW MIGHT THIS WORK IN PRACTICE?

Any experienced counsellor or psychotherapist knows that a client's presenting problem is often only an opening gambit. The real sources of a client's troubles, the so-called 'real problem', might not appear until later in the therapeutic process. The following two case studies show how two apparently very similar presenting problems were actually not very similar at all. In both cases the therapist had to make an assessment of each client's needs based on that individual's personal circumstances. That is why these two apparently very comparable cases were actually dealt with in two very different ways.

Case study 1.1   Working with a depressed client – a counselling
                  answer

Jean seemed to be very low – very fed up with her life. She had lost her appetite, slept at odd hours of the day, got very snappy with her family, and generally moped around. She felt sad and empty, and she just couldn't be bothered to keep up with her friends any more. Everything that had previously interested her now seemed to be just a waste of time. Life had become pointless. This

---

was why she had come along to see Grace, who worked for a local counselling service.

To begin with, Grace wondered if Jean was just depressed. On the surface at least, this looked to be a likely diagnosis. Perhaps Jean's doctor should be consulted? On the other hand, Grace was aware that there are number of psychotherapeutic approaches that are useful when working with depression. For example, should Grace suggest to Jean that they might see if some form of behaviour therapy might be helpful? What was the best thing to do?

Very sensibly, Grace decided to put off coming to any conclusions until she got to know Jean a bit better. As the introductory session progressed, Jean gradually began to talk about just how much she missed her mother. After some gentle probing Grace learned that Jean's mum had passed away a few months back. Jean eventually admitted that she still thought about her mum all the time. Her mum was gone and not gone all at the same time. Jean still felt totally shocked whenever she remembered that her mum was dead. Somehow Jean just couldn't get her mind around that dreadful reality.

It now seemed to Grace that Jean was not so much depressed as grieving – which has similar symptoms but a different cause. It turned out that what Jean really needed was support and a friendly ear. She needed to let out her feelings about missing her mum and about reshaping her life in a post-mum world. Grace offered Jean some sessions of supportive psychotherapy and Jean accepted. After a while Jean's life got back to normal. She hadn't been ill – she just needed to grieve properly.

In the next case study, another of Grace's clients, Hector, presents with what looks like a very similar set of symptoms. It would be easy to confuse Hector's situation with Jean's. Such an error might lead an inexperienced therapist to automatically offer the same sort of treatment in both cases. Fortunately for Hector, Grace is far too experienced to fall into that trap. The guiding principle illustrated in these two case studies is that if counsellors and psychotherapist 'rush in where angels fear to tread' then they will usually get things wrong. Wise practitioners assess, reassess and carry on revising their ideas all the time.

Case study 1.2   Working with a depressed client – a medical answer

Hector, another of Grace's clients, presented with some apparently very similar symptoms to Jean. He too was in a very low mood and very disconnected from life. The difference was that Hector had been like this for over a year. 'It can't be depression,' he told Grace. 'My doctor gives me antidepressants to stop anything like that.' Hector didn't think that medicine was the answer anyway: 'Pills don't solve your problems,' Hector said.

During the session Grace learned that this was not the first time that Hector had been 'down in the dumps', as he put it. He told Grace that he usually 'just got over it', as did his brother and his mother, who had both had similar problems over the years. Actually, Grace had a lot of difficulty in getting Hector to tell her about any of this or, indeed, to tell her anything much at all. Hector just didn't seem to be connecting with her. Grace wondered if this client might actually be clinically depressed. Perhaps Hector's GP should be consulted again.

Grace spent the next couple of sessions helping Hector to accept that he was sufficiently depressed to need some additional help. He needed to find the correct medication regime to try and give his mental functioning a bit of a 'lift'. Eventually Grace was able to persuade Hector to go back and see his GP. She urged him to tell the doctor that his current medication wasn't working – he needed something else. The doctor was, of course, able to suggest an alternative pill.

Fortunately, after the usual lead-in period, Hector's new medication seemed to be working. Now Hector's drug regime was helping him to feel a bit more positive. The new pills hadn't cured his depression, but they were certainly easing it a bit. Hector found himself much more willing, and much more able, to relate to Grace and to the therapeutic process. At last the counselling could begin.

EARLIER TIMES

Throughout history, humans have tried to understand mental distress (see reviews by Porter, 2003; Eghigian, 2010). Our ancestors were much less sensitive in their terminology than many of us are today. To them the mentally distressed were simply 'mad'. Some of the earlier attempts to explain madness are listed in Table 1.1.

Over the years, the idea that the mind was the source of madness began to gain ground, as did the conviction that the victim was to blame. Possession by evil spirits, moral weakness and similar 'blame the patient' explanations placed the responsibility for both the diseases and their cures on the victims. They were recalcitrant sinners, best locked away in institutions and shut off from society. That way, 'decent' people could avoid contamination. They could forget all about the mad. The mentally defective were cast out.

In these institutions, the mad were cruelly treated. They were whipped, beaten, starved and treated like animals. No differentiation was made between the mentally ill, the criminally insane or the socially disruptive. For example, women were committed for wanting to leave their husbands; men were committed for sedition; children were committed for being deformed. The mentally ill were accused of having abandoned themselves to the devil and to evil sorcerers. They were considered to be wilfully sinful. Punishment was the order of the day. These 'scoundrels' were persecuted without mercy.

When/Who	Cause	Treatment
Prehistoric	Evil spirits/pressures in the brain	Trepanning
Early Egypt	Loss of status or money	Talking it out; religion or suicide
Old Testament	Despair/incorrect thinking	Faith
Aeschylus	Demons	Exorcism
Socrates	Heaven sent	None – it's a blessing.
Aristotle	Melancholia	Music
Hippocrates	Natural medical causes	Abstain from excesses; diet and exercise
Celsus	Madness is madness	Entertaining stories; diversions; persuasion
Galen	Functions of the brain	Confrontation; humour; exercise

Table 1.1: Historical causes and treatment of madness

During the eighteenth century, conditions for the insane started to get a bit better (see review by Gask, 2004). A few asylums began to try to care properly for the mentally disturbed. In 1752 the Quakers opened the first-ever hospital that tried to treat the insane kindly, even constructively. By the mid-1800s many institutions were genuinely trying to cure the mentally afflicted. It is important to note that by the end of the nineteenth century the medical profession had attained a monopoly of the 'madness trade'. At that time, all psychological disturbances were believed to have medical or biological explanations, so these early doctor-therapists thought that they would be able to discover the appropriate biological cures for their patients. Psychotherapy, in the sense of the mind curing the mind, was largely undreamed of.

COMMENT

The cruelties of our forebears towards the mentally disturbed were no doubt based on fear and ignorance. It is very possible that political and social convenience played a part too. We can still see many regimes around the world that use psychiatric detention as a means of political control. Closer to home, the media often uses mental illness as a general purpose insult, even today. It can also be argued that some of the more humanistic opinion formers occasionally use offenders' supposed mental inadequacies as a general purpose excuse.

MORE RECENT TIMES

By the early twentieth century, popular ideas about madness had become to be questioned. During the First World War large numbers of so-called 'shell-shocked' soldiers were seen to be incapacitated by emotional and psychological problems. They were acting in some apparently abnormal ways. The cause of this 'madness' seemed to be their emotionally traumatic experiences on the battlefield (Shepherd, 2000). It was eventually reasoned that if a major psychological trauma such as war could cause such immediate and widespread symptoms, then it was possible that an accumulation of lesser psychological traumas (the sorts of events that might be found throughout everyday life) might produce similar effects. Perhaps mental illness, in its many guises, might be found anywhere in society. Madness need no longer be seen as a 'different country'. It might simply be an illness like any other.

Further developments came in the 1940s and 1950s when medications were discovered that seemed to help the mentally ill. To begin with, great hope was placed in these drugs. Had some new 'magic bullets' been discovered? Unfortunately, it was soon found that although these new drugs often helped, at least to begin with, they did not actually cure mental illnesses. Nevertheless, they were usually quite successful at reducing a lot of the distressing symptoms. Some of those medicines are still in use today.

A number of lucky discoveries revolutionised the treatment of the mentally ill. For example, in 1952, Henri Laborit found that chlorpromazine, a drug then used as an antihistamine, had a very calming effect on the more agitated of his patients who were awaiting surgery. Further research appeared to show that chlorpromazine could also be a useful treatment for schizophrenia. Some claim that it was the first 'world class' antipsychotic drug.

In 1987, Prozac (fluoxetine) began to be marketed as an antidepressant. This drug very quickly became a 'world leader'. The Prozac class of antidepressant medications are arguably the most widely used drugs in the world (Kirsch, 2009). Since then, many new medications have been discovered that seem to be useful for patients who show signs of mental dysfunction, and more new drugs are being found every day. The result is that many, probably most, of today's mentally ill patients no longer need to be shut away – they can be successfully cared for in their own homes and communities.

Nevertheless, we still do not really know the basic causes of most of the mental illnesses (see Healy, 2009). We often cannot even agree where to look for them. Many modern treatments are available, but arguments rage over their efficacy. The stigma of mental illness has not been eradicated, although the move to equate mental illness with physical illness has resulted in greater tolerance on some fronts. Nevertheless, from the social perspective we still have a long way to go. That is why all of us in the mental health trade – doctors, counsellors, psychotherapists, and everyone else – need a much better understanding of the human mind. It remains an essential area of study for everybody in the talking therapies.

STUDYING THE MIND

Clearly counsellors and psychotherapists need to have an appreciation of what the various investigations into the human mind have taught us so far. The generic term for this particular field of enquiry is *psychopathology*.

Psychopathology is the attempt to systematically study abnormal experience, cognition and behaviour (Oyebode, 2008). Many see it as a *medical approach* to psychological distress. However, this is not the case. Psychopathological explanations of human mental activity include the medical, the biological, the psychological, the psychotherapeutic, the social/sociological, and even the spiritual and the political. Indeed, one of the psychiatrists' diagnostic 'bibles', the *Diagnostic and Statistical Manual of Mental Disorders*, 4th Edition, or *DSM IV*, considers that all mental disorders have biological, psychological and social components to a greater or a lesser extent.

The discipline of psychopathology is further divided into the explanatory psychopathologies and the descriptive psychopathologies.

- The *explanatory psychopathologies* assume that there are ordered explanations for abnormal mental processes (psychodynamic, cognitive-behavioural, physical, etc.).
- The *descriptive psychopathologies* attempt to categorise and identify the abnormal processes by observing, and then classifying, the symptoms.

However, neither of these divisions of psychopathology tells us what is really going on inside the disturbed person. They are merely ways of speculating about *why* something might be happening and ways of describing *what* might be happening. This approach to understanding patients (phenomenology) is of particular interest to counsellors and psychotherapists. It is what we do best; it is how most of us usually relate to our clients. Put crudely, phenomenology is the study of events without necessarily ascribing provable causes to them. It is a way of theoretically exploring inner processes by investigating their external effects. That is what counsellors and psychotherapists do all the time. We can never be absolutely sure about what is really going on for our clients. The best that we can do is to make an educated guess.

As talking therapists, whether we realise it or not, we use interpretative, or best guess, phenomenology to try and 'get inside' the minds of our clients. However, the more sensible of us also put loads of caveats around our interpretations. Psychiatric diagnosis is littered with many embarrassing instances where this principle has been ignored. For example, there is the famous study (Rosenhan, 1973) in which sane people were misdiagnosed as being schizophrenic. All these fake 'madmen' did was to pretend to their doctors that they could hear three short words ('empty', 'hollow', 'thud') being said aloud.

However, before we smile knowingly at these 'arrogant' doctors and their 'obvious' short-sightedness, we might pause to think about some of our own certainties. Counsellors and psychotherapists, too, are fond of using jargon words in a very authoritative manner. We are quite capable of using terms such as 'transference', 'fixation' or 'congruence' as if they described real processes rather than only being 'as if' terms. We, too, think that we know how to explain depression or that we can truly appreciate regression. We, too, claim ownership of many psychotherapeutic 'certainties' as a result of our allegedly greater, 'expert' even, understanding of the human condition. However, are we really so clever? Do our professional 'certainties' have any real justification?

THE NEED FOR A PSYCHOPATHOLOGY

For many people, psychopathology is the study of the disorders of the mind. Clearly there are individuals whose behaviours and/or mental discomforts cause either themselves or those around them a great deal of distress. In extreme cases, such individuals can be so threatening to themselves or to others that they need to be physically or chemically separated from society.

Increasingly we are finding more and more evidence of significant bio-chemical or neurological dimensions to madness. However, few doctors today would argue that an exclusively medical model should be used in the treatment of the emotionally disturbed or even in the relief of the overtly insane. As counsellors and psychotherapists we need to be very aware of the 'package deal' approach to emotional and psychological well-being. We need to understand what we can usefully contribute to that package.

Perhaps we, as a society, would prefer a psychopathology that tells us that the disturbed, the dysfunctional, the insane or even the just eccentric are medically unwell. It is easier to blame the emotional pain that such troubled individuals inflict on themselves and on others as being a fault – albeit an involuntary one – in them rather than in us. It is also a good way of dealing with one's own fears as well, because by this means, the apparently irrational becomes rational and the frighteningly inexplicable is safely explained. The mentally unwell are abnormal; we are not. Better still, it is nobody's fault. For example, it is much more comfortable to describe child sexual abuse as being the province of 'sick' stranger paedophiles than it is to accept that over 80 per cent of such cruelty is perpetrated by so-called 'normal' family members (US Department of Health and Human Services, 2009; and many similar studies).

There is also a desperate need in us all for a medical explanation of mental abnormality; we need it for our own sakes. After all, it might not just be 'their' problem; one day it might be ours too. If it happens to us, then we certainly want a cure – quick. We don't want to waste time by learning how to take any personal responsibility; we just want to be made better – right now. If we are mentally ill, then some mentally effective medication ought to cure us – or so we desperately hope. Problem sorted.

So for the purposes of this book, we can conveniently take psychopathology as referring to the study of maladaptive behaviour or mental distress that somehow interferes with people's relationships with their own selves, with those around them, or with society generally. Therefore psychopathology is the scientific study of the mental disorders. *DSM IV* defines mental disorder as being a mental condition causing significant distress or disability. This includes disturbances in one or more areas of social or personal func-tioning provided that they do not have any other obvious explanations.

Of course, there are alternative definitions to that given in *DSM IV*. For example, the World Health Organization (WHO) says that a mental disorder is present when there is a clinically recognisable set of symptoms or behaviours that cause distress and interfere with personal functioning (*International Classification of Disease 10*, Chapter 5 – *ICD 10*, 2000). As we will see later on, most of the definitions of the mental disorders, either in general or in detail, are open to wide interpretation. Clearly, mental ill health is very difficult to define. Nevertheless, we have to try and do so. Workaday therapists right now meeting clients who might possibly have significant mental dysfunctions need some practical answers today, not some super-clever answers tomorrow. They want to know exactly what we mean by 'mental ill-health'.

HOW DO WE KNOW THAT SOMEONE IS MENTALLY ILL?

Unlike much in physical illness, in the case of mental illness there is a lot of dispute about its precise nature. Many physical illnesses can be explained objectively as a departure from a statistical normality. For example, your body's temperature might be above or below an agreed standard; your blood might or might not contain an acceptable level of white cells. These sorts of deviations from agreed norms can be measured and, if necessary, attempts can be made to correct them. However, in the case of mental ill health, it is difficult to find objective benchmarks from which abnormal deviations can be measured. Nevertheless the concept of 'mental illness' is the very foundation of the medical model of psychological 'disease'. By this standard 'mental illness' is therefore just another human 'disease', albeit one of the mind.

From a psychiatric point of view, if mental 'illness' is a departure from mental 'healthiness', then we need to have an idea of what 'good' mental health looks like. Defining this is far from simple. Do we look for the absence of disease? Is there an ideal state of mind? What is the average level of 'correct' mental functioning? Is there a range of acceptable levels? For example, is contentment necessarily healthy? Is the proper reaction to changes in mental functioning one of adaptation, resistance or resentment? Clearly, answering these, and the many related questions, is often going to be a very subjective process.

Obviously there is a wide range of behaviours and beliefs that by themselves may or may not indicate mental illness. It all seems to depend on the social context. For example, are hallucinations signs of mental ill health or are they really visitations from a different plane of existence? Are priests crazy if they think that they can talk to God or just mad if they think that God is talking back to them? Is the Archbishop of Canterbury a 'holy man' or a 'holy fool'?

DEFINING MENTAL ILL HEALTH

Defining mental ill health as being the absence of health is a circular argument – unhealthy people are ill until they are not; well people are not ill people, and so on. However, for most doctors and, indeed, for most of society, this is exactly what we do. We even go further and automatically define people who deviate enough from social norms as being mad. So are all social deviants really 'crazy'? For example, are serial killers insane? Possibly 'yes' if we are talking about Fred West or Harold Shipman but probably 'no' if we are taking about terrorists. Is homosexuality perverted? 'Yes' in the 1970s when *DSM III* defined homosexuality as a psychological malfunction, but 'no' in the 1990s when *DSM IV* deleted the very idea of such a 'mental disease'.

In the UK, we have a supposedly easy way of defining mental ill health. The government has told us what it is: The Mental Health Act 2007 says that a mental disorder is 'any disorder or disability of the mind' (Department of Health, 2007).

This is clearly a very vague definition of mental ill health. We can be fairly certain that it does not encompass all of the mental conditions listed in *DSM IV* or *ICD 10*. However, it probably does include the major psychiatric disorders (schizophrenia, personality disorders, anorexia, major depression, bipolar, and learning difficulties, although interestingly not alcohol or drug dependency) (see handbooks/reviews by Brown et al., 2009; Jones, 2009).

Perhaps we can approach the concept of mental ill health by looking more closely at the mental conditions that we commonly seem to agree are associated with it. Can we explain mental ill health by classifying and listing its various manifestations? In other words, we know the elephant is in the room, so let's stop theorising about it; let's measure it.

CLASSIFYING MENTAL ILLNESS

Modern psychiatric classifications of mental ill health are mostly derived from the medical models developed in the late nineteenth century by pioneers such as Kraepelin, Bleuler and their professional heirs. All these models assume that if we group together their apparently common characteristics, then we can adequately define each of the various syndromes, illnesses and other diagnostic categories that collectively make up the mental illnesses.

In more modern times, there are a number of classification systems used by health professionals to try and categorise mental illness. One is supplied by the World Health Organization. They published the 10th revision of the

International Classification of Diseases (*ICD 10*) in 1993. By itself, it is simply a coding system for diseases used for the collection of basic health statistics. *ICD 10*'s Chapter 5 describes the psychiatric conditions. In its complete format it is a complex document. However, the 'WHO Guide to Mental Health in Primary Care' format (*ICD 10*, 2000) is much more useful as diagnostic tool and as a treatment protocol adviser. Each mental disorder coded in *ICD 10* has its equivalent in many of the other systems.

Another major classification system is the Chinese Classification of Mental Disorders (CCMD). However, the CCMD recognises mental diseases such as exercise- and meditation-induced disorders and witchcraft psychosis that are unknown in Western medicine. It also recognises a number of mental conditions that are chiefly related to Chinese culture (Lee, 2001). Although of importance in China, if only in terms of the numbers of diagnoses made using it, the CCMD appears to be little used elsewhere.

Probably the classification system that will most often be encountered by UK therapists is the *Diagnostic and Statistical Manual of Mental Disorders* (*DSM*), which is published by the American Psychiatric Association. Unlike *ICD 10* and the CCMD systems, *DSM* is not merely a classification or a labelling system; it is also a set of diagnostic protocols. The current version is known as *DSM IV* as it is now in its fourth edition – it was first published in 1994. A new version, *DSM V*, is supposedly due to be released in May 2013.

The power of *DSM IV* comes from its provision of specific diagnostic criteria. Its supporters claim that this facility increases *DSM IV*'s reliability. However, the definitions of these criteria are mostly based on subjective clinical judgements and have not been fully validated by empirical research. Furthermore, these definitions have undergone, and will continue to undergo, considerable changes as psychiatric opinion evolves (see Sims, 2000). We will no doubt see further evidence of this in *DSM V*.

TREATING MENTAL ILL HEALTH

So far, we have been addressing the needs of the mentally disordered client, or patient, simply in terms of the medical and the psychotherapeutic approaches. Of course, there are actually quite a number of different ways of conceptualising mental discontent. This clearly means that there are likely to be a number of ways of conceptualising the treatment of the mental disorders. As we noted earlier, the modern tendency is to see the client/patient as a biological, psychological, social/sociological whole – the client 'in-the-round'. This composite, more comprehensive, approach to mental health – indeed to health generally – is more usually called the 'bio-psychosocial model' (see review by Richard, Quill and McDaniel, 2009). It is obviously essential that today's counsellors and psychotherapists should at least be aware of some of the more commonly used approaches to helping the mentally disordered, three of which are set out below.

1   Biological treatments – *pills for all?* As we have already seen, this is essentially a medical approach that views mental ill health as a disease. The expectation is that mental ill health results from organic dysfunctions either in, or affecting, the brain. Therefore 'madness' will eventually be explainable in terms of abnormal brain biochemistry, incorrect mental 'software' or even errors in the brain's 'hard wiring'. Put these problems right and the patient will improve. That is why there are so many psychotropic drugs (mental health medicines) on the market. However, in most cases of mental ill health, the connection between mental disorder and biological malfunction is far from clear (see Healy, 2009). The fact is that some pills appear to work only sometimes and only for some people (Healy, 2002). However, how they work and why they work remains very much disputed (Metzl, 2003; RCPsych, 2010a).

2   Psychological treatments – *the talking therapies?* Of course, these treatment styles mainly include the various counselling and psychotherapeutic approaches to mental discomfort. Taken overall, the psychological treatments are mainly based on ideas about how to:
    •   correct' sick' early-years psychological development;
    •   correct 'sick' self-perceptions and relationships with others;
    •   correct 'sick' thinking and behaving.
    If you want to learn more about these approaches, then read Claringbull (2010), McLeod (2009a), Woolfe et al. (2010) or one of the many other counselling and psychotherapy handbooks that are currently available.

3   Social/sociological treatments – *change the patient's circumstances?* Social scientists assume that the primary causes of emotional distress arise from stresses in society. These adverse factors, the sociologists claim, are the real 'emotional infections' that cause individuals to react in ways that appear, on the surface at least, to be due to some kind of mental illness. In other words, 'mad' societies create 'mad' people. It is argued by some that the sorts of social stressors that might be injurious to mental health include unemployment, educational inadequacy, poverty, personal isolation, and many other similar impoverished social conditions and environments. Social stress is the cause of the problem and so social stress relief is the cure. Therefore, the remedy for a social 'disease' is likely to come from an improvement in the sufferer's links with society or from improvements in society itself. Of course, there are major disputes about how such 'cures' might be brought about (see Golightly, 2008 and many others).

BY THE BY

As we all know from everyday life, there seems to be an infinite number of colloquial or slang phrases in use to describe poor mental functioning. Perhaps this is an indicator of just how much this topic both fascinates and repels people. Whether such phrases are offensive, amusing or even euphemistic is a matter I will leave up to you. Nevertheless, even many professionals, including counsellors and psychotherapists, have been heard to use them. Does this include you? Here are just a few of the many thousands of informal or slang phrases used to describe mental abnormality:

- mad as a hatter;
- got a screw loose;
- nutty as a fruit cake;
- bats in the belfry;
- lost the plot;
- loopy, potty, doolally;
- lost his/her marbles;
- basket case;
- bananas;
- away with the fairies;
- not playing with a full deck.

ACTIVITY 1.1

- How many different names for mental ill health (popular, technical, offensive, etc.) can you find? Try listing them as either 'helpful', 'harmful' or 'amusing'.
- Now explain your thinking.

COMMENT

Many people – including, no doubt, many therapists – unthinkingly use this sort of language to describe more or less anyone whose ideas seem odd to them. That is unlikely to change. Anyway, it might be only a matter of loose semantics. However, as mental health professionals, can we afford to be so careless in our use of descriptive expressions? Is using such language destructive to our professional purposes? Alternatively, if we are a bit too prissy, a bit too 'politically correct' in our attitudes, might we deter some otherwise potentially sympathetic supporters of our professional intentions?

CONCLUSIONS

Obviously 'good practice in working with others [other professionals] for the benefit of clients requires a knowledge of their role' (Daines, Gask and Howe, 2007, p16). Therefore it can be argued that counsellors and psychotherapists have much to gain if they are prepared to look over their discipline's parapets – if they are prepared to learn about the non-counselling approaches to mental health. Clearly it would be beneficial for everyone (clients and practitioners alike) if counsellors and psychotherapists were prepared to extend both their professional learning and their professional practices beyond the traditional boundaries of their parent disciplines. However, in order to gain confidence in so doing, they will need to learn not be afraid that they will have to defer to their alternatively skilled/differently trained professional colleagues. Ideally cross-disciplinary, professional, relationships should be ones of mutual professional support and respect, not one of professional surrender. In my own practice I happily take advantage of any of the sources of help that are available – GPs, psychiatrists, community mental health nurses, social workers, care workers, whoever. My clients benefit and so do I. For me, 'whatever works, works'.

No profession, and that includes the medics, always gets in right. No profession can claim exclusive ownership of any mental health treatment. For example, it is arguable that the medically unexplained symptoms that apparently take up large proportions of primary care time (Guthrie, 2008) might sometimes be investigated by non-medical (psychological?) means (Webb, 2010). This is an area where counsellors and psychotherapists could have an important role to play. If they are anything, psychotherapists are 'people people'. Therapists specialise in ensuring that clients are fully included, fully consulted and fully respected as responsible players in their own treatments.

Like all the other members of the caring professions, counsellors and psychotherapists have their own important roles to play in the care of the mentally distressed. This clearly includes activities within their own specialist disciplines; it also includes helping to reinforce, or even refocus, the other professional disciplines as or when necessary. In particular, when counsellors and psychotherapists are involved with clients who also need medical help, the basic choice does not need to be 'pills' or 'talk'. Sensible practitioners are always open to the possibility that the best course of action is very often 'pills' and 'talk'. After all, that is exactly what it says in the explanatory leaflets distributed with many of the common psychotropic drugs. Of course, this means that the talkers need to know what the pills do and the pill-givers need to know what the talkers do. That is what this book is all about.

CHAPTER SUMMARY

In this chapter we have:

- looked at what the medical approaches to mental health issues mean for counsellors and psychotherapists;
- started to understand just how complicated it can be to try and define the true nature of mental health;
- learned that mental health is a complex issue involving biological, psychological and sociological factors.

It is clear that understanding mental health issues is a complex business. Nevertheless, counsellors and psychotherapists have important roles to play in the various treatment packages. A key issue in mental health is deciding how to distinguish the ill from the well or, more basically, the normal from the abnormal. That is what the next chapter, 'Normalising the abnormal' is all about.

SUGGESTED FURTHER READING

Daines, B, Gask, L and Howe, A (2007) *Medical and psychiatric issues for counsellors.* London: Sage.

An excellent, easy to read, introductory textbook – Chapter 3 is particularly helpful in unpicking the therapist/GP relationship and has some useful tips on how to manage it.

Oyebode, F (2008) *Sims' symptoms in the mind: an introduction to descriptive psychopathology.* New York: Saunders (Elsevier).

A classic textbook that is a must – a bit geeky but well worth the effort. Section 1 will give you an excellent grounding in the core principles of psychopathology.

Pilgrim, D (2009) *Key concepts in mental health.* London: Sage.

An excellent overview of these topics that is set out in very readable 'bite-size' chunks. Part 3 contains a very good review of the major controversies in areas where psychopathology is in conflict with the public's opinions and prejudices.

Read, J and Saunders, P (2010) *A straight talking guide to the causes of mental health problems.* Ross-on-Wye: PCCS Books.

This is a useful book in that it puts clients to the forefront when making decisions about their own mental health. It is a sort of non-medical approach to the related medical issues, and reviews some interesting alternatives to conventional psychiatric treatments.

CHAPTER 2

Normalising the abnormal

CORE KNOWLEDGE

- Many of the medical models of mental ill health assume that the sufferer has become 'abnormal' and no longer conforms to supposedly 'normal' or 'healthy' standards.
- Ways to define abnormality include:
  - biological abnormality – physiological or metabolic dysfunctions or malfunctions;
  - psychological abnormality – emotional/behavioural dysfunctions;
  - moral abnormality – contravening socially acceptable ways of being;
  - social/sociological abnormality – adverse external pressures from the social environment, adverse relationships with society;
  - spiritual, socio-political, socio-biological, anthropological dysfunctions and disconnections;
    - Mental ill health (mental disorder) can be explained as the result of abnormalities in biological, psychological or social/sociological functioning
  - the *biopsychosocial model.*
- Modern developments in the medical and biological sciences suggest that biochemical, neurological and genetic explanations of mental disorder (mental abnormality) might become increasingly available.

ABNORMALITY AND MENTAL HEALTH

Some people sometimes behave in ways that others might call abnormal – we all do from time to time. What seems normal to me might seem weird to you, and vice versa. However, in the popular imagination 'abnormality' – at least in its more extreme forms – is closely linked to insanity. Very often these two terms are used interchangeably and indiscriminately (Haslam, Ban and Kaufmann, 2007). Sadly, abnormality is also often (mistakenly) equated with 'badness'. Historically, this has resulted in society shunning and excluding those who were considered to be abnormal (Porter, 2003). Even today, these unfortunates, allegedly the 'mad' and the 'bad', are all too often denied social contact, human rights, employment, or even simple respect. However, to equate abnormality with illness or badness can often be misguided, unhelpful and, in most cases, just plain wrong.

As we noted in Chapter 1, only a very small number of people with formally diagnosed mental abnormalities ('mental illnesses') actually are a positive danger to themselves or others. The majority offend no one and lead apparently perfectly ordinary lives in their communities (Elbogen and Johnson, 2009). Couched in psychiatric terminology, a clinically significant mental abnormality means only that someone has a clinically diagnosed mental disorder or disability. That is all that it means. It is only a medico/legal technical term – it is not a reason to turn your back on someone.

Obviously, many people prefer to take a medical view on all aspects of health. The underlying principle is that the sick are deviating in some way from the medically *normal*. In other words, they are medically *abnormal*. Clearly the hope is that if the physically sick can regain their physiological normality, then they will be healthy once again (Silagy et al., 2005). It follows that from the medical point of view, the mentally abnormal are sick, too (Pilgrim, 2002). Perhaps they, too, can get better.

So if we can find out how the mentally unwell (the mentally abnormal) became ill, we might be able to do something about it. It is actually quite a simple idea: normality = good; abnormality = bad; if something is bad, then fix it. However, first we have to decide what we actually mean by 'abnormal'. That is not so simple, and it is where our problems begin.

WHAT IS ABNORMALITY?

For counsellors and psychotherapists, defining abnormality is not just an interesting intellectual pastime. They often need to come to some workaday conclusions about their clients/patients' behaviour and the quality of their psychological functioning. Obviously therapists would find it helpful if they had some practical rules of thumb to guide them through the normal/abnormal maze. The problem is that there are many ways in which to define abnormality. Most counselling and psychotherapeutic definitions ultimately depend on the purposes of both the therapist and the client (Oyebode, 2008). As ever, the answer to a question – in this case, the question of normality – probably depends on who is asking it.

We will consider four of the more common explanations of abnormality. Doubtlessly you can think of others.

Explanation 1: Abnormality and statistical infrequency

In purely statistical terms, some behaviours are clearly abnormal. Let us look at an example. Sadomasochism is clearly statistically abnormal in that only a small minority of people engage in it (Kleinplatz and Moser, 2007). This is a mathematical observation; it is not a moral judgement. However, in modern Britain, do we still view minority sexual practices as being abnormal? Probably not, but we certainly did do so up until 1994. Before then, *DSM III* told us that many forms of so-called 'kinky sex' (the paraphilias) were treatable psychiatric conditions. Even today, would our judgements about minority sexual interests differ if we were religious fundamentalists or if we came from one of the more puritanical political regimes? They probably would, but remember that *DSM IV* now tells us that 'abnormal' (minority) sexual behaviours are no longer to be considered as mental disorders.

The problem with a simple yes/no or in/out mathematical definition of abnormality is that it tells us nothing about the quality of the statistical deviation being examined. After all, most behaviour lies on a moral continuum and is rarely absolute. We can, of course, decide to choose cut-off points at which certain levels of behaviour are no longer acceptable. However, we would probably have a lot of difficulty in agreeing where those cut-off points should be.

Making statistical judgements is easy; making judgements about what is acceptable (and what is not) is much harder. We might use judgements about the degree of deviance from statistical normality to decide on the acceptability of someone's behaviour. If we do so, we immediately hit a consistency problem because we are not always intolerant of significant behavioural deviance – we sometimes actually encourage it. In other words, we can be biased, and certainly inconsistent, in our tolerance (or not) of deviance. In some situations, people whose behaviour is very different from the norm are not criticised at all – they are actually publicly applauded. For example, we admire high achievers such as champion athletes, famous artists and outstanding scientists. Statistically, they are in a small minority, but we do not condemn them – many people would like to be just like them. However, in other cases of statistical deviance – child abusers, for example – our intolerance is absolute. In terms of numbers, they too may be in a minority, but socially they are permanent outcasts.

Explanation 2: Abnormality and moral standards

All societies set up moral rules for behaviour and punish those who do not conform to them (Bicchieri, 2005). However, some social theorists would argue that moral 'abnormality', sometimes expressed as 'madness', is only a labelling system designed to denigrate social rebels. This means that morals might well change as society evolves. For example, in very recent times in the UK, allegedly promiscuous ('immoral') females were often sent to the 'madhouse' (Porter, 2003). Today, we view female sexual activity from a very different moral standpoint. Of course, some moral codes seem to be more inviolable than others. For instance, murder is usually viewed as being immoral and wrong in most societies.

There is a major problem with using moral standards to define normality. It is that these standards often vary over time and place. For instance, it is clear that a social and moral revolution has stormed through this country over the last 25 years or so (Brown, 2008). Even the language has changed; for example, unmarried, co-habiting couples seemingly no longer 'live in sin' – they simply 'live together'. How many of our earlier 'moral certainties' (Beck, 1992) have vanished? What new certainties have arisen? Possibly only those people with the unquestioning convictions that come from rigidly organised official belief systems can really believe that they absolutely know right from wrong: very comforting for them – very dangerous for the rest of us.

As counsellors and psychotherapists, we have a further problem if we use accepted moral standards as a way of conceptualising the abnormal. By this definition it is easy to slip into the notion that extreme social deviance equates to such a level of moral abnormality that it is really a sign of mental ill health. Such a definition, if generally accepted, would allow those who carry out particularly nasty crimes to try and plead not guilty by reason of insanity. They could claim that what they have done is so weird that they need help and not punishment. There have been some spectacularly successful uses (or abuses?) of this defence. Lorena Bobbitt successfully claimed temporary insanity when she emasculated her husband with a kitchen knife while he slept. Christopher Clunis successfully claimed that his psychiatric history meant that he was not responsible for his murder of newly married musician Jonathan Zito. These sorts of crimes often provoke intense moral debate: are the accused really mad, are they actually bad, or are they simply sad?

Explanation 3: Abnormality and expected behaviour

We all of us have to distinguish between normal and abnormal behaviour on a regular basis. Fortunately we do not have to do so about all the people we come across during our daily lives. After all, if we had to make judge-ments about all the apparently – in our terms – aberrant behaviour that occurs in our immediate worlds, then we would do little else.

In fact, what many of us usually do, either as individuals or as therapists, is to make judgements just about the behaviours of people who we know about. We can usually ignore strangers and bit-players in our lives – those who are just passing through. In the case of the people that we know, we usually have some preconceptions about what to expect from them. How does that person normally behave? What is she normally like? Because we know what to expect from people we are familiar with, if they unexpectedly change in ways that disturb us, then we might conclude that something has happened – that something is wrong. Sometimes, sudden significant deviations from the expected, from the normal, can be useful indicators of mental ill health. The danger, of course, is that such an 'out of the blue' change in someone might actually be a perfectly understandable reaction to a sudden shift in that person's circumstances. Not all sudden changes are caused by mental instability.

Explanation 4: Abnormality and suffering or dysfunction

Take one example of suffering that leads to dysfunction. People with acute anxiety conditions often suffer from high levels of inner dread. Such terrors can cause them to become socially and personally dysfunctional. Their fears, no matter how irrational, can psychologically imprison them and keep them apart from the rest of us. Are their fears a sign of abnormality or are they just a symptom of something being very wrong? After all, even extreme anxiety might simply be a normal or rational reaction to extremely worrying life events. In other words, it can be normal to be abnormal.

Clearly it can be argued that, by itself, suffering does not necessarily equate to abnormality. Therefore even if we detect such symptoms in our clients, it does not necessarily indicate emotional ill health. Someone suffering from a 'broken heart' might simply be grieving for a lost relationship. Someone who has recently become bereaved is probably just very sad and not medically depressed at all.

It also seems that, apparent dysfunctions can fool us into making false diagnoses. For example, someone who is refusing to eat might be dysfunctionally anorexic or might be on a hunger strike. Usually, it is only when self-imposed behavioural changes become sufficiently abnormal to cause self-harm that we consider them to be pathological. So are hunger-strikers crazy or rational political activists? What do you think?

We can endlessly debate whether or not personal dysfunctions, suffering, or simply inner disquiets are the results or the causes of mental ill health. However, as far as *DSM IV* and *ICD 10* are both concerned, these are all indicators that something might be wrong mentally.

ACTIVITY 2.1

- Draw up a list of behaviours that you (or people you know) commonly exhibit. Place all these behaviours on one of two lists. The normal activities go on List 1 and all the abnormal ones go on List 2. *You* decide what's normal and what's abnormal.
- Now write down some alternative interpretations of each of those behaviours that would let you put it on the other list. Did you, or those other people, seem to become more insane or less so?

COMMENT

Defining abnormality is not only a difficult process but also a very subjective one. Clearly answers to the 'what is abnormal behaviour' question will vary from person to person and with time and place. Nevertheless, important judgements about people, their futures and their treatments, are routinely made by mental health professionals, often using some regrettably subjective evaluation processes. Making such life-changing judgements about people is an awesome responsibility.

EXTREMISM AND ABNORMALITY

Madness, especially if defined as abnormality, is not just confined to individuals. Groups and organisations (large or small) can also be considered deviant or on the 'lunatic fringe'. Usually, this is because of their radically different beliefs and practices (Hood, Hill and Williamson, 2005; Abbott, 2009). Of course, sometimes those allegedly 'insane' individuals and groups come in from the cold and become accepted mainstream opinion. No longer mad, perhaps they become not so bad, or at least respected. An excellent example of this can be seen in the history of women's rights in the UK. In the nineteenth century campaigning suffragettes were popularly believed to be deranged; in the twenty-first century we are more likely to think that anyone wanting to deny women the right to vote is insane.

On the other hand, some of the extremist groups or cults that can be found on the outer fringes of society probably are 'mad and bad' (see Jordison, 2005). The outrageous behaviours and exploits of such people often stem from a need to act out their extreme beliefs. For them it's OK; they can do literally anything because their 'inspired' leader, their god or their 'special' knowledge tells them so. They know that they are not abnormal; it is the rest of us who have got it all wrong. That is probably why such fundamentalist group abnormalities include feelings of exclusivity and superiority, and extreme intolerance towards those holding opposing viewpoints (see Lalich, 2004 for an interesting account).

However, before we dismiss such extremists as being irrational, it is worth noting that we can find similarly absolutist standpoints in many of today's mainstream, apparently socially acceptable, belief systems – women must never be priests; experimenting on animals is always wrong; abortion is murder, etc. Are these ideas acceptable or insane?

Case study 2.1   Was Hermione's client mentally abnormal or just different?

Albert had recently lost his wife. He had been referred to Hermione, an integrative counsellor, by his GP, although Albert wasn't really sure why. As a matter of routine, early during the assessment session Hermione asked Albert if he was on any medication. 'Not really,' he replied. The counselling session continued and again the subject of medication came up. 'Well, all I actually take is a bit of lithium,' Albert told Hermione in a rather throwaway manner.

   This admission rang alarm bells for Hermione. That was because she knew that in the UK lithium compounds are mainly used to treat the bipolar disorders. Fortunately, as Hermione had a good relationship with the GP, she was able to find out more about her client's mental health history, having first got Albert's consent, of course. It turned out that Albert had been under the care of a consultant psychiatrist for some time. Hermione felt that she probably could not (perhaps should not) continue to work with Albert without the consultant's agreement.

   Again with Albert's consent, Hermione contacted the consultant, who explained that Albert's condition had been stable for some time now. In the psychiatrist's opinion, Albert's life had returned to normal, with all the ups and downs that everyday life has for all of us. There could therefore be no objection to Albert receiving counselling to help him deal with life's problems, such as bereavement – his emotional needs were just the same as anyone else's.

   Hermione was now happy to continue to counsel her now 'normal' client in her usual way. She could focus on Albert the bereaved client. She could forget Albert the guy with a major mental health problem. The alarm bells went silent.

ABNORMALITY AND MODELS OF MENTAL HEALTH

Of course, making judgements about abnormality is more than just an issue for those whose take on mental health comes from the medical standpoint. It is a problem in most approaches to mental health, medical or otherwise. This is because it can be argued that many, if not most, models of mental health assume that mental dysfunction results from some kind of abnormality (biological, social/sociological, psychological, etc.). Of course, abnormality is not a problem for those who believe that madness is just another phase of human existence and not a mental disease. For them there is no such thing as madness and therefore no such thing as mental abnormality (see Szasz, 1984; Warme, 2006; Szasz, 2010).

This book is largely focused on the medical and psychiatric approaches to mental health. However, counsellors and psychotherapists must always be aware that there are a number of ways of modelling mental health. Which one is the most useful will depend on each client's particular circumstances. It would probably be helpful if we now take a brief overview of the main-stream models of mental health that are likely to be of concern to the workaday therapist.

Abnormal physiology – the biological model

The biological model of mental health is essentially an approach that views mental disorder as a symptom of biological abnormalities or illnesses. However, it seems that so far we have not been able to generally agree about which sorts of biological abnormalities cause which sorts of mental health problems (Healy, 2009). For example, blocking the brain's dopamine system with antipsychotic drugs seems to help many patients with schizophrenia-type symptoms (Ellison, 1994). However, this does not necessarily mean that abnormally high dopamine production causes schizophrenia. It might be that patients whose dopamine levels have been artificially lowered can no longer be bothered to respond to the urges of their schizophrenic symptoms. Their illness is the same; it is just their reactions that have changed. This could mean that the root cause of schizophrenia is not an abnormality in the dopamine system. Is this particular biological model wrong?

An alternative biological approach to the biochemical imbalance/organic abnormality concept is to investigate possible genetic deficiencies. Are there structural problems in the brains of the mentally disordered? It seems that almost every day there are claims that genetic markers have been discovered for all sorts of mental conditions. However, these genetic theories remain the subject of considerable debate and, at best, such studies show linkages and not proven causes (see Read, Mosher and Rentall, 2004; Minkel, 2009).

Nevertheless, let us suppose that we do eventually discover genetic inade-quacies for at least some of the mental disorders. What could we do about these abnormalities? What should we do about them? Do we ignore them? Do we rectify them? Do we breed them out? Do we cull the victims? Which is extremism and which is treatment? What would you do?

If madness truly is a biological malfunction, then becoming ill is very unlikely to be the sufferer's fault, and the mentally disordered are therefore probably not responsible for their actions – they cannot be blamed for being ill. Nevertheless, the mentally sick appear to act irrationally and in unpredictable ways, and this causes us to fear them. We do not like the unknown or the unknowable. It might therefore be argued that it is in the interests of the patient and society that we should make choices on behalf of the mentally ill. If they cannot help themselves, should we take over their lives? This question is examined in more depth in Chapter 9.

REFLECTION POINT

You have a male client whose mental health has been causing you concern from some time. His life is becoming more and more chaotic, and his thinking and behaviour patterns are getting more and more irrational. He tells you: 'If I can't have my bitch of a wife and my kids, then nor will anyone else.'

- Is he mad or evil? What will you do next?

COMMENT

You are in a 'damned if you do and damned if you don't' situation. If your client is truly evil, then clearly breaking confidence to protect his family is essential. If he is dangerously disturbed (mad), then equally you cannot keep silent. However, what if your client is just impotently posturing? You might be unnecessarily destroying a potentially beneficial therapeutic relationship. A subsequent complaint against you to your professional association could even result in a disciplinary sanction.

Abnormal emotional development – the psychological model

Historically, the psychological models of mental health have depended on the three traditional explanations of emotional development (person-centred, psychodynamic, cognitive-behavioural) (see Claringbull, 2010). Put crudely, errors at any stage of these developments might result in emotional and psychological damage that could lead to a psychological disorder – to a mental health issue. Modern psychotherapeutic theory tends to dismiss any single personality theory as being the only way to explain a client's problems. Today's therapists are increasingly willing to try to integrate the traditional explanations of personality with any or all of the other theories (traits and skills; learning styles; socio-political, etc.). The intention is to create a complex, overarching theory of personality that can be tailored to suit each individual client. This means that the treatments offered are also tailored to the needs of the needs of each individual patient. A comparison of these psychological theories of emotional development and their associated treatment methodologies is set out in Table 2.1.

Model	Psycho-dynamic	Person-centred	Cognitive-behavioural	Integrative
Problem	Errors in early-years emotional development.	Unfulfilled self-actualisation (the drive to satisfy emotional and spiritual needs).	Incorrect learning from life's experiences.	Errors in any aspect of personality and lifestyle development.
Abnormality	Later-years emotional and psychological problems.	Blocked, externally focused, personal development. Inadequate or misunderstood current relationships with self and others.	Adoption of unhelpful cognitive (thinking) and behavioural patterns.	Psychological and emotional problems in any area of life (personal, work, social, relationships, etc.).
Therapy	Reprocess early-years experiences. Explore an evolving relationship with a therapist in terms of how it is influenced by past experiences and earlier relationships	Attain a better understanding of self and others. This is done by entering into an ongoing, open, and honest therapeutic relationship with a counsellor in the 'here and now'.	Experiment with new ways of reacting to life events. Learn new and more helpful patterns of thinking and acting.	Any combination of any of the appropriate psychological therapies – whatever works, works.

Table 2.1: Explanations of emotional development issues

Abnormal personal and social environments – the social and/or sociological model

Many sociologists and social work theorists assume that abnormal social conditions are influential factors in the emergence of emotional distress (e.g. Huxley and Thornicroft, 2003; Golightly, 2008; and many others). In other words, if the quality of people's social environments deteriorate, then so does the quality of their mental health. Therefore:

- normal social environments – good housing, financial security, access to education and adequate healthcare, safety, communal support, and so on – promote good mental health;
- abnormal social environments – poor living standards, insecurity, isolation, injustice, inadequate healthcare, poor diet, discrimination, and so on – undermine mental health.

Let us take marital and relationship dissolution as an example of social stress affecting mental health. A number of studies have suggested that separated or divorced people (and their dependants) are more prone to mental health problems than are married or partnered people (Richards, Hardy and Wadsworth, 1997; Lorenz et al., 2006; Bracke et al., 2010). In the UK, psychologically distressed relationships even have their own special 'doctors' – for example, Relate counsellors and family therapists. So is the stress that might result from divorce and separation a diagnosable mental disorder or just the expected result of an adverse social situation? Does this apparently adverse psychological dysfunction (stress) arise from relationship break-ups or does it cause them?

It seems arguable that some kinds of psychological discomfort and emotional distress might at the very least be made worse by impoverished social conditions. However, whether poor social environments are the causes or the results of poor mental health is a far from settled question. Put simply, do we create society or does society create us? If we assume that mental health problems do indeed vary as social conditions vary, then we might also wonder if there is actually such a condition as mental ill health. Perhaps human mental problems are merely understandable individual reactions to sick social situations.

Other models

There are a number of other standpoints from which we could choose to view mental health/ill health. Some are socio-political (e.g. feminism, anarchism, oppression); some are anthropological (e.g. we are out of tune with our evolutionary social origins); some are socio-biological (e.g. we are in conflict with our ecological origins).

One very important take on mental health, and a viewpoint that is of importance in many parts of the world, is that mental disorders result from inner spiritual or religious conflicts. These might be due to matters of faith, personal religious crises, or even assumed demonic possession. In these cases, is mental ill health simply a visitation from God?

It is obviously important that counsellors and psychotherapists are aware of these alternative models of mental health – there may be clients who come to see us who genuinely believe that such matters lie at the root of their problems. So do we try and work with these clients or do we refer them on? Is there a need for a priest-therapist, a therapist-activist or an exorcist?

A TABLE OF MENTAL HEALTH TREATMENTS

Clearly, there are a number of ways of modelling mental health. Each model has its supporters; each has its detractors. It is therefore unsurprising that there are also a number of treatment methods available. Many counsellors and psychotherapists, especially those who have progressed beyond single school models of psychotherapy, will choose the treatment style for their clients that seems appropriate at any given time. Table 2.2 overleaf lists most of the more commonly used methods.

Case study 2.2   Psychotherapist or priest?

Bill practised as an eclectic psychotherapist and normally worked in a brief-intervention, solution-focused style. Unusually for him, he had been treating Irene for a long time – several months, in fact.

Over the last few weeks, Irene had been talking a lot about her mother, who had died several years previously. Mother and daughter had been estranged, and Irene had refused to attend her mother's bedside during her final days. The problem was that Irene now had a constant feeling that her mother was always close by and angry with her. Irene felt haunted – literally. She had come to believe that by allowing the estrangement to fester she had somehow sinned against her mother. It seemed that her mother's spirit wouldn't be going away until Irene's sins were forgiven. Irene was desperate for confession and absolution.

Irene was a religious person. Bill was not, and he did not feel very comfortable about dealing with spiritual issues during therapy. He referred Irene to a local vicar – no good; he referred Irene to a local spiritualist preacher – no good; he suggested some of the alternative faith practitioners – no good.

Irene kept asking for someone in authority to forgive her – then all would be well again. Finally, Bill – feeling rather harassed and stressed – simply told Irene, 'I forgive you.' 'At last,' she said. 'Now Mum will leave me alone.' Irene's psychotherapy could go forward – normal service had been resumed.

Mental health approach	Biological	Psychological	Sociological	Spiritual
Causes	Biochemical imbalances Neurological malfunction Genetic defects	Early-years issues Actualisation and relationship issues Angst Maladaptive learning	Social stress Environmental stress Personal stress Injustice and oppression Inadequate resources	Spiritual conflict Conflicts of faith and conscience Loss of faith Possession
Result	Medically diagnosable mental disorders: *Psychosis* *Neurosis* *Mood disorders* *Anxiety disorders* *Personality disorders* *Dementia* *Learning disorders* *etc.*	Feelings of emotional and psychological disquiet/discomfort Inadequate current relationships Maladaptive thinking and behaviour	Poor mental health Feelings of insecurity Disconnection from society and social norms (anomie) Poor functioning	Spiritual discomfort Spiritual crisis Loss of personal moral control
Treatment	Drugs Electro-convulsive therapy (ECT) Therapeutic activities Psychosurgery	Counselling and psychotherapy *(psychodynamic; humanistic/person-centred; integrative, etc.)* Cognitive-behavioural therapy (CBT) Exercise Lifestyle changes	Change individual's connections to society Change society Empowerment Improvements in the social environment Political/social activism	Spiritual counselling Prayer and meditation Religious conversion Contact with a 'higher power' Exorcism

Table 2.2: Common mental health treatment methods

THE BIOPSYCHOSOCIAL APPROACH TO MENTAL HEALTH

From the dawn of psychiatry in the late nineteenth century until the mid-twentieth century, the medical model of mental disturbance prevailed (Pilgrim, 2002; Claringbull, 2010). However, over the years it became apparent that mental ill health could also be caused, or at least worsened, by other important contributory factors (Meyer, 1952). Theorists such as Brown and Harris (1978) argued that if psychological and sociological factors could affect physical health, then it was likely that they could also have an impact on mental health, and by the late 1980s, investigators were proposing a more complete, integrated, model of mental health, one that combined its medical, psychological and social components (Engel, 1980).

That combined approach, the biopsychosocial model, fitted both the then popular theories about the origins of mental disturbance and the then so-called progressive or eclectic social politics and opinion about the needs and roles of wider society (Pilgrim, 2002). A holistic approach to all of life, including mental life, was then, and probably still is, the name of the game. It is an approach that certainly gelled with the views of those who took a more comprehensive view of the interdependence of psychiatry, psychotherapy and social work (see Goldberg and Huxley, 1992; Falloon and Fadden, 1993).

Today, in much of psychiatry, in much of psychotherapy – indeed, in much of mental health practice generally – the biopsychosocial model of mental disorder remains a 'brand leader'. However, modern medical research is providing us with an ever expanding understanding of how the brain functions. This means that we are learning more and more about how biochemistry, neurophysiology and genetics affect mental health. It is possible that a new, exclusively medical model of mental health may emerge. It is even possible that the medical profession may eventually be able to use the power of these new developments to find some new and guaranteed cures for the mental disorders. In such an event, doctors might be able to regain the dominance that they enjoyed 100 years ago – what goes around, comes around. Perhaps the end of the biopsychosocial model of mental health is in sight (Ghaemi, 2009).

This possibility is, of course, exciting for the medics. Nevertheless, at present neither they nor any other profession, including counselling and psychotherapy, have any exclusive answers for clients presenting with psychological (mental health) issues. The mental disorders seem to have a complex series of causes and an equally complex supply of remedies. Mental health issues are clearly multidimensional, multifactored concerns. The trick that counsellors and psychotherapists need to master is to find out which factor to tackle first. Perhaps a more useful model of mental health, and the ways to treat mental ill health, might look like Figure 2.1.

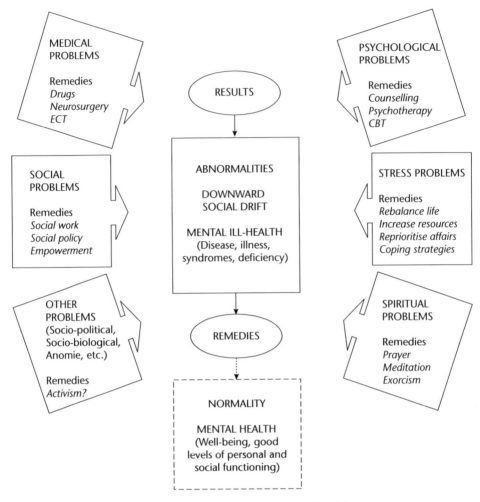

Figure 2.1: A model of mental health

COMMENT

If a comprehensive biological explanation of madness, together with a comprehensive ability to remedy it, is ever achieved, then the power of those administering it could be overwhelming. The counselling and psycho-therapy profession might even find itself being sidelined and becoming a socially subversive movement. Is the ultimate in mental health a society in which happiness depends on mass mind control by a minority of managing intellects?

CHAPTER SUMMARY

In this chapter we have learned that defining just what a mental abnor-mality actually is seems to be a very complex undertaking. It is certain that none of the disciplines that are currently concerned with helping the mentally abnormal/unhealthy, the psychologically disturbed and the emotionally troubled has monopoly on the truth. They are all much better at explaining why their rivals are wrong than they are at demonstrating that their own ideas are right. Indeed, they all seem to relish telling horror stories about the alleged malpractices and incompetencies of the competing professions (e.g. Masson, 1992). The fact is that – as we noted in Chapter 1 – none of the practitioners in any of the mental health disciplines can offer a comprehensive, all-embracing explanation of mental abnormality within their own professional discourses, let alone judge the explanations offered by their rivals.

We have also seen that the modern tendency, at least in the National Health Service, is to offer a range of professional activities to the mentally dis-ordered. These include medicine, psychology, psychotherapy, social work and counselling (and anything else to hand or currently fashionable). In other words, the NHS will use any take on abnormality that seems to help right here, right now. This is an obviously flexible, cross-disciplinary attitude in thinking not only about mental abnormality but also about how to help the mentally disordered. Perhaps counsellors and psychotherapists might find it useful to adopt such a wide-ranging approach in their everyday professional activities.

Lastly, we have been made aware that making judgements about clients is difficult. However, we cannot usually avoid doing so, either formally or informally. Therefore, we need to find out how to carry out client evaluations as objectively as possible. After all, at base, client assessment is about helping the client to see things more clearly. It is not about causing more confusion. Assessment is clearly a difficult process to get right – if, indeed, we ever can. How to assess someone's mental health seems likely to be as much an art as it is a science. In the next chapter we will be 'assessing assessment'.

SUGGESTED FURTHER READING

Gask, L (2004) *A short introduction to psychiatry.* London: Sage.

A nice easy read – very helpful in telling you about what psychiatrists actually do and where they actually do it. Chapter 1 'Historical context' provides a fascinating account of psychiatry's emergence as an independent discipline.

Gould, N (2009) *Mental health social work in context.* Exeter: Learning Matters.

An engaging text that offers a well-argued critical discussion of biopsycho-social approaches to mental health problems. Chapter 1 'Perspectives on mental health' will give you a good foundation on which to build your enquiries into mental health issues generally.

Tew, J (2005) *Social perspectives in mental health: developing social models to understand and work with mental distress.* London: Jessica Kingsley.

A well set out text that takes an interdisciplinary approach to modern mental health practice. Chapter 3 'Social approaches to madness and distress' is particularly useful.

Client assessment

CORE KNOWLEDGE

- Some therapists disagree with client assessment because they believe that it might obstruct the client/therapist relationship and that it demeans clients by labelling them.
- Some therapists approve of assessment because they believe that it provides useful information about clients and helps with treatment planning and outcome monitoring.
- Assessment could/should include the presenting problem, the client's personal and family history, health information, drug and alcohol usage, and a risk assessment.
- ICD 10 (*International Classification of Diseases – Version 10*) supplies labelling codes for the mental disorders.
- DSM IV (*Diagnostic and Statistical Manual, 4th edition*) is a system of classification protocols that includes all the mental disorders.

INTRODUCTION

It seems reasonable to suggest that many (perhaps even most) clients go along to see counsellors and psychotherapists because they are looking for some sort of help. If that is true, then it is arguable that in order to assist their clients, therapists need answers to two questions. First, what is wrong? Second, what sort of help is necessary?

So is that it? Is that 'assessment in a nutshell'? Well, no, because there is considerable debate about what assessment actually is and what it is for. The fact is that many therapists are unhappy with the very idea of assessment (see review in Milner and O'Byrne, 2003). They fear that assessment might distort the emerging client/therapist relationship. Indeed, some practitioners deny that assessment has any place at all in the talking therapies.

These 'anti-assessors' argue that assessment is only client labelling. That, they say, is disempowering for the client (Smail, 2005). They claim that assessment demeans clients by reducing them to a cipher. They allege that assessment establishes a false therapist/client hierarchy; one that owes more to therapist power-grabbing than to client need.

The 'pro-assessors' (Finn, 2007) disagree and argue that assessment should be an essential piece of kit in any therapist's toolbox. This is because they think that therapists need to find out all that they can about their clients so that they can work out how best to help them. They believe that the more therapists know the more they can do.

Clearly, some counsellors and psychotherapists will use assessment, and others will not. That is a matter of individual choice. However, throughout the caring professions generally, assessment is widely used. It is a fact of therapeutic life. Therefore, whatever our personal positions, we still need to understand assessment. We need to know how assessment is carried out, what the pitfalls are, and what the strengths and weaknesses of the process are. We need to know when to assess, and, just as importantly, we need to know when not to assess. This is what this chapter is about.

DIFFERENT PROFESSIONS – DIFFERENT ASSESSMENT NEEDS?

Some theorists argue that counselling and psychotherapy are actually different callings with different objectives. For example, McLeod (1999b, p12) claims that 'counselling chooses to view the person in a social, cultural and organisational context'. If that is true, then assessing a 'counselling client' in isolation would indeed be meaningless. It would show us only one facet of that client.

McLeod (1999b, p12) also argues that 'mainstream approaches to psycho therapy . . . operate on the basis of an individualised concept of the person'. If that were true, then assessing a 'psychotherapy patient' in isolation would be valuable – even essential. We might learn enough of that patient's individual story to be able to offer some appropriate, personally tailored assistance.

So if counselling and psychotherapy are indeed two different callings, then it might be that counselling does not need assessment but psychotherapy does. However, other theorists such as Claringbull (2010), Feltham and Horton (2006), and John and Rita Sommers-Flanagan (2004) reject the idea that psychotherapy and counselling are professionally divergent. They say that the two professions are more or less two sides of the same therapeutic coin; the differences, if any, are minuscule. If that is true, then techniques that are useful in one of these two co-disciplines are likely to be equally useful in the other, and that includes client assessment. Of course, claiming that assessment is a *useful* therapeutic tool does not mean that it has to be a *universal* therapeutic tool. The wise practitioner knows that the 'do or do not' and 'now or later' decisions about assessment need to be preceded by the 'why now' and 'for what purpose' questions.

IS CLIENT ASSESSMENT UNAVOIDABLE?

It can be argued that client assessment is built into the very fabric of counselling. It might perhaps be unacknowledged, but it cannot be avoided. After all, many practitioners will have chosen to adopt a particular model of therapy early on in their careers. If they remain exclusively loyal to their original choices, then it is likely that that choice will influence the ways in which they work with their clients. In all probability, psychodynamicists will usually analyse, humanists will usually empathise, and behaviourists will usually sympathise. In other words, each of them is adopting their own 'one size fits all' philosophy. In effect, this is 'diagnosing in advance' – 'we know what's likely to be wrong with you and we know how we are going to fix it'.

Therefore, it is arguable that no matter what name we give the process, counsellors and psychotherapists cannot avoid evaluating (assessing?) their clients and forming hypotheses about what makes them tick. This happens even if they do not realise that they are doing it. So it seems that assessment may well be unavoidable.

PRE-ASSESSMENT

Pre-processed or not, it is quite likely that assessment starts before the therapist and the client ever get together. They might have had some direct or indirect contacts by telephone, email or voicemail. Possibly a referring letter has been sent, or perhaps a colleague has passed along some information about the client. Before they ever meet, the therapist and the client are both gathering, or imagining, all sorts of snippets of information about each other.

It seems very likely, deliberately or not, that therapists will arrive at some pre-meeting assumptions (assessments?) about their clients – a sort of 'fantasy client'. Of course, sensible practitioners will be aware that clients are pre-assessing them too – that they are 'shopping around', perhaps for a 'fantasy therapist' (Withers, 2007). Like much in life, 'first impressions count'. Will you meet your client's expectations? Does your client meet yours?

WHAT TO INCLUDE IN AN ASSESSMENT

Some therapists argue that clients need to be viewed as a composite whole. This includes not only their personal histories but also what has gone on, or what is going on around them. In other words, assessment should be as comprehensive as practicality allows (Marquis, 2007).

The following list sets out some of the main areas of their clients' lives that therapists might find it helpful to know more about.

- *The presenting problem*: Why now? Is it recent or long term? Has it changed over time? Is it the real issue? True or false, the important question is: 'Why is this particular story being told at this particular time?'
- *Family history*: We sometimes need to know almost as much about significant family members as we do about our clients. Some clients are indeed 'chips off the old block'.
- *Personal history*: Critical life events, significant relationships, education, work history, psychiatric/psychological history, medical treatments past and present can all be important.
- *Drugs and alcohol*: Gaining information about the client's history of legal and illegal drug use is vital. This includes 'nil returns' because even abstinence tells its own story. Never forget, there is the potential in all our clients (including 'dear little old ladies') to have a history, or even a current habit, of drug and/or alcohol misuse. Therapists and assessors who shy away from directly challenging or confronting clients about substance abuse issues are doing their clients a disservice.
- *Risk*: An assessment of the client's likelihood of self-harming, or of being a danger to others, is always necessary. Even a 'no-risk' finding is of note. Therapists who ignore possible dangers to their clients or to others chance being held professionally and personally liable for any unfortunate outcomes.

DIAGNOSIS OR ASSESSMENT?

If you are not medically qualified, do be careful how you use the term 'diagnosis'. This is especially important if you are preparing official documents and reports. Mental health diagnosis is the province of appropriately trained doctors. Therapists are not medical diagnosticians. However, many forms of counselling and psychotherapeutic assessment are very akin to diagnosis. Like the medics, we too want to find out what the problem is, how to classify it, and how to treat it.

It is essential to remember that many of the symptoms that might indicate mental disorders are also signs of physical disorders. For example, a rapid heart rhythm might be caused by anxiety. On the other hand, it might be caused by disease. If there is any doubt, then the client should be encouraged to see a doctor.

However, along with the clear benefits that accurate assessment can bring (proper treatment planning, etc.) there are some potential downsides. For example, just how accurate are our client assessments? Are the classification systems that we use to arrive at our professional judgements even valid? Szasz (1991) argues that because mental disorders do not have a demonstrable pathology they cannot be illnesses and so classification is actually impossible.

Another example of a downside comes from the problems that careless diagnostic labelling can cause. Mislabelling has distorted, even destroyed, the lives of some psychiatric patients (see Masson, 1992).

Yet another example of a downside to assessment comes from issues around diagnostic confidentiality. Assessments and/or diagnoses are often permanently placed on official records. Depending on where those records are stored, they may be accessed by all sorts of people, including the clients themselves, and there is a danger of unauthorised or improper use of the diagnostician's evaluations.

REFLECTION POINT

- You are a workplace counsellor seeing a female client who is starting to become aggressive, anxious and very self-absorbed. She is also becoming unreasonably suspicious of everybody around her. Possibly she is developing a psychotic disorder. You are working in a safety-sensitive industry, and you are obliged to report safety concerns to your clients' managers. You do so in this case, and a note is placed in your client's personal files. Later, you discover that this client's symptoms were actually caused by a bad reaction to a drug that she was taking to relieve a heart condition. That has been sorted out and she is fine now. The problem is that she remains under suspicion at work. What have you done?

COMMENT

One simple misdiagnosis or careless assessment can have a huge knock-on effect throughout a person's life. In this case, your mistake might have permanently damaged your client's career. Therapists clearly have a vital duty to be as conscientious as possible when assessing their clients and, equally importantly, when deciding how to use their assessments. Careless talk really does cost lives.

REASONS NOT TO ASSESS

Clearly giving a name or a classification to a client's apparent mental health condition is a very convenient way to describe what seems to be going on for that person. Classification can be a useful form of professional shorthand provided it does not degenerate into professional jargon. The danger is that our assessments, which at best are only well-intentioned hypotheses, might become mistaken for absolute, authoritative fact. Our convenient therapeutic 'classi*fictions*' can surreptitiously become unquestioned diagnostic 'truths'. It can be difficult for clients to shake off the labels that we might unthinkingly stick on them. That is one reason why some counsellors refuse to assess under any circumstances. They believe that such a labelling process can strip the client of the necessary dignity levels that they believe are necessary to underpin eventual emotional growth.

Under some circumstances assessment might not be advisable due to the client's current mental health situation. Inappropriately applied, assessment might do more harm than good. It might actually serve to reinforce the original symptoms. Sometimes psychological defences are there for a purpose. For example, in trauma cases assessment usually includes a review of the triggering events. However, some victims may be so traumatised, so emotionally fractured by what happened that such an assessment might cause them further damage. In certain other cases (some obsessive-compulsive disorders, a few of the personality disorders, some anxiety states, and so on), inopportune assessment could actually worsen the problem by seeming to legitimise, and so apparently normalise, the patient's symptoms – 'it's OK, it's not my fault, everybody does it, I'm not ill'. Obviously, if a client is extremely mentally disturbed, extremely psychologically fragmented, then assessment might not only be ill-advised, it might be impractical or even impossible.

PRACTICAL ASSESSMENT – TALKING THE TALK

There are a number of ways in which counsellors and psychotherapists can choose to go about assessing their clients.

The formal/informal choice

Some therapists might choose to have a formal assessment session with a checklist to fill in – a sort of 'white coat and clipboard' approach. Doing it this way has the advantage of getting the assessment process all sorted out before the counselling proper starts. After all, for many counsellors Session 1 can be a bit of an 'admin day' anyway. There are consent forms to sign, names and addresses to be recorded, GP details to be noted, information leaflets to be handed over, payment arrangements to set up, etc. Another advantage of having a formal, clipboard-style assessment process is that important issues are unlikely to be overlooked. All the necessary questions are there on the assessment form. The blank spaces are just waiting to be filled.

However, it might be that it is this very formality, this very rigidity, that is rather off-putting for both therapist and client alike. Some would say that such an assessment interferes with the client/counsellor relationship. It might appear, on the surface at least, to set some firm, possibly artificial, boundaries to the therapeutic relationship – therapists question; clients answer. For many practitioners this is just not how counselling works. There can definitely be an authoritarian feel about such a formally stylised assessment procedure. After such an 'I'm the expert' beginning, some practitioners would argue that therapists might find it difficult to help their clients to find their own independent voices and to grow emotionally.

The static/rolling decision

Does assessment take place on fixed occasions, say Sessions 1, 5 and 10? Or does it take place on an 'as and when' basis? Clearly the fixed basis helps therapists to find out just how their clients are doing at regular intervals. However, what about any additional information discovered between the assessment sessions? Is it to be ignored until the 'proper' time?

Using a rolling assessment approach clearly has the advantage of eventually optimising the information to be gained. It helps to flesh out any basic details gathered earlier. There are also more opportunities to fill in any gaps. However, an informal 'as and when' approach does require therapists to remember to obtain enough information to permit adequate assessments to be made when required. Equally importantly, they also have to remember enough about what they have been told to be able to properly complete their client notes. For some therapists, the informal rolling approach to client assessment means keeping a sort of imaginary checklist in their heads, or having a real one secreted nearby.

PRACTICAL ASSESSMENT – WALKING THE WALK

Whatever method or style of assessment you choose, there are still a lot of areas of the client's life that you might feel need investigation. This is always assuming that you have the time, or that doing so seems appropriate. Experienced therapists will know that assessments are very likely to change as the therapy progresses. In effect, our assessments may well need re-assessing. It seems that, in practice, assessment is necessarily a very fluid and a very tentative process. Figure 3.1 is a sample of a typical assessment checklist sheet. Please feel free to use it, adapt it or devise your own.

CLINICAL ASSESSMENT SHEET

PRESENTING PROBLEM (using client's own words)

Why now?

HISTORY OF PRESENTING PROBLEM AND RELEVANT PSYCHOSOCIAL HISTORY

Strengths and resources

Previous attempts at solutions and outcomes

Use of psychological / psychotherapeutic services

MEDICAL HISTORY AND ALL CURRENT MEDICATION

THE MIRACLE QUESTION – how will the client know that the situation is significantly better?

WORK IMPACTS

CULTURAL / RELIGIOUS FACTORS

DOMESTIC VIOLENCE / CHILD ABUSE / SEXUAL ABUSE
Previous   Current   Potential

SELF-HARM / HARM TO OTHERS

Previously planned   Previously activated   Currently planned   Currently activated

GENERAL PRESENTATION
Personal   Mood   Speech   Intellectual functions

ALCOHOL / DRUGS HISTORY
Areas of life affected   Substance(s)   Quantities   When

CLINICAL DIAGNOSIS
Axis 1   Axis 2   Axis 3   Axis 4   Axis 5
                                                                              Current / Previous GAFs

THERAPEUTIC PLAN
Intention   Method   Measurement

COMMUNICATIONS NEEDED WITH EXTERNAL AGENCIES

ANY OTHER RELEVANT FACTORS AND INFORMATION

Figure 3.1: Clinical assessment sheet

PRE-TREATMENT AND POST-TREATMENT ASSESSMENT MEASURES

Over the years, psychologists have devised a wide range of questionnaire-based tests that can be used to assess a client's current mental health function. Counsellors and psychotherapists might also find that these psychometric tests can give them some useful insights into what is going on for their clients. If you decide to use any of these measures, always bear in mind that they ultimately depend on self-reports and subjective evaluations. For example, clients might be asked to state whether they have felt bad about themselves 'not at all', 'occasionally', 'a lot of the time' or 'most of the time'. Our clients choose the appropriate reply. No one specifies what those terms really mean. Clearly the value actually chosen depends largely on the client's personal opinions.

Unlike, say, a gas meter or a speed camera, psychometric tests cannot provide precise measurements. We cannot say that someone is 93.2 per cent depressed. We cannot even say that Mr A is twice as depressed as Mrs B. However, what we can say is that according to whichever test it is that we are using, Mr A's score last month was, say, 20 and this month it has dropped to, say, 10. Therefore, he seems to be getting better. Actually, we can say more than that. Most of these tests have been standardised against national averages. Perhaps researchers have found that across the nation most depressed people score 15 or more on this particular test. Therefore Mr A's initial score of 20 allows us to conclude that at least some of his symptoms are centred on depression.

Psychometric tests have some other potential benefits. Clearly they can help us get a measure on how clients are progressing during their therapy. They can help the clients to feel more validated too. Possibly some clients find it comforting to see that their 'disease' is 'officially recognised' and that it can be given an authoritative-sounding grading. Presumably, this process might be especially gratifying if a series of measurements indicate a positive trend. The clients somehow feel justified in having sought help. Sometimes, being formally diagnosed even seems to make them feel hopeful. Perhaps it is the not knowing that scares them the most.

Obviously, finding a negative trend is also very useful clinically: it might indicate that the client is getting worse, and we certainly need to know that. This deterioration might be because the original diagnosis was inaccurate or that the chosen therapeutic approach is the wrong one. If this is so, then we need to rapidly revise our therapeutic planning.

There might be another important reason why the tests suggest that this client is getting no better. The original diagnosis might have been correct; the initial treatment choice might actually have been the right one; but what might be wrong is the therapist. It might be the case that the therapist is simply incompetent. That is a sobering thought. Therapists might be prepared (even if reluctantly) to psychometrically measure their clients, but they very rarely measure themselves. What if therapists too had to achieve 'good' performance scores? What if counsellors and psychotherapists had to justify their professional competences against measured, outcome-based criteria? What if they too had to pass regular fitness-to-practice tests? What if failing those tests resulted in professional sanctions? Scared? You should be – regulation is coming.

SOME COMMON ASSESSMENT TOOLS

Counsellors and psychotherapists are quite likely to come across one or more of the following mental health assessment tools. They all use subjective rating scales such as 'sometimes', 'occasionally', 'often'. All of those listed here, and most of the many other available tests, can be found on the internet. Some are free to download. Some providers demand that you obtain their consent to use their products. Yet other providers require you to pay a fee or undertake special training. Many of the available assessment tools are self-administered by the patients themselves. Clearly therapists must make sure that their clients are competent to carry out such a task.

- *Generalised Anxiety Disorder Assessment (GAD 7)*. This test measures a patient's anxiety levels using seven questions such as, 'Over the last 2 weeks, how often have you been bothered by feeling nervous, anxious or on edge?'
- *Patient Health Questionnaire (PHQ)*. The PHQ is a series of tests used in primary care to diagnose most of the routinely encountered mental disorders. The PHQ 9 version tests for depression by using nine questions such as 'Over the last 2 weeks have you had little interest or pleasure in doing things?'
- *Beck Depression Inventory (BDI)*. This test has been found to be very useful in research studies although it can be equally informative for practitioners.
- *General Health Questionnaire (GHQ)*. This is a general measure of individual distress. It is a self-administered screen and tests a patient's ability to function normally. It is available in formats of 60, 30, 28 and 12 questions. For example, GHQ 28 assesses levels of somatic symptoms, anxiety, depression and social dysfunction.
- *Hospital Anxiety and Depression Scale (HADS)*. This speaks for itself – and it is quick and easy to use.
- *Clinical Outcomes in Routine Evaluation (CORE)*. This is probably the most commonly used therapeutic progress and outcome measure used in counselling today. It comes in 18- and 34-question formats. CORE assesses clients along four personal dimensions or 'domains'. These

are: subjective well-being; problems/symptoms; life functioning; risk/harm. Each client's score is compared to cut-off points derived from testing the general population. Scores above these points indicate a need for clinical concern.

ACTIVITY 3.1

Assume that all counsellors and psychotherapists have to pass regular 'fitness-to-practice' tests.

- Draw up a list of suitable assessment criteria.
- Devise some tests to check if the therapists are meeting those criteria.
- Devise a list of remedial actions to be taken by therapists who fail the tests.
- Devise a list of sanctions for use in cases of non-compliance.

COMMENT

At present, there is no national regulation process in place to officially license counsellors and psychotherapists. Anyone can call themselves a counsellor or a psychotherapist and set themselves up in a consulting room. Unfortunately, all sorts of people do just that. Nearly every profession has some sort of a quality-controlled continuing personal development system in place to ensure that its practitioners remain competent to practise their trade. Counselling and psychotherapy does not. Some therapists would argue that statutory regulation would mean the end of individual freedoms. Others demand better consumer protection for the client population. This debate is likely to be ongoing for some time yet.

Case study 3.1   Assessments can confirm suspicions

Tom had had two sessions with Jackie, who was a psychotherapist with the local community mental health service. The GP had referred Tom because his chronic anxiety condition did not seem to be responding very well to treatment.

Jackie had carried out a routine psychological assessment on Tom when they first met, and nothing had particularly stood out. There was certainly nothing obvious that was fuelling Tom's anxiety attacks. The GP had diagnosed general anxiety disorder (GAD), and that seemed to be a reasonable conclusion. However, during session three, Tom mentioned that some eight months ago he had been involved in a car crash. At that time, the paramedics had thought that Tom might be quite seriously injured and so they had rushed him off to hospital. Fortunately,

Tom's injuries were not too bad and not life-threatening. It had all been a bit scary, but after some treatment Tom was soon discharged.

Tom told Jackie that the incident was too minor to be important and that he was now completely over it. However, there was something in the very vivid way that Tom was describing the car crash that alerted Jackie's suspicions. Was there a possibility that Tom's supposed GAD was actually unrecognised post-traumatic stress disorder (PTSD)? There and then, Jackie carried out an Impact of Events Scale (IES) test on Tom and found a positive score. IES is a very quick screen for PTSD, and a positive result makes carrying out a full PTSD inventory worth the doing. After she had carried out the inventory, Jackie's suspicions were confirmed. Tom was indeed suffering from PTSD. Jackie knew that this disorder can continue to generate high anxiety levels for years if untreated. Medication can only ease the symptoms – it cannot cure the condition. This explained why the pills were not working.

Jackie now had enough information to be able to help Tom with some more suitable therapy techniques, methods that were targeted at trauma relief. Her pro-active use of some appropriate psychological assessment techniques had paid off.

MENTAL DISORDER CLASSIFICATION SYSTEMS

There are a number of classification systems used by health professionals to categorise mental illness. For counsellors and psychotherapists, probably the two most important are *ICD 10* and *DSM IV*.

ICD 10

International Classification of Diseases, Revision 10 (usually known as *ICD 10*) is simply a coding system for illnesses that is used for the collection of basic health statistics. It was first published by the World Health Organization in 1993. The codes for the mental disorders are listed under *ICD 10* in Chapter 5. The various *ICD 10* codings are really just another sort of labelling. For instance, depression as a stand-alone disorder is coded as F32. However, if the depressive symptoms are actually due to other mental disorders, then different codes are used. For example, depression can also be a result of alcohol misuse (F10) or a symptom of a psychotic disorder (F23).

A much more useful subsidiary version of *ICD 10* is the *WHO Guide to Mental Health in Primary Care*, published in 2000. This is usually known as *ICD 10 PHC*. The advantage of this version is that it provides GPs with some useful screening guides for the common mental disorders. It also provides treatment recommendations for most of the disorders and gives advice about when to make a specialist referral.

The *ICD 10 PHC* screening guides are easy to use. For example, the depression checklist simply asks GPs if the patient has had any of the following:

- low mood or sadness;
- loss of interest or pleasure;
- decreased energy or increased fatigue.

If the answer is 'yes' to any of these questions and if the patient also answers 'yes' to four out of eight supplementary questions about sleep loss, appetite loss, poor concentration, diminished bodily movement, libido, confidence, self-harm, and excessive guilt, then depression might be indicated. *ICD 10 PHC* (pp55–59) then goes on to help the doctor to decide if medication is necessary, what sorts of advice to offer the patient and whether referral to a counsellor seems sensible. There is even a useful list of agencies and contacts that the patient can access for some additional help.

DSM IV

DSM IV is the classification system that most therapists will encounter at some time in their professional lives. Its full title is the *Diagnostic and Statistical Manual of Mental Disorders, 4th edition*. It was published by the American Psychiatric Association in 1994. A fifth edition is supposedly due in May 2013. As mentioned previously, unlike *ICD 10*, *DSM IV* is not merely a classification or a labelling system; it is also a complete set of diagnostic protocols for all the mental health disorders or conditions.

DSM IV bypasses the difficult issue of 'mental abnormality' that we examined in Chapter 2. It avoids this term altogether by instead using the concept of 'mental disorder'. If we refer to *DSM IV*, we learn that:

> *In DSM IV, each of the mental disorders is conceptualised as a clinically significant syndrome or pattern that occurs in an individual and that is associated with present distress (e.g. a painful symptom), or disability (i.e. impairment in one or more important areas of functioning) or with a significantly increased risk of suffering death, pain, disability or an important loss of freedom. In addition, this syndrome or pattern must not be merely an expectable and culturally sanctioned response to a particular event, for example the death of a loved one. Whatever its original cause, it must currently be considered a manifestation of a behavioural, psychological or a biological dysfunction in the individual. Neither deviant behaviour (e.g. political, religious or sexual) nor conflicts that are primarily between the individual and society are mental disorders unless the deviance or conflict is a symptom of a dysfunction in the individual, as described above.*

> (DSM IV, 1994a, ppxxi–xxii and xxv)

It is to be noted that by this definition mental disorders are only diagnosed in 'the individual' – only in the patient. *DSM IV* addresses only the 'insane' individual, not the insanity in society. Because *DSM IV* is a very important – probably the most important – classification system, we will now look at it in a bit more detail.

DSM IV – DIAGNOSIS

Diagnoses using *DSM IV* are made along a multi-axial assessment system. There are five such axes. The reason that these five axes were adopted is partly because they were found to be convenient and partly because it was recognised that mental health issues are really complex biopsychosocial problems. Therefore any system that classifies mental health must include a way of allowing for all the relevant potential biological, psychological and social/sociological factors. The system also allows for a number of very useful get-out clauses when either there is no diagnosis (nothing wrong or can't find it) or when the practitioner simply does not know what is happening (and does not want to admit it).

The five *DSM* axes

Axis 1
- clinical disorders;
- other conditions that may be a focus of clinical attention.

These are, more or less, the disorders that most of us think of when the subject of mental illness comes up, e.g. depression, anxiety, bipolar disorder, schizophrenia, eating problems, compulsions, and so on.

DSM IV presents us with lists of symptoms that have been associated with each of the disorders listed on Axis 1. A particular disorder can be diagnosed if enough boxes have been ticked on one of the lists. As the number of ticks made on a disorder's 'symptom menu' increases, then so too does the likelihood that a particular diagnosis is correct. For example, in order to diagnose a bipolar disorder (*DSM* Code 296), a 'manic episode' has to have occurred. For a manic episode to have happened, it is necessary that the patient reports having at least three of the seven symptoms listed in *DSM IV* on page 332. Immediately we can see a serious weakness in the system. In order to tick our boxes we have to rely on our patient's obviously subjective self-reports or our own subjective observations. What we do not have, what we cannot get, is direct, independent, objective, verifiable evidence. So, are we diagnosing reality or is this another case of 'as if'?

Axis 2
- personality disorders;
- mental retardation.

These are the disorders that are supposedly inherent in someone's make-up – usually from birth. They are long-standing and are supposedly just as much a natural part of that person as gender or shoe size. This means that until recently, at least, Axis 2 disorders have been largely considered to be untreatable. However, this rather absolutist position is increasingly coming under attack (Bateman and Fonagy, 2000; Adshead and Jacob, 2007). It seems that some specialist treatments, such as dialectic behaviour therapy, might be of some help in certain Axis 2 conditions such as borderline personality disorder (Palmer, 2002; Livesley, 2003). There have even been claims that mood stabilising drugs such as valproic acid or gabapentin might be of help in such cases (see Healy, 2009). Additionally, there is currently some interest in finding out if any of the antipsychotics or the psycho-stimulants might also be effective for some Axis 2 disorders.

It will be interesting to see if *DSM V* reclassifies any of the Axis 2 personality disorders as Axis 1 conditions. Presumably if it does so, then we can infer that any such condition is now considered potentially treatable. As with Axis 1 disorders, Axis 2 classifications are carried out by tick-boxing symptom lists. For example, in order to diagnose schizotypal personality disorder (*DSM* Code 301.83) it is necessary that at least five of nine associated symptoms are present. A list of these symptoms can be found in *DSM IV* on page 645.

Axis 3
- general medical conditions

As we know, quite a number of medical conditions can cause mental abnormalities. For example, in some cases the mental abnormality may arise from a physical deterioration (brain tumours, Alzheimer's dementia, Korsakoff's syndrome, etc.). In other cases the mental abnormality might arise from the effects of illegal or prescription drugs. In yet other cases, physical disease might cause mental abnormalities (hyperthyroidism, endocrine dysfunctions, etc.). It is possible that more or less every medical condition can, in the right circumstances, have some sort of a psychological side-effect. For instance, many viral diseases will result in patients becoming depressed – at least in the short term.

Axis 4
- psychosocial or environmental problems

These are many complicating issues that can arise out of a patient's personal, social or localised environmental background. If they are likely to impact on the patient's mental health, then clearly such problems must be taken into consideration when making a diagnosis. After all, there might be nothing wrong with the patient. It might actually be that it is the patient's circumstances that are causing the trouble. These include: personal issues (bereavement, relationship break-up, illiteracy, sexual abuse, etc.); social problems (unemployment, poverty, social exclusion, etc.); discrimination (sexuality, class, appearance, ethnicity, etc.); and oppression (injustice, torture, political exclusion, etc.). The list is virtually endless.

Axis 5
  • Global Assessment of Functioning – GAF Scale

This evaluates someone's psychological, social and occupational functioning along a series of performance criteria. The range begins at 100 (superior performance in all aspects of life) and descends in stages to 1 (barely sustainable existence). Clearly, positioning someone on the GAF Scale is highly subjective. However, its main purpose is not to measure the patient in absolute terms but to measure changes in functioning. It is how today's assessment differs from last week's, last month's, last year's that is clinically important, not precisely where the patient is on the GAF Scale at any one time.

DSM IV – DIAGNOSTIC RULES

  • Check that:
    – the disorder is not due to the direct effects of a substance – particularly alcohol. This is Rule Number 1 for every patient. I will never forget getting a referral from an eminent consultant psychiatrist whose headed notepaper proudly proclaimed his claimed expertise in addictions. This 'expert' had not noticed that his patient was drinking a bottle of whisky every day;
    – the disorder is not due to the direct effects of a general medical condition – when did your client last see a doctor?
    – the disorder causes clinically significant distress or impairment in social, occupational or other important areas of functioning. This again is a matter of subjective opinion – even when based on assumed professional experience. I once counselled a client who had come along to talk about a problem with her teenage daughter. It turned out that this client had been subjected to a particularly horrifying rape some years back in her own teens. Despite my initial doubts, I had to accept her claim that she had finally got over the rape; it was no longer an issue for her; she had dealt with it. This client only wanted to work on her issues with her daughter. That is what we did, and that is what seemed to help her. So who had the best take on what her 'clinically

significant' distress was? Me and my subjective opinions or my client and her inner self-knowledge and convictions?

- Disorders due to general medical conditions or cognitive function disorders are the diagnosis of choice above all other diagnoses. For example, a client presenting with excessive repetitive behaviour is unlikely to be diagnosed as having obsessive-compulsive disorder if, say, Huntington's Chorea has been diagnosed during an earlier examination.
- Use as few diagnoses as possible. In other words, try and find a single diagnosis that explains all the symptoms rather than arrive at a series of diagnoses on a one disorder per symptom basis. Simple is better than complex.
- Consider the first occurring disorder and then the most chronic disorder. If 'A' occurred first, it might have caused 'B'. On the other hand, 'B' might now be so dominating that it has become a problem on its own. For example, many years ago a client might have developed post-traumatic stress disorder (PTSD) after experiencing a traumatic event – perhaps a train crash. Over the ensuing years that original PTSD might have caused the client to also develop agoraphobia. If the client's main problem is still the PTSD, then that should be treated first. The agoraphobia can be attended to later. Alternatively, is the agoraphobia now so debilitating that the patient cannot deal with any other issues in life, including the PTSD? If the answer is 'yes', then the agoraphobia should be addressed first and the PTSD can be dealt with later.
- Always look at the past and present mental health histories of a client's family members. No matter what your take is on the nature/nurture debate, the family background can still provide vital information. This is true even if there is no significant history. 'Nil results' are actually important clues in our search for what makes our clients tick.
- On Axes 1 and 2, if there is no diagnosis, then '*DSM* Code V71.09' is always used. I do not really know why, but it certainly looks more impressive than just saying nothing. So:
  - If you are not yet sure what to diagnose, then you can use '*DSM* Code 300.9' (unspecified mental disorder – non-psychotic).
  - In case of doubt, you can always put off making a diagnosis until you know a bit more about the client. This decision is coded '*DSM* 799.9'.
- It might be that you believe that a particular disorder is present. However, you might not be sure about the actual subtype. You can bypass the niceties by diagnosing a 'Not Otherwise Specified' (NOS) condition. For example, people with imaginary defects in their appearance might be diagnosed with body dysmorphic disorder (*DSM* Code 300.7). However, if the condition cannot be properly differentiated from others in the somatoform category, short-term

hypochondria for instance, then somatoform disorder NOS (*DSM* Code 300.81) would be used – in other words, 'we know you've got it but we can't prove it'.

DSM IV – A CRITIQUE

There are many possible ways to criticise any manual-based approach to defining mental ill health (Oyebode, 2008). *DSM IV* is no exception – here are some examples.

- The definitions used are arbitrary. The supposed boundaries between the various disorders are imposed and artificial. These definitions do not take into account subtle differences in human experience. For example, words such as 'often' or 'rarely' when used to define the frequency of mental events often cannot really tell us anything about the true inner levels of distress actually being felt by our clients.
- Mental events cannot be directly observed. We know only what the individual chooses to tell us or to show us. Very often we are getting only a small part of the story. This makes the diagnostic task really a bit like trying to define a giraffe in the dark when we can only touch the tip of its tail.
- It is claimed that *DSM IV* is objective and that it has overcome the biases and prejudices of its users. However, those who carried out the *DSM IV* classifications were themselves probably, perhaps inevitably, influenced by their earlier training. Furthermore, is it possible that some of the illness-based definitions of mental dysfunction owe more to political need or social acceptability than they do to diagnostic reality? For example, might religious extremism be classified as a 'culturally sanctioned response' (and not a sign of psychosis) for sound medical reasons or for political expediency?
- *DSM IV* focuses on the individual's symptomology and on ways to relieve the individual's distress. However, put into a social context, these symptoms might be a very normal reaction to society's stresses and pressures. For example, does a depressed single mother living in a tower block on a run-down estate need Prozac or rehousing? Is this mother depressed in the clinical sense or is she simply overwhelmed by her environment? If your answer is to nod knowingly, sneer at the GP, and to plump for rehousing, then just check that you too have not fallen into the auto-categorisation trap. She might be delighted with her housing but suffering from a malfunction in her serotonin system. Pills might be the answer after all.
- To be of any real value, diagnosis has to be reliable, and it must also be meaningful and valid. The difficulties and problems confounding diagnosis in general medicine are well known. After all, a headache

might indicate a hangover or it might indicate a brain tumour. In the case of psychiatric diagnosis these difficulties are far worse. Study after study has shown that psychiatric diagnosticians, when faced with the same symptom clusters, come up with different diagnoses (see review by Canino and Allegria, 2008). Not only that but the validity of assigning symptom clusters to various 'mental diseases' has also been shown to be highly subjective and open to wide variations (Kendal and Jablensky, 2003; and many others). Again and again we are faced with problems of diagnostic bias when addressing the concept of psychological disturbance or the notion of mental ill health.

CHAPTER SUMMARY

It seems that assessment is a complex business. That has certainly been the message set out in this chapter. There is fierce debate about assessment in terms of principle and in terms of therapeutic expediency. There are arguments about assessment in terms of type and style, when and where, and, of course, why. Clearly there is much to be gained from skilfully carried out assessments that therapists can use to the benefit of their clients. Equally there is much to lose from inappropriately or inexpertly handled assessments if they become therapeutically destructive. Obviously, in the final analysis, choices about the place and value of assessment in the therapy room are matters for each individual counsellor and psychotherapist. Or are they?

The fact is that increasingly we are living in a results-centred world. If therapists want to claim that they get adequate results, then they might well find themselves having to prove it. This is especially so in the National Health Service when 'value for money' and 'evidence-based practice' are universal buzzwords. Counsellors and psychotherapists in the NHS, in employee welfare schemes, in the voluntary sector or, indeed, anywhere are not immune from hard-headed, commercial, evaluations of their work. If therapists want to claim a respected place in society, then they will have to show that they deserve one. They will have to prove their worth. The talking therapies will have to demonstrate that public and private investment in their services pays off. In other words, they will have to produce sufficient supportive data to back up their claims. After all, the bean counters must have something to count.

So if therapists want to get enough useful facts and figures together, to justify their professional existence, they will have to be prepared to measure their effectiveness. In order to do that they will increasingly have to get involved in pre-therapy assessments and post-therapy outcome evaluations. It rather looks as if client assessment (and therapist assessment too) is here to stay in the counselling and psychotherapy world.

In this chapter, we have learned how to assess clients. The next thing we need to do is to learn a bit about what these assessments might mean and where they might be taking us.

- What does it mean to us as therapists, if we conclude that a client probably has a certain psychological condition or mental disorder?
- What are these various disorders and what can we do about them?

In the next four chapters you will learn about depression, anxiety, schizophrenia, bipolar disorder and personality disorder. You will also learn how to manage clients who you suspect might be troubled by any of these problems.

SUGGESTED FURTHER READING

Bager-Charleson, S and van Rijn, B (2011) *Understanding Assessment in Counselling and Psychotherapy.* Exeter: Learning Matters.

The authors have produced a very readable book that provides a great deal of indispensable additional information about assessment. This is essential reading because client assessment is all too often a neglected topic in counselling and psychotherapy training. Readers are offered a sound theoretical basis for assessment and the book is packed with experience-based information and extensive case studies that illustrate the practicalities of applying theory to client work. The sections on the role of the assessor and on treatment planning are of particular relevance to the everyday, practical therapist.

DSM IV (1994a) *Diagnostic and Statistical Manual of Mental Disorders, 4th edition (DSM IV)* Washington DC: APA Publishing.

A highly technical text. You do not have to read it page by page, but you do have to have a copy to hand – always. The 'Introduction' and 'Use of the manual' sections are particularly helpful.

DSM IV (1994b) *Quick Reference to the Diagnostic Criteria from DSM IV.* Washington DC: APA Publishing.

A 'pocket book' version; much easier to use and to handle – the pull-out checklists at the front are well worth a careful inspection.

ICD 10 (2000) *The WHO guide to mental health in primary care.* London: RSM Press.

A more readable, must-have handbook. A good guide to specialist agencies.

Milner, J and O'Byrne, P (2003) *Assessment in counselling: theory, practice and decision-making.* Basingstoke: Palgrave Macmillan.

A very authoritative read. The authors are experienced practitioners of assessment at Northorpe Hall Child and Family Trust. The chapter on assessment is particularly instructive.

CHAPTER 4

Understanding depression

CORE KNOWLEDGE

- The core symptom of depression is *anhedonia* – a lessened ability to experience pleasure or joy. Depression is a *unipolar mood disorder.*
- There are a number of different and conflicting explanations of depression:
  - biological – caused by biochemical imbalances;
  - cognitive – result of negative thinking about the self;
  - behavioural – absence of positive behaviour reinforcers;
  - sociological – result of the sickness in society;
  - psychoanalytic – fantasised loss, anger turned inwards, inner conflicts.
- UK treatment protocols recommend a stepped approach to the management of depression:
  - Step 1: Low mood. *Do nothing, the condition will probably self-remit.*
  - Step 2: Mild depression. *Guided self-help and short-term counselling and psychotherapy.*
  - Step 3: Moderate depression. *Medication and longer-term counselling and psychotherapy.*
  - Step 4: Severe depression. *Complex medical and psychological treatments.*
  - Step 5: Extremely severe depression. *Hospitalisation and advanced care.*
- In order to diagnose depression using *DSM IV*:
  - a mood episode must have occurred (enough symptoms are present);
  - the other associated symptomology is present. Then one of the four depressive disorders is selected.

INTRODUCTION

Counsellors and psychotherapists will often meet clients who are depressed. That is a routine fact of therapeutic life. Depending on how the statistics are interpreted, it can be argued that at any given time up to 1 in 10 of us suffers from some sort of depression (US National Survey on Drug Use and Health, 2005; National Health Service Information Centre, 2007). Various studies by the World Health Organization indicate that roughly similar figures can be found around the world (www.who.int/research). It seems that globally depression is at pandemic levels.

The symptoms of depression (originally known as melancholia) vary widely and so, too, does their severity. Depression can range from just feeling very fed up (lowered mood) to a totally debilitating condition in which the sufferer is unable to function, to connect with normal life, and might even experience delusions. Depression can even be fatal, because in a worst case situation, suicide is always a possibility.

Over the years, many different ideas have been put forward about what depression actually is and what causes it. For much of the last century, depression was usually considered to be either of biological origin or, alternatively, a reaction to imposed stress (Parker, 2000). Today, the distinction between internally caused depression (endogenous) and externally caused depression (exogenous) is largely passed over. Nowadays, depression is generally considered to be one of the mood disorders (see *DSM IV* or *ICD 10*). This class of mental disorder includes the various types of depression and the bipolar disorders (manic depression). Modern evidence suggests that someone who appears only to be depressed has a *unipolar* disorder whereas someone who has both depressed and manic episodes has a *bipolar* disorder (Forty et al., 2008).

Many modern biological theorists argue that depression is either caused by or causes a biochemical imbalance in the brain's neurotransmitters (see review by Healy, 2009). An inadequacy in serotonin levels is usually considered to be the main culprit – at least, that is today's fashionable position (Den Boer, 2006). Doubtlessly that will change.

Therapists should particularly note the 'caused by' or 'causes' distinction. On the one hand, depression might be caused by external factors (ended relationships, problems at work, strife, etc.); the resulting stress might cause changes in brain biochemistry and the victim becomes depressed. On the other hand, internal factors such as changes in brain biochemistry might lower a person's ability to cope with their lives. Again, the victim becomes depressed. The 'causes/is caused' debate is more than just another chicken and egg puzzle. As long as this question remains unanswered, or appears to be unanswerable, it remains possible to argue in support of either the medical or the non-medical explanations of depression – or both.

WHAT IS DEPRESSION?

This is a wide open question. The more cynical among us might even argue that depression is simply a mythical condition invented by the sellers of antidepressants. That is certainly the position of some of the 'anti-drug' campaigners (Kirsch, 2009). However, for the many people who experience any of the symptoms generally found on the *DSM IV* 'depression menu', their distress is far from being an interesting academic debate. Their suffering is real. So if any of them find that their pills work – and many do (Daines, Gask and Howe, 2007) – then they 'know' that they have had depression. After all, they have just been cured by antidepressants.

Medically, depression is relatively easy to diagnose. Tick enough boxes on a diagnostic checklist and patients can be labelled as 'depressed'. They are 'sick'. Counsellors and psychotherapists, on the other hand, are more likely to explain depression as an emotional condition than to view it as a diagnosable illness. For them, depression is not a disease; it is a 'dis-ease'. Therefore, for many talking therapists depression is neither normal nor abnormal; it is just a way of being. If it is an unhelpful way of being, then psychotherapy is there to help the client make the necessary changes.

It is hard to arrive at an exact definition of depression. Any attempt to do so is as likely to cause an argument as it is to settle one. Clearly, depression can be an intermittent condition or a condition that can at least be temporarily overcome. After all, as any internet search will tell us, many of the great achievers have allegedly suffered from it. The list is endless and allegedly includes Edgar Allen Poe, Winston Churchill, Sylvia Plath, Gustav Mahler, Virginia Woolf and many others. Depression might have caused them psychological pain, but it did not stop them being extremely success-ful in their various spheres. For example, see Wolpert (1999), who has provided a fascinating personal review that shows us how his own career as a very successful, world-class scientist has been dogged by depression.

ANHEDONIA

There seems to be a consensus that *anhedonia* is the root symptom of depression (Gilbert, 2007). Anhedonia is usually defined as being a general loss of interest and motivation together with an inability to experience pleasure – a sort of 'flatness' of mood. We have all been there. Interestingly, it appears that very often both our negative and our active emotions are flattened in depression. This means, for example, that although we might not feel particularly happy, we probably will not get overly angry either (Rottenberg and Gotlib, 2004). So it is not just that we are fed up; we do not really care about what is happening at all.

THE SIGNS OF DEPRESSION

Depression has been called a dimensional change from normal sadness or misery (Gilbert, 2007). So what is the distinction between depression and just being 'down in the dumps'? It is probably something to do with the degree of effect. Depression is usually viewed as being a level of melancholy that significantly interrupts, even prevents, a person's ability to function across a wide range of essential activities. The concept of depression as a life-disrupter underpins most of the ways in which this disorder is diagnosed.

The Royal College of Psychiatrists, for example, says that someone who experiences five or six of the following symptoms is probably depressed:

- generally feels unhappy;
- loses interest in most things in life – doesn't enjoy anything much;
- can't make decisions;
- can't cope very well;
- feels tired all the time;
- can't keep still – restless and nervous;
- suffers sudden weight loss or gain;
- has disturbed sleep – can't get to sleep and early hours wakening;
- has no sex drive;
- lacks confidence;
- feels generally no good any more – no use to anyone;
- avoids people – especially friends;
- feels very ratty;
- feels worse at particular times, often in the mornings;
- feels as though they would be better off dead.

(RCPsych, 2008a)

Psychologists also tend to assess depression by considering how people are functioning in specific areas of their lives (emotional, motivational, cognitive, etc.). These are what Gilbert (2002 and 2004) has called the biological, psychological and social aspects of depression. Table 4.1 is another 'depression menu' – this one has been based on Gilbert's (2007) proposal. Again, the more ticks the more we can assume that the patient is likely to be depressed.

REFLECTION POINT

- Does depression really exist? If so, what does this term mean to you?
- What is there about the condition known as 'depression' that distinguishes it from any of the other mental disorders? In other words, are depressed people different from the rest of us is some definable way?

Life area	Diminished functioning
Emotional	Sadness No sense of pleasure Tearfulness Hopelessness Guilt Worthlessness
Motivational	Increased dependency Low energy Fatigue Apathy Poor concentration Loss of interest
Cognitive	Negative expectations Negative self-concept Exaggerated view of difficulties Self-blame Indecisive Thoughts about death/suicidal ideation Preoccupation with health
Behavioural	Social withdrawal Cease engaging with interests and pastimes Diminished activity
Biological	Sleep increase/reduction Appetite and weight increase/reduction Reduced libido Daily mood cycles

Table 4.1: The symptoms of depression

COMMENT

It can often be very difficult to distinguish between depression and normal reactions to life's many downsides. At the extreme end of the depression continuum the condition is clearly present in its clinical sense. When the symptoms are milder, then sometimes depression is almost too easy a diagnosis. Is it possible that depression is a twentieth-century disease? Were people depressed in earlier times or were they just much tougher than we are? However, for a condition that some claim is mythical, depression seems to cause an awful lot of people an awful lot of grief.

A PSYCHOANALYTIC TAKE ON DEPRESSION

Freud argued in his 1917 monologue *Mourning and Loss* that depression results from loss. He argued that depression is a more severe (and more lasting) debilitating emotional state than mourning (grief). In the classic psychoanalytic world, grief is deemed to be a *conscious* reaction to a known loss whereas depression is seen as being an *unconscious* reaction to loss generally. Therefore, in the case of depression, although the victims are aware of their emotional suffering, they are supposedly unaware of its true causes (see Leader, 2009).

The loss that Freud refers to might be real – perhaps a close relative has died. Alternatively the loss might be fantasised or symbolic – perhaps an orphan has 'lost' a fantasised 'super-parent', or maybe a recently discharged soldier, having 'lost' his regiment, has also lost all that his army 'family' has meant to him.

In psychoanalytic theory, the depressed person allegedly regresses to an earlier developmental stage and tries to deal with the loss by internalising it – by internalising the lost person or symbolic object. It is also assumed that the victim has conflicting feelings of love and hatred towards the subject of the loss: 'I love you so much but you died and abandoned me. I hate you for doing that.' Therefore, when the loss is internalised, the anger too is also turned inwards. This resulting love/hate ambivalence triggers unconsciously held inner conflicts – or so the psychoanalysts say.

All this means that in psychodynamic-speak depression is caused by the sufferer's anger being driven inwards. The assumption is that this inwards-directed anger becomes self-anger and that this triggers the self-denigrations and self-criticisms that underpin depression (see review in Bush, Rudden and Shapiro, 2004 or Holmes, 2002).

Inwardly directed anger is not the only psychodynamic explanation of depression. For example, some psychoanalysts concentrate on the idea that depression results from people's falsely exaggerated notions of how they should be (ego ideal) and from falsely low assessments of how they actually are: 'I ought to be strong but actually I'm a coward'. Unconsciously contrasting these internalised (and unreal) assumptions produces the inner conflicts that fuel the depression. 'I'm not good enough.' 'Who says so?' 'I do.' Yet other psychodynamic models of depression rely on conflicts around interpersonal attachments and losses, especially in infancy (Bowlby, 1991; Mooney, 2009). The psychodynamic debate goes ever on.

A COGNITIVE TAKE ON DEPRESSION

Beck (1967, 1991) suggested that depression is supposedly caused by nega-tive events that occur either before or during its onset. According to this model, both the depressed person and the 'normal' person might have negative thoughts about some aspects of themselves and the world about them. The difference lies in how those thoughts are processed and managed.

According to Beck and his followers, in many situations 'normal' people (the non-depressed) can probably correct their negative thinking by finding that it has no base in reality. For example, an internal belief that 'I am stupid' might be reversed by passing an exam. In another example, a belief that 'I'm scared of lifts' might be overcome when a forgotten childhood experi-ence of being locked in a small room has been remembered and reassessed. However, for depressed people these negative cognitions become reinforced and exaggerated. This means that the depression becomes a self-fuelling, downward spiral: 'Yes I am stupid; I've just made another mistake' or 'Every time I get into a lift I get more and more scared.' This distorted thinking, however, is not irrational; it has causes. The job of the cognitive therapist is to help the client to discover these causes, to challenge them and to encourage the client to unpick them (see Beck and Alford, 2009).

Some cognitive theorists bow to the psychodynamic model by believing that the tendency towards negative cognitions is often acquired through internalised early-years experiences. Others simply argue that depression is triggered by life events that somehow affect a person who, for whatever reason, is predisposed to negative cognitions. The original cause is unim-portant; it is the result that matters. Yet other theorists argue that depression results from maladaptive social learning: 'Experience tells me that it will always be a rotten old world.' Some theorists even argue that depression is not by itself pathological; it is merely a justifiable reaction to over-whelmingly adverse circumstances such as poverty or ill health. Whatever the cause, they claim that the resulting negative thinking spreads through the whole of the victim's life.

It seems that as far as the cognitive therapists are concerned, the root causes of depression are not all that important but the cures are. Therefore, the core purpose of cognitive therapy is simply to relieve, or even reverse, the client's unhelpful thought patterns (Clark, Beck and Alford, 1999). Results are more important than theory.

A BEHAVIOURAL TAKE ON DEPRESSION

Unlike much of conditioning theory, the behavioural model of depression does not depend on the assumption that maladaptive psychological reinforcers encourage negative thinking or depressive responses. Instead it is argued that it is the absence of positive reinforcers that results in lowered performance and a withdrawn attitude (see review by Abreu and Santos, 2008).

So imagine yourself confined to a boring, uncomfortable room on a miserable day with no diversions or entertainment available and nothing much to look forward to. How would you feel? Most of us would get pretty fed up, or – in diagnostic parlance – 'depressed'. According to the behavioural theory of depression, it is not the negative room that is depressing you; it is the absence of anything positive about it that is getting you down. Take a different example: suppose you are working really hard at doing a good job for somebody, but no matter how hard you try, your work is criticised. After a while you would probably get pretty fed up and just stop trying any more. So, say the behaviourists, the answer to depression is straightforward. Simply set up lifestyle regimes that encourage and reward. In other words, as the old song tells us, 'just direct your feet to the sunny side of the street'.

A SOCIOLOGICAL TAKE ON DEPRESSION

Some sociologists (Barry and Yuill, 2008, for example) take the view that much of mental illness, including depression, is actually the sickness of society appearing as sickness in the individual. In other words, people themselves are not really sick; they just carry the sickness of what is going on around them. It is a 'diseased' world that is making some people appear to be behaving abnormally – apparently 'mentally disordered'. It is argued, therefore, that we should not waste our time trying to treat the individual. At best that could be only palliative. What we really need to do is to address the root cause of the problem, and that root cause is the supposed sickness in society.

The sociologists claim that sociological 'sicknesses' can affect the individual in two ways.

- Someone might be directly affected by personally depressing or distressing events (bereavement, divorce, homelessness, etc.).
- Someone might indirectly become dispirited by negative forces in the social environment (injustice, oppression, etc.).

Whatever the reason, sometimes people get to a point in their lives where they have 'just had enough'.

On an individual basis, personal events that cause depression are sometimes termed 'exit events'. Examples include redundancy, rejection and personal failures. Interestingly, apparently 'happy' events can have some very depressing side effects, too. These happy events include, for instance, moving to a better house, going on holiday, and changing to better employment. Often there is some lingering regret for what has gone before.

If therapists do accept the sociological model of depression, then it is difficult to see what treatments they might offer. Therapists are usually concerned with individual clients and not with the general social structure. However, this need not be a reason for counsellors and psychotherapists to ignore this model. What if sometimes it is indeed the case that social pressures have triggered the depression that an individual client is presenting? Does this mean that therapists should persuade such clients to address the social issues that affect them personally? For example, should someone in poor accommodation be encouraged to participate in a political campaign for better housing? If it is really the case that identifiable faults in society are the causes of depression, then might therapists better employ themselves as social activists? Should they forget mumbling 'Mmm' or 'I hear you' and start shouting 'Right on' and 'We shall not be moved'?

A BIOLOGICAL TAKE ON DEPRESSION

The biological take on depression is deceptively simple. A particular something has gone wrong with how the brain works, and the outcome is the mental illness that we call 'depression' – problem solved. Find out what has gone wrong and then find out how to put it right – job done. Even better, as by luck we seem to have discovered that certain medical treatments apparently relieve – even cure – depression, then we have got there already. However, the reality is that trying to understand what these serendipitous discoveries actually mean is actually the point where our apparently simple biological take on depression starts to get rather complicated.

Over the years we have developed a number of drugs that seem to help quite a lot of depressed patients. Once we had found that they appear to work, we then went on to try and explain how they work. This has led theorists to speculate that these drugs have specific effects on certain brain functions. In particular, they have focused on the brain's biochemistry. The result is an increasingly more detailed understanding of neurological and biochemical structures in the brain. So according to the supporters of the biological take on depression, what we now need to do is to get a better understanding the brain's biochemistry. When our knowledge in this area is sufficiently complete, we will be able to arrive at a comprehensive understanding of the biological take on depression. At least that is the hope.

Our modern ideas about the biology of depression started to emerge during the mid-twentieth century. This was when two new types of antidepressant medication were discovered (Healy, 1998):

- the tricyclic class of antidepressants (amitriptyline, imipramine, dothiepin, etc.) – the term 'tricyclic' merely describes the basic chemical structure of these drugs;
- the monoamine oxidase inhibitor antidepressants (MAOIs such as phenelzine and tranylcypromine).

It has been argued that these two drugs correct imbalances in two important brain chemicals, the neurotransmitters noradrenaline and serotonin. From a biological point of view, therefore, many theorists claim that depression is specifically caused by these particular biochemical imbalances (see Healy, 2009, for a very readable review of this theory). This view was reinforced when the Prozac class of drugs was discovered. These drugs (fluoxetine, citalopram, Seroxat, Cipramil etc.) are known as the selective serotonin reuptake inhibitors or SSRIs. That is because they too act on brain chemistry and supposedly correct serotonin imbalances.

The more recent discovery of another class of antidepressant drugs that also seem to influence brain chemistry offers yet more support to the bio-chemical imbalance theory of depression. These are the serotonin–noradrenaline reuptake inhibitors or SNRIs (venlafaxine, duloxetine, etc.). Again, see Healy (2009) for an explanation of this topic.

A very different medical approach to the treatment of depression also supports the brain chemistry deficit model. It can be shown that for some types of depression electro-convulsive therapy (ECT) can offer some relief (UK ECT Review Group, 2003). No one really knows why this works (when it works). However, there is some limited evidence that ECT either stimulates the production of the necessary 'antidepressant' neurotransmitters or makes those already present in the brain work better (RCPsych, 2008b).

In sum, the biological explanation of depression assumes that the bio-chemical workings of the brain have gone wrong. In particular, it is argued that this error is the result of an imbalance (usually a lessening) in the activities of two important neurotransmitters (noradrenaline and serotonin). Although the biochemistry is complex, the solution seems simple. If people are depressed, then just boost their biochemical systems. Why not just give them a 'neurotransmitter sandwich'? If only it really was that simple.

So does antidepressant medication work? If it does, then it is arguable that depression is indeed caused by a biological imbalance in the brain. Unfortunately the jury is still out on that one. According to the American Food and Drugs Agency (cited in Healy, 2009, pp56–57), antidepressants seem to work about 50 per cent of the time. This finding is in part confirmed by Khan et al. (2002) whose meta-analysis found that about 48 per cent of mildly depressed patients improved with medication, although this 'cure' rate did increase as the severity of the disorder increased.

So it seems that the more depressed you are the more likely that an antidepressant will be effective. This idea is supported by Fournier et al. (2010) who found that antidepressant medication is significantly effective for the more severely depressed patients. Alternatively, according to Kirsch (2009) antidepressants do not work at all. Kirsch claims that any alleged benefits are actually due to the placebo effect. For Kirsch, antidepressants are nothing more than fake curatives that address a fantasy disorder.

The fact is there are many studies supposedly 'proving' and 'disproving' the benefits of antidepressant drugs – 'you pays your money and you takes your choice'. Probably the best that we can say for now is that biochemical imbalances might be at least part of the explanation of depression. What we do know is that many other treatments also help to relieve depression – even 'cure' it perhaps. These include psychotherapy, exercise, diet change and reducing alcohol intake (RCPsych, 2008a).

Of course, it is always possible that these treatments also have an impact on brain biochemistry but in ways that are yet to be discovered. It might even be that some of the alleged 'depressive defects' in brain chemistry are self-repairing. We do know that many depressed patients get better without any treatment at all (National Institute for Health and Clinical Excellence, 2004; Stein and Wilkinson, 2007). So if medical treatment as such is often not necessary, then perhaps depression is not a medical (biological) condition after all. Who knows?

In sum, it seems that the biological explanation of depression is also bedevilled by the 'cause or effect' puzzle. Even if we could successfully manipulate brain chemistry in order to eliminate depression, would we have simply relieved an unpleasant symptom of a deeper problem or would we have genuinely struck at the problem's fundamental cause? Perhaps this question is really only of academic importance. After all, what really matters is that the patients get better. When the pills work, they work, and depression seems to be a biological condition; when they don't work, it seems to be something else.

ACTIVITY 4.1

- Think back to a time when you felt very sad and dispirited. Make a list of the ways in which you thought about yourself and about your life at that time. Then draw up a list of the ways in which you acted.
- Now think back to a time in your life when you or someone you know was probably depressed in the clinical sense of the word. Make another list of your own or that person's thoughts and actions.

- Finally, try comparing the two lists. How different is being in a low mood to having a depressive mental disorder? Is it truly different? Is depression a specific condition or is it just a more extreme feeling of being fed up with everything?

COMMENT

When matters get personal, what to someone else might seem to be only a bit of a downer, soon starts to seem to us like a more major mental health problem – 'I'm not just worried; I'm clinically depressed'. So, with the great benefit of hindsight, looking back, perhaps some of our own 'depressions' were not really classifiable as mental disorders. The learning point here comes when we reassess our original self-diagnoses. Were we really depressed or just feeling a bit low? Our problem as practitioners is, of course, that we are meeting our clients in their 'here-and-now'. Hindsight is unavailable.

BEFORE TREATMENT STARTS

Before counsellors and psychotherapists start treatment planning for their depressed clients they will do well to remember Rules Number 1 and Number 2 in the *DSM IV* diagnostic system (see Chapter 3).

> *Rule 1 Check that the disorder is not due to the direct effects of a substance – particularly alcohol.*

If a depressed client is currently using harmful levels of alcohol or drugs, then a decision needs to be taken about whether or not this is the time to start any form of counselling or psychotherapy. Perhaps a referral on to an addictions agency would be better?

> *Rule 2 Check that the disorder is not due to the direct effects of a general medical condition.*

If this is a possibility, then obviously a doctor must be consulted. As we now know, depression, or at least depressive symptomology, can be caused by certain illnesses. Sometimes it is necessary to defer psychotherapy until a doctor gives an 'all clear'.

Remember: 'If in doubt, check it out.' If you do not know or if you are not sure, ask – do not be shy. If necessary, ask your client some direct questions – not 'Do you drink a lot?' but 'Exactly how much do you drink each week – how many bottles of what, pints of what, etc.?'

Table 4.2 contains a non-exhaustive list of some common 'non-psychiatric' reasons why somebody might appear to be depressed.

Cause	Examples
Prescription drugs	beta-blockers oral contraceptives L-dopa (for Parkinson's disease) phenytoin (used in epilepsy) chemotherapy withdrawing from amphetamines withdrawing from appetite suppressants steroids – hydrocortisone, etc. verapamil, diltiazem, amlodipine, etc. (for cardiac and similar conditions) Accutane (used for acne) . . . and many other medications
Illnesses	dementia brain tumour Parkinson's disease multiple sclerosis influenza many viral diseases glandular fever vitamin deficiency thyroid conditions certain cancers many life-threatening/terminal illnesses . . . and many other medical conditions
Other drugs	alcohol (a major cause of depression) cannabis (especially 'skunk' etc.) LSD narcotics withdrawal

Table 4.2: Non-psychiatric causes of depression

TREATING DEPRESSION

As we know, there is a large number of conflicting explanations of the causes of depression. It is therefore not surprising to find that there is also a wide range of treatments available. When we looked at client assessment in Chapter 3, the general conclusion was that assessment and any emerging ideas about treatment should be adapted to fit the needs of each client. Indeed, as far as counsellors and psychotherapists are concerned, this is also the clinical approach favoured by therapists who have moved towards integrated practice.

In this chapter, therefore, treatment planning will follow the *stepped care approach* suggested by the National Institute for Health and Clinical Excellence (NICE) *Guideline 23* (*Depression: management of depression in primary and secondary care*, NICE, 2004). It is the guideline that most primary care doctors (GPs) use. You can get the latest version of this guideline from www.nice.org.uk. However, the NICE recommendations are based on the assumption that the patient is being managed by a GP. I have therefore modified them to better suit counselling and psychotherapy practice. As you will see, therapists who use the approach suggested in this book will easily be able to employ their own preferred methods of working with depressed clients.

Treatment – step 1

At this level, the client presents in a generally low mood. If any of the measures listed in Chapter 3 are employed (HADS, BDI, PHQ9, etc.) then a very low score is likely. In any case, Eysenck's original (1952) observation that most people with mild depression recover over time, treated or not, still holds true (see the Garfield/Eysenck debate in Dryden and Feltham, 1992, pp100–34). In other words, depressed clients often get better without any special help, and placebos seem to be as effective as active drugs (van Schaik et al., 2002; Khan, Redding and Brown, 2007).

So, by this standard, the treatment for depression is very simple: do nothing. This is especially so in the case of borderline depression levels. All that the therapist needs to do is to keep a watching brief on the client's depression levels while the supportive counselling proceeds. However, sometimes it might seem advisable to encourage the client to take up some of the self-help methods that will be discussed in Step 2.

Treatment – step 2

At this level the client is presenting with mild depression; assessment measure scores will be starting to rise. Nevertheless, should a GP be involved at this stage, it is unlikely that an antidepressant will be prescribed. This is the point where the particular skills of counsellors and psychotherapists can be especially helpful – after all, therapists are very good at 'people management', though they might prefer to call it 'empowerment' rather than 'management'.

First, therapists can use their people skills to encourage their clients/patients to try some of the self-help treatments. In particular, they can offer support to those of their clients who are experimenting with any of these techniques. Self-help for clients with depression includes:

- cutting out or reducing alcohol;
- stopping illegal drug use;
- eating healthily and/or controlling weight;
- getting active – taking some exercise, going out for a walk, doing something;
- making action plans to actively tackle life's routine problems;
- carrying out those action plans;
- talking to people about their problems and worries;
- getting their work/home-life balance in order;
- reading self-help books;
- accessing self-help websites;
- joining self-help groups;
- doing anything else that looks like it might help.

Second, therapists can use their assessment skills to start planning some low-level psychotherapy with their clients. They can also use their people management skills to persuade their clients to try out such forms of therapy. Potentially helpful treatments at this stage might include the brief intervention and solution focused therapies. Low-intensity cognitive-behavioural therapy, brief psychodynamic therapy, or perhaps limited-sessions-only versions of any of the commonly used counselling and psychotherapy techniques. They all have their uses.

Treatment – step 3

At this level, the client/patient is exhibiting the symptoms of moderate depression. This is the level of depression where some argue that medication can be effective for something like 50–60 per cent of such patients (Daines, Gask and Howe, 2007). Therapists might well consider either referring their clients to a GP or perhaps encouraging them to use properly any already prescribed antidepressants. This does not mean that psychotherapy has to stop. Often the best treatment is pills *and* talk.

This is also the depth of depression where the longer-term psychotherapies might be usefully employed. These include any of the mainstream approaches to counselling and psychotherapy together with high-intensity cognitive-behavioural therapy.

Treatment – step 4

At this level the client is showing signs of severe depression. Usually a referral to specialist mental health teams is necessary, normally through the client's GP. There is increasing risk of self-harm or worse, and complex medical and psychological treatments are indicated. Especially skilled counsellors and psychotherapists might be able to contribute to this process, but of course the primary responsibility for client care will be held by the specialist team leader who will usually be a psychiatrist.

Treatment – step 5

At this level the patient is severely/extremely mentally disordered. Treatment will be provided by mental health crisis teams and will often include urgent hospitalisation followed by specialist care in the community. It is very unlikely that counsellors and psychotherapists will have any role to play in the early stages of this sort of intervention. However, they might be able to assist at a later stage, perhaps once the immediate crisis has been dealt with.

Technical assessment of depression

If you are interested in carrying out a technical assessment of depression, then this is how it works if you use *DSM IV*. Remember that in *DSM IV*, depression is only one of the mood disorders. There are ten mood disorders, including the bipolar disorders (see *DSM IV*, pp317–18). Four of these disorders can be classified as 'depression'. Here we are concerned only with the depressive disorders.

There are three stages in the diagnosis of depression. They are:

Stage 1
Before any of the mood disorders can be diagnosed, a relevant *mood episode* must have occurred (see *DSM IV*, p327). In the case of depression we want to know if the patient has had the type of lowered mood known as a *major depressive episode*. In order to do this we need to know if five or more of the following symptoms have been present for the same two-week period. They must represent a noticeable change in previous function and must include either a depressed mood or a loss of interest or pleasure (or both):

- depressed mood;
- loss of interest or pleasure;
- appetite up/down; weight loss/gain;
- insomnia or hypersomnia;
- psychomotor agitation or retardation;
- fatigue or loss of energy;
- feelings of worthlessness;
- loss of concentration;
- thoughts about death/suicide – no active ideation.

These symptoms must be of a nature to cause clinically significant distress or impairment and they must not be due to other causes such as bereavement or major personal loss.

continued overleaf

Stage 2
If a major depressive episode has occurred, then check that there is no history of manic episodes (see *DSM IV* p332), mixed episodes (see *DSM IV* p335) or hypomanic episodes (see *DSM IV* p338). Provided that none of those other mood episodes has occurred, then one of the following two depressive disorders can be diagnosed:

1 major depressive disorder – single episode: only one depressive event (see *DSM IV* p344);
2 major depressive disorder – recurrent: two or more depressive events (see *DSM IV* p345).

If the client is in a generally and persistently low mood but without fully fulfilling the criteria for a major depressive episode, then one of the following two diagnoses might be made:

1 dysthymic disorder – the client has been in a depressed or low mood more often than not over the last two years (see *DSM IV* p349). No major depressive episode has occurred but two or more of the following symptoms have usually been present:
    • reduced/increased appetite;
    • reduced/increased sleeping;
    • low energy or fatigue;
    • low self-esteem;
    • difficulty with concentration and decision-making;
    • hopelessness.
2 depressive disorder Not Otherwise Specified – the usual convenient 'catch all' for the difficult to diagnose cases (see *DSM IV* p350).

Stage 3
Finally the *mood specifiers* are identified that describe either the most recent episode or the course of recurrent episodes, for example, mild, moderate, severe, with melancholic features, with seasonal pattern (see *DSM IV* p318).

Job done
That's all there is to it – it is only check-box science really and anyone who can follow a cookery book can follow *DSM IV*. Actually *DSM IV* is easier – you cannot burn anything. Given that we have always got our old friend 'Not Otherwise Specified', we cannot really go far wrong. Of course, the easy bit is arriving at a diagnosis. The hard bit is deciding what to do next – deciding, that is, where you come in.

Case study 4.1   Tailoring therapy to the client's needs

Chris started his counselling with Irene because he felt that his marriage was heading south. He was rather gloomy, both about his relationship and about his future. Nothing was much fun any more. During session 2, Chris seemed to be in an even lower mood than he had been in session 1. Although Irene had started to assess Chris from the beginning, she had not yet checked out his depression levels, so at this session, she asked him the questions in the GP's checklist (*ICD 10 PHC*) and found that she could definitely tick three of the boxes and that there were also a couple of 'maybes'. Irene asked Chris if he had ever seen anyone about his emotional health and got a vague reply that hinted at an occasional use of antidepressants over the years. She decided just to keep an eye on things for now. Chris's depression had presumably got better in the past and might well do so again this time.

Chris's therapy, supposedly for his relationship problems, continued. By session 4 Chris's mood was definitely much lower. He seemed to be losing interest in life. Irene got him to complete a Beck Depression Inventory questionnaire – he scored 20. As this score indicated borderline level (almost moderate level) clinical depression, she felt that some additional help might be indicated.

Irene managed to convince Chris that he ought to go and see his GP. He popped into the surgery, and the GP decided to try him on Seroxat. Irene and Chris carried on working together for the next three sessions. The problem was that Chris's depression didn't seem to be getting any better. If anything it was getting worse. Irene got Chris to complete another BDI. This time Chris scored 30. He was obviously well into the moderate depression range and looking like he would soon be at the severe depression level. Irene was now very concerned for her client. With his permission, she contacted his GP surgery and discussed her findings with the duty doctor. The doctor agreed to refer Chris urgently to the local community mental health service.

Irene did not see Chris for the next four weeks. When Chris did make contact once again, Irene learned that he had been hospitalised. He was still under the CMH team's care, and they were encouraging him to start seeing Irene again. Now the counselling could start.

CHAPTER SUMMARY

Depression can be a complex mental disorder. Equally, deciding on the best way to work with a depressed client can be a complex process. This is why a stepped approach can be so helpful. We begin with the attitude that depression is 'just one of those things' and opt for 'masterly inaction'. If the depression deepens, we can adopt more complicated explanations of the cause of the disorder and more advanced methods of treating it. In the worst cases, depression can become an extremely serious condition indeed and one that needs the full resources of hospital-based psychiatric services.

It seems that as far as depression goes, different treatments seem to work with different people. Many experienced therapists will be aware of the benefits of a 'suck it and see' approach to most of their client work. In the case of depression, this seems to be the reality whether we are talking about medication, about psychotherapy, about self-help or about any other form of treatment. For example, as far as medication is concerned, some anti-depressants seem to work better for some people than for others. Fluoxetine might work fine for Mr A but make Mrs B far worse. Then again citalopram might suit Mrs B yet cause Miss C to develop some unacceptable side effects. The problem is that we do not know in advance which drug is going to suit which client.

Fortunately, in many cases the clients seem to get better no matter what sort of treatment is offered. Perhaps they sometimes actually get better despite their helpers and not because of them. In any event, recovery need not be the end of someone's depression history because unfortunately some people will be subject to recurrent episodes of depression for much of their lives. This is why encouraging sufferers to self-help and to self-monitor can be so important. It is also why counsellors and psychotherapists are likely to have an important and ongoing part to play in combating this most insidious mental disorder.

SUGGESTED FURTHER READING

Brampton, S (2009) *Shoot the damn dog: a memoir of depression.* London: Bloomsbury.

A must for anyone coping with depression, or living with someone who suffers from it – the author tells us her own story in a painfully honest, warts and all style that can only be admired.

Gilbert, P (2007) *Psychotherapy and counselling for depression,* 3rd edition. London: Sage.

A good, all-round review of the topic – a little biased to the behavioural approaches, but this book has something to offer everyone. Part 1 provides an excellent review of the biopsychosocial approach to depression.

Gilbert, P (2009) *Overcoming depression: a guide to recovery with a self-help programme.* London: Robinson.

This book will change your understanding of depression and psychology with a biological/evolutionary/social explanation of depression. Parts 2 and 3 are invaluable guides to the practicalities of treating depression.

Power, M (ed.) (2004) *Mood disorders: a handbook of science and practice.* Chichester: Wiley.

A comprehensive, heavyweight tome – it is all you will want to know about depression but it is not a book for the faint-hearted. Of particular value are the various contributions from leading authorities on this topic.

Wolpert, L (1999) *A malignant sadness: the anatomy of depression,* London: Simon & Schuster.

A very vivid, very personal account of depression plus an interesting overview of the condition from a worldwide perspective.

CHAPTER 5

Understanding anxiety

CORE KNOWLEDGE

- Everybody gets anxious from time to time. It is part of the human 'fight or flight' survival mechanism and includes both psychological and physical symptoms.
- The anxiety disorders include:
  - panic disorder;
  - agoraphobia;
  - generalised anxiety disorder (GAD);
  - obsessive-compulsive disorder (OCD);
  - social anxiety disorder;
  - phobias;
  - post-traumatic stress disorder (PTSD).
- Anxiety treatments include cognitive-behavioural therapy, medication, counselling and psychotherapy, self-help and exercise.

INTRODUCTION

We all get anxious; we have all been there; there is nothing new about anxiety. There is not even anything particularly new about calling modern times 'the age of anxiety' – W. H. Auden did so in his well-known 1942 poem. Leonard Bernstein did so in an equally famous symphony composed in 1949. More recently, Madeleine Bunting did so in her column in the *Guardian* as did Scioli and Biller (2009) in their book *Hope in the age of anxiety*. It is not even a particularly original idea to view anxiety as a medical issue. Tone (2008) tells us about the history of the early attempts by doctors to medicalise anxiety. These primitive essays into treating anxiety ranged from the esoteric to the compassionate. For example, Rush's 1811 'Tranquillising Chair' (see Hunter and McAlpine, 1963) looks rather like a bondage nightmare. On the other hand, Connolly's 1830 vision suggested that asylums should be relaxing places, as 'tranquil havens where humanity, if anywhere on earth, shall reign supreme' (Bynum, Porter and Shepherd, 1984).

Anxiety seems to be yet another of the modern psychological pandemics. It is certainly on the increase. Today's young people appear to have far higher levels of anxiety than their parents had when they were teenagers (Twenge, 2000). The Royal College of Psychiatrists (RCPsych, 2010b) tells us that about 10 per cent of the modern population suffer from troubling levels of this condition. Tone (2008) claims that in 2006 alone, some 40 million Americans were diagnosed as having clinical levels of anxiety. The UK Centre for Anxiety Disorders and Trauma (http://psychology.iop.kcl.ac.uk/cadat/ – click on 'Panic disorder') estimated that in 2009 between 1 per cent and 4 per cent of all adults experienced clinically significant levels of anxiety that required treatment. They also found that typical onset ages were commonly in the late teens or in the late twenties. It also seems that once developed, anxiety – or at least a vulnerability to anxiety – can sometimes be a life-long condition.

It appears that the numbers of patients with anxiety who look to their doctors for help is high, too (up to 15 per cent of all primary care patients in one UK study), and yet in about 50 per cent of such cases the symptoms are not recognised by doctors (Munk-Jorgensen at al., 2006; Martin-Merino et al., 2010). However, the good news about anxiety is that it can often be successfully treated, or at least significantly relieved (Butler et al., 2006; Acarturk et al., 2009; Roy-Byrne et al., 2010). The even better news is that counsellors and psychotherapists can usually help most of their clients who suffer from anxiety. Very often this means incorporating some fairly straightforward cognitive-behavioural techniques into the 'therapy package'.

GOOD ANXIETY

Not all anxiety is bad for you. It all depends on the circumstances. Some levels of anxiety can help you to perform better (Lazarus, 1966). It works like this. Suppose that life's demands on you are increasing. The pressure is on. Perhaps the boss wants you to take on some extra responsibilities. Possibly you might be trying to fit a part-time study programme into your normal weekly regime. In order to achieve more, you have to 'fire yourself up' a bit more. As a result, both your body and your mind start to zip along a bit faster. In other words you are in a state of increased arousal. You feel more 'stretched' or 'stressed – but in a good way. In fact, this 'good anxiety' concept is so powerful that adaptations of it are used to improve athletic prowess and to maximise performance generally (e.g. the Catastrophe Model – Hardy and Fazey, 1987; the Multi-Dimensional Anxiety Model – Martens et al., 1990).

BAD ANXIETY

Sometimes anxiety gets too intense. It might be going on for far too long. Perhaps someone is getting anxious a bit too often, especially when there is no obvious need. In these sorts of circumstances anxiety is clearly a 'bad thing'. By the way, it is worth noting that terms such as 'stress', 'arousal' and 'anxiety' tend to get mixed up. That is because both physiologically and psychologically each of these terms is associated with the others, and therefore each can appear to be a symptom of the others. If you get too fired up, then 'good zip' turns to 'bad arousal'. That stresses you and causes 'bad anxiety'.

GETTING OVERWHELMED BY ANXIETY

The argument is that anxiety and/or arousal are not necessarily threats. It is how the individual deals with them that counts (see Aldwin, 2007). Just enough and you zip along nicely; too much and you are in danger of having an emotional train crash.

It is usually argued that adverse anxiety is a condition that arises when stress and anxiety start to overwhelm people's capacity to cope. It interferes with their ability to manage both life's demands on them and their own demands on themselves (see Viner's 1999 review of Selye's original 1935 theory). If the pressure gets too much to bear, then people lose the ability to get by. They can no longer manage their lives and find themselves getting over-whelmed. It is rather like the idea of a stressed acrobat balancing on an emotional 'pressure tightrope' – see Figure 5.1. Put simply, when demands outstrip their resources, people lose their balance (their psychological

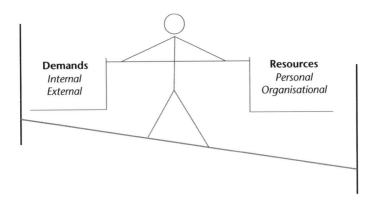

Demands

Internal	Messages we tell ourselves (I'm always OK, etc.); expectations we place upon ourselves (I must succeed, etc.)
External	The responses/requirements that other people and life's events impose on us

Resources

Personal	Coping strategies, physical health, emotional strength, etc.
Organisational	Support systems, relationships, social networks, helpers, carers, etc.

Figure 5.1: The balancing act of psychological equilibrium

equilibrium). They fall off the tightrope. If this happens often enough, or for long enough, then the victims might become anxious in the clinical sense of the word.

WHAT HAPPENS WHEN 'GOOD' BECOMES 'BAD'

Another way of understanding the benefits (and the damage) that excessive anxiety can bring is to have a look at updated versions of the arousal/anxiety versus performance curve. Modern versions of this curve are based on the original law proposed by Yerkes and Dodson (1908). Briefly, the Yerkes-Dodson law states that performance increases with arousal (or with arousal expressed as anxiety). That is good for the individual – beneficial even – until a cut-off point is reached. At that point, the arousal (or the anxiety) is so intense that it starts to overwhelm the person, and performance starts to drop off. The good anxiety has become bad anxiety. If the pressure gets too much, then eventually the victim will break down emotionally and fail psychologically. Burn-out threatens. Figure 5.2 will give you an idea about how this works.

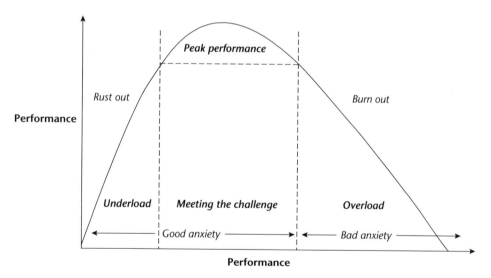

Figure 5.2: Arousal/anxiety versus performance curve

WHAT IS BAD ANXIETY?

Emotionally, anxiety feels a bit like worry or fear. Physically it feels uncomfortable in all sorts of ways. According to the Royal College of Psychiatrists (*Anxieties and phobias*, RCPsych, 2010b), the symptoms of anxiety, as a clinical condition or as a mental disorder, can be observed in either the mind or in the body, or both; some of them are listed in Table 5.1.

In the mind	In the body
Feeling generally worried	Palpitations – fast/irregular heartbeat
Feeling tired	Sweating
Losing concentration	Pallor
Irritability	Dry mouth
Disturbed sleep	Trembling
Feeling in a low mood	Numbness/tingling at extremities
	Tense/painful muscles
	Over-breathing/breathing fast
	Feeling dizzy
	Indigestion
	Frequent need for the toilet
	Feeling sick/stomach pain

Table 5.1: Symptoms of anxiety

It is very important to note that any of the symptoms listed in Table 5.1 can be caused by certain physical illnesses (thyroid problems, diabetes, etc.). As always, *if in doubt, get it checked out.* On the other hand, already anxious clients can sometimes mistakenly believe that the symptoms of their disorder are actually signs of serious illness. Clearly, worrying about such a possibility will make their anxiety symptoms much worse. A vicious, downward, cycle is set up and their anxieties are aggravated.

Whatever the cause, excessive anxiety can eventually lead to people suffering from one of the diagnosable anxiety disorders.

THE ANXIETY DISORDERS

Strictly speaking, the symptoms listed in Table 5.1 do not indicate adverse levels of anxiety – at least, not at a clinical level or as a mental disorder. They are only the symptoms of a panic attack (*DSM IV*, p395). There is nothing wrong or unusual about having a panic attack. We all have them. Sometimes we have them with good reason and sometimes without. For most of us, and on most occasions, the panic passes and life returns to normal.

Sometimes, however, these sorts of symptoms become all-pervasive and chronic. At this level, anxiety is starting to disrupt normal life. This is when one of the clinically significant types of anxiety, the 'bad' versions, might be developing. As you might expect, there are a number of differing anxiety disorders. You can find out more about them from the Anxiety Disorders Association of America's website (www.adaa.org). We will also get to a more technical way of diagnosing the anxiety disorders later in this chapter.

Just for now, however, we will note that the various sorts of clinically significant anxiety that counsellors and psychotherapists are likely to come across include the following types.

Panic disorder

When someone has frequent panic attacks and there are no obvious rational explanations, then that person may be suffering from a panic disorder.

Agoraphobia

When the panic is associated with a fear that escape might be impossible (from crowded places, public transport, queues, escalators, etc.), then the sufferer may be agoraphobic. Because such patients often also fear being unable to access urgent help when needed, they are often afraid of being alone outside their homes. That is why agoraphobia is sometimes misunderstood as simply being a fear of open spaces. Agoraphobia is usually diagnosed if the person deliberately shuns such 'trapping' situations, even if doing so is personally detrimental. For example, this might mean that the sufferer might try and avoid going out shopping or misses out on an enjoyable social occasion for fear of travelling there.

Generalised anxiety disorder (GAD)

People with GAD usually over-worry in an excessive and unwarranted manner about all sorts of anticipated disasters and about everyday problems, too. They usually realise that their worrying has got out of control and is probably unrealistic. GAD sufferers also often experience the physical symptoms associated with panic attacks. Although GAD can start off as a minor inconvenience, at more serious levels it can wreck a person's lifestyle and make carrying out the most mundane of tasks more or less impossible.

Obsessive-compulsive disorder (OCD)

The *obsessions* can include any form of intrusive thinking that disrupts someone's life. Such thoughts might include excessive worrying about hygiene, excessive concern for order and neatness, a fear that one's unstoppable bad thoughts might hurt someone else, and many other personally overwhelming thought patterns (cognitions). The sufferer is usually fully aware of the irrationality of this type of maladaptive thinking but is unable to stop.

The *compulsions* can include almost any endlessly repeated activity. Again the key is that sufferers are aware of the irrationality of this kind of behaviour but they just cannot stop themselves. Even when the endlessly repeated behaviour is damaging – for example, excessive hand washing that is causing sores and lesions – the victim still cannot stop. These maladaptive behaviours include such actions such as repeatedly cleaning things, repeatedly checking that doors are locked or that the gas/electricity is turned off, and so on. These compulsions might involve saying/thinking certain mantras, repeating certain rituals to 'keep the gremlins away', and many other similarly repetitive actions.

Again, although victims are aware that such excessive thinking and behaving (obsessions and compulsions) is damaging, they cannot help themselves. They cannot act any differently. This remains the case even when their OCD is severely disrupting normal life.

Social anxiety disorder

When panic attacks frequently occur during social interactions, formal or informal, then the sufferer might be experiencing social anxiety disorder. Examples include a dread of speaking at gatherings, being afraid of meeting new people or of asking questions in a classroom. The underlying fear seems to be something to do with a fear of drawing attention to yourself in a social setting. If you have to do so, you risk being adversely judged by other people.

Specific phobias

These are the irrational fears of particular events, situations and objects. In some circumstances they can cause panic attacks that are so disturbing that normal life is severely disrupted. These fears are specific to a particular stimulus. Clearly their impact varies according to the sufferer's circumstances. For example, zoo keepers who develop a fear of animals or aircrew who develop a fear of flying have got serious problems. Someone with a mild fear of lifts can probably cope by always using the stairs. A person with a fear of open water but who lives in the desert probably has little to worry about.

The list of supposedly specific phobias is literally endless; more are being named every day. Anyone can be afraid of absolutely anything, real or fantasy. All you need to be a 'phobia hound' is a good English/Greek dictionary and lots of imagination. You will find an extensive list of phobias – and one that is regularly updated – at http://phobialist.com/.

Post-traumatic stress disorder (PTSD)

People who have experienced a very traumatic situation, one in which they genuinely feared death or serious harm, either for themselves or for someone else, might develop PTSD. This disorder is characterised by the sufferers being unable to stop themselves from having seriously intrusive and disruptive thoughts, feelings, and flashbacks about the traumatic event. They usually experience panic symptoms when reminded of the critical event in any way. Very often PTSD suffers go to great lengths to avoid such reminders. These sorts of symptoms can totally interrupt normal life and normal relationships. PTSD can last for many years after the original precipitating event.

REFLECTION POINT

- Do you ever throw spilt salt over your shoulder to prevent 'bad luck'? Do you refuse to walk under a ladder or try to avoid walking on the cracks in the pavement? How do you feel about black cats or spotting two magpies? Got any similar little foibles? What are they? OCD, harmless quirk, or what? What about Friday the 13th or Hallowe'en – scary and dangerous or just a bit of fun?

COMMENT

Anxious thoughts and behaviours are part of everyday life. We all have our individual little rituals and our own 'funny little ways'. Sometimes anxiety is easily explainable – examination fear, first night nerves, and so on. Other times its causes are far from clear – fear of fear, etc. However, sometimes anxiety, explicable or not, passes beyond the 'collywobbles' and becomes debilitating. Indeed, it can be so disruptive as to totally destroy the sufferer's life. People with minor anxieties can usually 'snap out of it' or ignore them; people with major anxieties only wish that they could too. This is the point where anxiety becomes a mental disorder and needs to be treated in some way.

A COGNITIVE-BEHAVIOURAL THEORY OF ANXIETY

The cognitive-behavioural (thinking-doing) explanation of people's personalities and their psychological problems simply connects ideas about how people think (Kelly, 1955; Ellis, 1962) with ideas about the ways that they behave (Skinner, 1953; Bandura, 1977). It also connects people's thinking and behaving with the ways that they feel emotionally (Beck et al., 1985). So, put simply, when thinking 'goes wrong' then behaviour 'goes wrong', and emotions 'go wrong', too. One of these 'wrong' emotions is anxiety. The basic principle is that thoughts, behaviours and emotions all interact with each other (see the review in Claringbull, 2010, pp65–85). These interactions also affect our bodies. When our bodies 'go wrong' too, we experience the physical symptoms of anxiety.

This is what happens: when our thinking identifies a threat, we refer to our heightened levels of response as indicating a state of anxiety. As we noted above, anxiety is usually seen as having cognitive, physical, emotional and behavioural components (Seligman, Walker and Rosenhan, 2001). They say it works like this:

> *Thinking identifies a danger. This causes the body/mind to get ready to act rapidly or urgently (flight or fight). Increases in heart rate, blood pressure, sweating and similar physiological 'tune-ups' are all activated. Emotionally, a feeling of fear is triggered and all sorts of automatic avoidance/defensive behaviours (flinching, withdrawing, attacking, etc.) are set in motion.*

There is nothing wrong with this sort of anxiety – nothing 'crazy' about it. After all, fleeing, deflecting or resisting real danger is an essential survival mechanism. It is only when these reactions become maladaptive that anxiety becomes of clinical importance. Anxiety becomes harmful when our routine responses get 'stuck in a groove' and are triggered inappropriately. We might sees threats when there are none and become worried unnecessarily. Equally we might act physically and wind ourselves up when there is no need. These phantom triggers and threats might be false psychological demands or they might be incorrect perceptions of personal danger.

Let us take an example. Perhaps a mistaken idea that everything must be perfect at all times might compel us to put endless effort into achieving the impossible. Our inevitable failures might well make us feel very worried about failing again. In another example, someone might experience an increased heart rate, possibly due to working too hard on a hot day. This could be misinterpreted and cause the person to fear an imminent heart attack. Obviously all these sorts of false alarms can make any of us feel extremely anxious. It can therefore be argued that anxiety is an interlinked psychological and physiological condition that shows itself in someone's ways of behaving and thinking – see Figure 5.3.

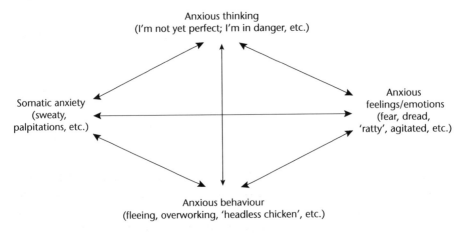

Figure 5.3: Anxious thoughts and behaviours

TRAIT OR STATE?

Cognitive-behavioural theorists argue that anxiety (as an adverse clinical condition) arises when people's worries get out of hand. It might be that if some people are overly anxious, it is because they were made that way. Is anxiety actually an inborn emotional *trait*? In fact, those who support the trait theories of personality usually view inherent anxiety as one of the important human dimensions. This is not a new idea (see the review by Digman, 1990). After all, most of us probably know someone who we would describe as 'always having been a bit nervy'.

On the other hand, perhaps some people have a tendency to get anxious because life's events have pushed them that way. Perhaps anxiety is an emotional *state*. This is the view of many theorists who usually suggest that anxiety is fuelled by incorrect thinking or unfortunate experiences (Eysenck, 1992; Beck, 1995; Veale, 2008; and many others).

A PSYCHODYNAMIC THEORY OF ANXIETY

For the Freudians, anxiety is the result of internal psychological conflicts. They claim it arises when the rational part of the mind cannot balance the demands of the primitive or primal mind with the needs of the conscience. Therefore, from a psychodynamic point of view anxiety is a result of struggles involving the Id, the Ego and the Superego (see review by LaPlanche and Pontalis, 1988). The Id yells 'gimme NOW', the Superego retorts 'rules are rules', and the Ego tries to intervene – 'let's be sensible about this'.

Anxiety is emotionally uncomfortable and therefore best avoided. The psychological mechanisms that help us to fight off anxiety are called the defence mechanisms (denial, repression, displacement, intellectualisation, symptom conversion, etc.). Freud (1926, reissued 1990) proposed that there are three kinds of anxiety. Each causes psychological conflict and therefore each is of interest to the psychoanalyst. These are:

- neurotic anxiety – the unconscious worry that we will disobey 'the rules' and so incur punishment;
- reality anxiety – a fear of real, or supposedly real, events;
- moral anxiety – a fear of contravening one's own moral integrity.

In Freudian terms, the symptoms of anxiety reflect these internal conflicts and the psychological defence mechanisms that are used to suppress them. The alleged purpose of psychodynamic therapy for anxiety is to help the patient resolve such inner conflicts by bringing them into the patient's everyday awareness (Luborsky, 2001).

ANXIETY SENSITIVITY

It might be that some people are more predisposed to anxiety than others. This is why Reiss and McNally (1985) suggested that some of us are either born with, or have acquired, 'anxiety sensitivity'. This is the fear of the physical sensations of anxiety such as palpitations, sweating, and so on – a sort of 'fear of feeling afraid'. Such people appear to have an ingrained belief that these sensations will inevitably have overwhelming physical, social or psychological consequences (see the review in Taylor, 1999). In other words, people who are anxiety sensitive are liable to catastrophically misinterpret what is happening to them (McNally, 1999). Put simply, anxiety sensitivity makes people much more likely to become anxious at inappropriate times or when there is no genuine need (Zahradnik et al., 2009) – 'I've got a pain in my toe; it must be foot cancer; I'm going to die.'

TREATMENT PRINCIPLES FOR ANXIETY

Many theorists (Beck et al., 1985; Eysenck, 1992; Butler, Fennell and Hackman, 2008) argue that anxiety exists along two, intimately connected, dimensions. These are:

- a *cognitive dimension* – worrying thoughts and adverse thinking patterns ('I'm about to fail'; 'I know it'll go wrong'; 'nothing good ever happens for me');
- a *somatic dimension* – worrying physical symptoms such as becoming aware of increases in breathing rates or muscle tension; there are also other physical symptoms that are unlikely to be immediately noticed, such as variations in the body's biochemistry.

These two dimensions of the anxiety disorders are usually the targets (either individually or in combination) of most of the currently popular approaches to anxiety disorder management (see review by Sims and Snaith, 1998). We shall now take a look at some examples of the more commonly practised medical and psychological treatment methods.

TREATMENT METHODS FOR ANXIETY

Medical treatment

The National Institute for Health and Clinical Excellence *Guideline 22* (NICE, 2007) strongly recommends practitioner-guided patient self-help as a first step in the treatment of anxiety. It then goes on to suggest that in the more severe cases, a limited use of one of the benzodiazepines such as diazepam (Valium) or oxazepam (Serenid). These drugs will usually calm the mind, if only temporarily, but due to their presumed addictive nature, NICE recommends that they should not be used for more than two or three weeks. However, not everybody agrees that the benzodiazepines are really quite so addictive (see Healy, 2009).

When a longer-term use of mind-calming medication seems necessary, then one of the antidepressants that also have sedative properties might be useful (NICE, 2007). These include some of the Prozac class of drugs (SSRIs such as citalopram), the venlafaxine class (SNRIs such as Zispin), the tricyclic drugs (dothiepin, etc.) or the serotonin enhancers (buspirone, etc.). These drugs are all further discussed in Chapter 8.

In cases where calming the somatic effects of anxiety is the more urgent need, then body-calming drugs such as the beta-blockers (propranolol, etc.) are believed to sometimes relieve shaking and palpitations.

One thing that many medical practitioners are in agreement about is that the pills will usually only relieve the effects of anxiety. Dealing with its causes is quite another matter. That is why the National Institute for Health and Clinical Excellence (NICE, 2007) and the Royal College of Psychiatrists (RCPsych, 2010b) firmly support both self-help and the psychotherapies as important ways of teaching patients how to deal with their anxiety disorders for themselves.

Self-help
Self-help does not mean leaving clients to their own devices. They will need information about their condition and some guidance towards ways of helping themselves. These include:

- understanding that anxiety is a normal part of life – if a client has a particular problem that is a major source of worry (a difficulty at work, for example), then resolving that problem (talking to the boss, consulting the union, etc.) might be the best way forward – anti-anxiety medications are unlikely to help;
- joining a self-help group – it can be a great relief for anxious clients to find that they are not alone and to get the support of other people with similar problems;
- exercise – 'a healthy mind in a healthy body' is not just a slogan; it's a fact; physical exercise diverts the worrisome thinking, releases 'feel good' dopamine into the brain and generally makes people feel better about themselves;
- talking over problems with friends or family – it is a powerful form of emotional release and personal support; chatting your problems away is much healthier than shutting your problems away;
- reading self-help books – this is what psychotherapists call 'bibliotherapy', which means that reading helps clients if they can find out for themselves about how to 'wind down';

- computerised CBT – there are some excellent self-therapy websites on the internet; clients who are able to make use of them often report beneficial effects.

Cognitive-behavioural therapy (CBT)

There is a reason why so much emphasis has been given in this chapter to the cognitive-behavioural understanding of anxiety. It is because in the NHS, and increasingly elsewhere too, CBT is very much the favoured treatment for anxiety. It is simple, often effective, and certainly fast. Learning how to apply CBT is easy – in other words, it is cheap to provide (see review in Claringbull, 2010). That does not mean that CBT is always the best treatment or that it is always guaranteed to work. However, the reality is that government policy is very likely to ensure that CBT becomes increasingly the psychological 'flavour of the month' (Department of Health, 2001a and 2001b). Whatever your own view of CBT might be, one thing is certain – it is here to stay.

The basic, upfront aims of CBT are simple. As we know, anxiety has both a physical and a psychological dimension. CBT can be targeted at either or both of these aspects (Grant et al., 2008). Just to emphasise the obvious, CBT targets maladaptive *cognitive* processes and it is also aimed at unhelpful *behavioural* processes.

The cognitive bit
Anxious people can get into distorted, even harmful, thought patterns (cognitions). They might have ingrained, almost automatic but essentially incorrect and unhelpful thinking processes. CBT seeks to challenge these 'negative automatic thoughts' or 'NATs' (see Willson and Branch, 2006). An important concept in CBT is that a person's own particular ways of thinking come between an activating event and a person's reaction to that event (Ellis, 2001; Dryden, 2005). For example, if I see someone laughing I might automatically think 'he's sneering at me' – I might get angry. Change that intervening thought to 'he's laughing at my joke' and I will probably laugh too. There are many other useful cognitive therapeutic techniques available (see reviews by Leahy, 2003; Westbrook, Kennerly and Kirk, 2007; and many others).

The behavioural bit
Unhelpful or maladaptive behaviours might originate from either incorrect internal responses or self-disruptive actions and activities. For example, you might find yourself starting to over-breathe (hyperventilate) or feeling an urgent need to go to the lavatory whenever you have to go to a production meeting at work. In order to avoid those sorts of unpleasant feelings, you might start to avoid such get-togethers. This could put your job in

jeopardy. A common CBT technique used in these sorts of cases is called 'desensitisation'. The sufferers are taught to quell their inner turmoil by using one of the many mind/body relaxation techniques. Another approach involves encouraging sufferers to face their fears by gradual exposure to their 'panic triggers' and so slowly learn that they need not be so terrifying after all.

Grant et al. (2008), Wills (2008) and many other practitioner-authors will provide you with lots of much more detailed information on the many ways to use CBT with clients. Case Study 5.1 will give you an idea about how all this can sometimes work.

Case study 5.1   How Rita relaxed her way out of her fears

Rita was a busy architect. Her latest project involved attending progress meetings with the clients whenever they felt it necessary. The problem was that going to these meetings was making Rita more and more anxious. Rita did not know why this was happening, but she was scared that one day she would embarrass herself by having to run out in the middle of a meeting – a professional disaster.

Rita consulted Kirstie, a CBT-trained psychotherapist. After hearing all about Rita's problem, Kirstie explained to Rita that her anxiety was hitting her from two directions. First, there was the sense of dread and fear that was flooding her mind. Second, and at the same time, her body was being automatically revved up as her pulse rate climbed, her blood pressure rose, sweating started and so on. Kirstie's plan was to show Rita how to calm her body and then how to let that calming effect spread into her mind.

Kirstie knew that Rita's anxiety was unlikely to hit her suddenly, just out of the blue. There was almost certainly a build-up, one step at a time, over the days and hours preceding the meeting. Kirstie planned to use a technique known as 'hierarchical desensitisation' to deal with Rita's problem. Kirstie got Rita to tell her how her anxiety grew at various stages from when she first learned that a meeting had been called to when it actually took place. Rita was asked to rate the level of anxiety that she felt at each stage on a 1 to 10 scale (10 = 'disaster'). Together, Rita and Kirstie were able to build a sort of 'anxiety staircase'. Rita's anxiety build-up can be seen in Figure 5.4.

Kirstie next taught Rita how to progressively relax her whole body, one group of muscles at a time. Rita found that each time she did this her whole being, mind and body, became calmer and calmer.

Rita practised her relaxing for a week or so. Then, as they sat together in the therapy room, Kirstie asked Rita to relax herself right down. She then got Rita to imagine the scenarios listed in Figure 5.4, starting with the bottom step (the five days before the meeting stage). Kirstie asked Rita to rate her real-life anxiety level, there and then in the counselling room, while she was still imagining stage 1. 'It's

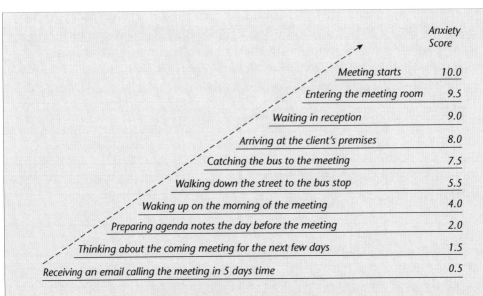

	Anxiety Score
Meeting starts	10.0
Entering the meeting room	9.5
Waiting in reception	9.0
Arriving at the client's premises	8.0
Catching the bus to the meeting	7.5
Walking down the street to the bus stop	5.5
Waking up on the morning of the meeting	4.0
Preparing agenda notes the day before the meeting	2.0
Thinking about the coming meeting for the next few days	1.5
Receiving an email calling the meeting in 5 days time	0.5

Figure 5.4: Rita's anxiety staircase

about a half; maybe a 1,' Rita replied. 'OK,' said Kirstie. 'Now breathe in, hold it, feel the tension, breathe the tension out and relax.' Rita did so. 'How's your anxiety now?' asked Kirstie. 'Better,' said Rita. Over the next two sessions they worked their way up the anxiety staircase until Rita could more calmly imagine stage 10, and, although not fully relaxed, she certainly felt able to cope.

Kirstie then asked Rita if she now felt able to do all this in reality. 'Yes, I do,' replied Rita, 'and I've just found out that a meeting has been called for next week.' 'Great – give it a go,' said Kirstie. Rita practised her relaxing every day, right up to the meeting. On the actual day, much to her surprise and certainly to her delight, Rita found herself managing very well. She found herself getting better and better, ever more competent, at subsequent meetings. Rita's career is back on track.

Psychotherapy and counselling

Some counsellors and psychotherapists might wonder what part their own particular chosen styles of therapeutic practice can play in the treatment of anxiety. Might the person-centred, psychodynamic, gestalt, existential and similar therapies be of any help? It is possible that any of them might have an eventual role in helping clients to discover any root developmental or intra-personal causes relating to their anxiety conditions (Claringbull, 2010). Wampold (2001) provides some useful information about the general relative effectiveness of the various talking therapies that is a helpful contribution to this discussion. What he actually says is that they are all usually about as effective as each other. Therefore it does not really matter which approach is chosen. However, before any longer-term therapy is ever thought about, it remains the case that both the Royal College of Psychiatrists and the American Psychiatric Association are firm in the belief that attending to the clients' current fears is the first priority.

There are, of course, many who would argue against focusing on the 'immediate-use', solution-focused therapies. They would probably claim that the symptom reduction/management therapies (CBT, psychopharmacology, self-help, and so on) might only serve to mask the real problem. In other words, truly effective treatment needs to be an in-depth, individually created process. If this is not done, so their argument goes, then the original anxiety condition will simply reappear at a later time. Whether or not this argument is sound will doubtlessly remain one of psychotherapy's perennial debates.

In any event, there are some more important questions to be asked when considering using any of the non-CBT talking therapies with an anxious client. These are the 'how to' and 'when to' issues. We must avoid making our clients worse. For example, the insistence of Rogerian therapists that clients can be best helped by trying to anchor their feelings in the 'here and now' might actually be harmful to a PTSD client whose overwhelming terrors are still being experienced in the present. This is because such an intervention risks retraumatising an already severely damaged client. As ever, the therapeutic needs of the anxious client must be carefully assessed before any type of treatment is started.

ACTIVITY 5.1

- Possibly you have already got your own view on what your preferred treatment for anxiety would be. Even if you are not currently practising as a counsellor or a therapist, you probably feel instinctively drawn to one or other of the many therapeutic/treatment approaches. Make your choice.
- Next make a list of all the reasons why your preferred style of anxiety 'cure' might not work. How might it harm your client? How might it make your client worse? Might it have no effect either way?
- Now think of someone, or even a small group of people, who might share your therapeutic preferences. Write down a list of reasons why they ought to consider revising their ideas. What would make them change their minds? Play the 'devil's advocate'.

COMMENT

It is difficult to find any modern evidence-backed authority that supports any psychological treatment for anxiety that is not based on CBT principles, or at least on cognitive theory. For some clients it is only when CBT has allayed their anxieties that any deeper problems might start to come to the surface. It is therefore arguable that it is in the patients' best interests that CBT should be provided only by comprehensively trained counsellors and psychotherapists, by practitioners who are professionally equipped to work across the full range of client need, as it emerges.

Technical assessment of anxiety

If you are interested in carrying out a technical assessment of anxiety, then the diagnostic rules listed on the following pages will show you how it works using *DSM IV*. The following lists are summaries and extracts – consult *DSM IV* for full and precise details.

Panic attacks and agoraphobia (DSM IV, pp395–97)
Neither of these two conditions is a diagnosable psychiatric disorder on its own. However, before an anxiety disorder can be diagnosed, one or both of these two conditions must be present.

1 Panic attack (*DSM IV*, p395): four or more of the following symptoms are required for a diagnosis:
   - palpitations, tachycardia etc.;
   - sweating;
   - trembling or shaking;
   - feeling of choking;
   - chest pain/discomfort;
   - nausea or abdominal distress;
   - feeling dizzy/lightheaded/faint;
   - fear of dying;
   - feelings of unreality/detachment;
   - fear of losing control/going crazy;
   - chills/hot flushes;
   - numbness of tingling feelings;
   - sensation of breath shortage or smothering.
2 Agoraphobia (*DSM IV*, pp396–97): the following must be present:
   - anxiety about being in places from which escape might be difficult or embarrassing or in which help might not be available;
   - avoidance of such restrictive situations or endurance of them with marked distress levels.

If, as well as suffering from panic attacks or from agoraphobia, certain additional criteria are also present, then an anxiety disorder may be diagnosed. The anxiety disorders are:

Panic disorder without agoraphobia (DSM IV, p402)
- Recurrent panic attacks with persistent fear of future attacks; worry about the implications of an attack or its consequences, (losing control, going 'crazy', etc.); evidence of resultant significant behaviour changes.

Agoraphobia without panic disorder (DSM IV, pp403–04)
- As above, replacing 'panic attack' with 'agoraphobia'.

Panic disorder with agoraphobia (DSM IV, pp402–03)
- As above, including both panic attack and agoraphobia.

Specific phobia (DSM IV, pp410–11)
- There is marked or persistent fear that is excessive or unreasonable.
- Exposure to the phobic stimulus provokes an immediate anxiety response.
- The person recognises that the fear is excessive or unreasonable.
- The phobic situation is avoided or endured with intense anxiety or distress.
- The avoidance, anxious anticipation, or distress in the feared situation(s) interferes significantly with normal routine etc.

Social phobia or social anxiety disorder (DSM IV, pp416–17)
- As with specific phobia, except that it refers to a fear of social or performance situations in which the person is exposed to unfamiliar people or to possible scrutiny by others.

Obsessive-compulsive disorder (DSM IV, pp422–23)
- The victim suffers from either obsessions or compulsions.
- Obsessions:
  - recurrent or persistent thoughts, impulses or images that are experienced at some time during the disturbance as intrusive and inappropriate and that cause marked anxiety or distress;
  - thoughts, impulses and images that are not simply excessive worries about real-life problems;
  - attempts by the person to suppress or ignore such thoughts;
  - recognition by the person that the obsessional thoughts are self-generated.
- Compulsions:
  - repetitive behaviours that the person feels driven to perform in response to an obsession or to rules that must be applied rigidly;
  - behaviours aimed at preventing or reducing distress and/or at preventing some dreadful event or situation; these behaviours are not realistic.
- The person recognises that the obsession or the compulsion is excessive or unreasonable.
- Marked distress is caused that significantly interferes with normal routine.

continued overleaf

Post-traumatic stress disorder (DSM IV, *pp427–29*)
- The victim was exposed to a traumatic event that threatened or was believed to threaten death or serious injury to self or others. The reality does not matter – it is what the victim believed at the time that counts.
- The traumatic event is persistently re-experienced mentally – intrusive thoughts, flashbacks, dreams, etc.
- The victim persistently avoids stimuli or reminders associated with the event.
- There are symptoms of persistent arousal.
- The disturbance has lasted for at least four weeks – and may not occur until long after the triggering event.
- The disturbance causes clinically significant distress or impairment in social, occupational, or other important areas of functioning.

Acute stress disorder (DSM IV, *pp431–32*)
- The victim was exposed to a traumatic event that threatened or was believed to threaten death or serious injury to self or others, plus most of the above PTSD symptoms but to a lesser degree.
- The symptoms last less than four weeks.

Generalised anxiety disorder (DSM IV, *pp435–36*)
- Excessive anxiety and worry.
- Difficulty in controlling the worry.
- Three or more of the following:
  - restlessness/feeling keyed up/on edge;
  - easily fatigued;
  - muscle tension;
  - difficulty in concentrating;
  - irritability;
  - sleep disturbance.

Anxiety disorder due to a medical condition (DSM IV, *p439*)
- Evidence in the victim's medical history – a matter for a doctor.

Substance-induced anxiety disorder (DSM IV, *pp443–44*)
- Evidence of legal or illegal maladaptive substance use, including prescribed drugs – another matter for a doctor to begin with and possibly a task for a counsellor or a psychotherapist in due course.

Remember – you have always got the 'Not Otherwise Specified' option to fall back on.

PSYCHOLOGICAL TESTS FOR ANXIETY

Here is a selection. You can find the following (and plenty more) on the internet – some are free and some have to be paid for.

- Beck Anxiety Inventory is a self-administered 21-item scale that measures the intensity of the patient's feelings in respect of the common symptoms of anxiety. Using this inventory requires a licence.
- Anxiety Sensitivity Index is a 16-item questionnaire that was devised by Stephen Reiss as a measuring tool for research into his core idea that some people are more sensitive to depression than others. Using this Index also requires a licence.
- Hamilton Anxiety Rating Scale (HAM-A) is a therapist-administered, 14-item rating scale that measures the severity of a person's anxiety symptoms.

CHAPTER SUMMARY

Anxiety appears in many guises in modern society. Is it a social 'sickness' caused by the age we live in? Is it a learned or acquired condition that results from social and personal pressures? Is it truly a stand-alone mental disorder or is it one of our modern 'manufactured complaints' that helps the drug companies to sell their pills?

We do know that anxiety as such is not an abnormality. Anxiety can be a useful 'spur to excellence' in some situations. We also know that some people's lives are severely disrupted by anxiety and that their very existence can become an ordeal. At the end of the day, when counsellors and psychotherapists are faced with clients presenting with clinical levels of anxiety, much of this debate becomes irrelevant. The clients need help; therapists are there to provide it. So, too, are the doctors.

The good news for talking therapists is that there are some readily available, simple to learn therapies that can be offered to clients – treatments that will at least bring symptom relief. There are other, longer-term therapeutic approaches available if necessary. As with so much in today's therapeutic world, it may be that practitioners need to come out of their single model comfort zones and be receptive to new therapeutic ideas in order to best help their clients. Perhaps all that counsellors and psychotherapists really need to do is to make their anxious clients feel better right away? Is that enough? Is it really that easy?

SUGGESTED FURTHER READING

Beck, A, Emerey, G and Greenberg, R (1985) *Anxiety disorders and phobias: a cognitive perspective* – republished 2005. New York: Basic Books.

A 'golden oldie' – a bit dated but well worth a read.

National Institute for Health and Clinical Excellence (2007) *Guideline 22, Anxiety* – amended April 2007, www.nice.org.uk – then type in 'anxiety'.

Read this guideline and find out what GPs do about anxiety.

Tone, A (2008) *The age of anxiety: a history of America's turbulent affair with tranquillisers.* New York: Basic Books.

This is a fascinating history of anxiety together with a comprehensive account of anxiety as a modern phenomenon. Chapter 9 provides a useful critique of the modern medical treatments for anxiety.

Willson, R and Branch, R (2006) *Cognitive behavioural therapy for dummies.* Chichester: Wiley.

An excellent introduction to CBT – Chapter 9 provides some excellent advice on suitable treatments for anxious clients.

CHAPTER 6

Understanding schizophrenia

> **CORE KNOWLEDGE**
>
> - Schizophrenia is a mental disorder that causes its victims to become psycho-logically and functionally disconnected both within themselves and from the world around them. It does *not* mean that its sufferers have split personalities.
> - Schizophrenia has *positive symptoms,* so called because they cause thoughts and behaviours to happen. These include delusions, hallucinations, distorted thinking, disorganised speech and disorganised behaviour. It also has *negative symptoms,* so called because they halt or flatten existing thought and behaviour.
> - In *DSM IV* there are five subtypes of schizophrenia (paranoid, disorganised, catatonic, undifferentiated, residual). *ICD 10* adds two more types (post-schizophrenic depression, simple schizophrenia).
> - The most common methods for treating schizophrenia are centred on medication. This includes the *typical* antipsychotic drugs (believed to act on the positive symptoms) and the *atypical* antipsychotic drugs (believed to act on the negative symptoms).

INTRODUCTION

Back in the nineteenth century, psychiatric pioneers such as Philippe Pinel and Emil Kraepelin thought that the mental disorder that we now know as schizophrenia was a form of premature dementia or 'dementia praecox' (Heinrichs, 2003). They believed that it was caused by irreversible early brain deterioration. However, by 1908 Eugen Bleuler had realised that some of these patients actually recovered and that therefore this form of dementia could not be the result of permanent physical brain degeneration (Porter and Berrios, 1995). Bleuler then decided that his alleged prematurely demented patients were actually experiencing mental disconnections within themselves. Their perceptions, thinking, memories and general mental functioning no longer appeared to be internally integrated. He called this condition 'schizophrenia' (schizo = split; phrenia = mind).

In Bleuler's view, the thinking patterns, feelings, actions and intentions of his schizophrenic patients no longer seemed to form a composite whole (Porter, 2003). They were disconnected from reality and from each other. These are the sorts of functional splits that Bleuler was referring to. He did *not* suggest that his patients had 'split personalities'. Actually, there is such a condition, but it is rather rare – it is one of the dissociative disorders.

Schizophrenia has had a long history of controversy. The disputes about its causes and its cures continue to this day. The anti-psychiatry movement has even argued that there is no such condition (see review by Nasser, 1995). According to the 'antis', the schizophrenia debate is at best an irrelevancy and at worst a conspiracy by 'megalomaniac psychiatrists'. Be that as it may, for the first half of the last century schizophrenia was often considered to be an inborn, and therefore incurable defect (the Freudians took a different view, of course – see below). From the 1950s onwards, opinion changed, and schizophrenia began to be thought of as being a potentially treatable mental illness. This change was very much influenced by the discovery of the antipsychotic drugs, the first of which was chlorpromazine.

Argument about schizophrenia's proper diagnosis continues, and a number of diagnostic/classification systems have been proposed. These include the First Rank Symptoms (Schneider, 1959), the St Louis Criteria (Feighner et al., 1972), the Research Criteria (Spitzer, Endicott and Robins, 1975), and many others. Nowadays, the diagnosis of schizophrenia largely depends on the criteria set out in either *DSM IV* or *ICD 10* (these criteria are further explained later in this chapter).

WHAT IS SCHIZOPHRENIA?

Schizophrenia is a mental disorder that causes destructive disturbances in thoughts, emotions and behaviours. The diagnosis of schizophrenia is a challenge for clinicians. There are no objective tests and so diagnosis is based on patient self-report plus the clinician's interpretations of the sufferer's observed behaviours. The usual characteristics of schizophrenia include:

- the *positive symptoms*, so called because they cause reactions (delusions, hallucinations, distorted thinking, disorganised speech, disorganised behaviour, etc.);
- the *negative symptoms*, so called because they flatten behaviour (cannot be bothered with anything, apathy, social withdrawal, no energy, emotionally 'flat', cannot concentrate, no motivation, etc.)
- serious social and/or occupational dysfunction (declining scores on the Global Assessment of Functioning Scale (*DSM IV*, p32), destroyed/strained relationships, job loss, diminished participation in all activities, etc.)
- long lasting (six months or more, often lifelong or persistent).

Once schizophrenia has been diagnosed, *DSM IV* further divides it into five subtypes: paranoid; disorganised; catatonic; undifferentiated; residual. *ICD 10* adds a further two subtypes: post-schizophrenic depression; simple schizophrenia. There is a more detailed explanation of all this later in this chapter.

As well as schizophrenia as such, there are some lesser forms of the psychotic mental disorders that have similar although less intense schizophrenia-like characteristics – a sort of 'schizo lite', if you prefer. These include:

- schizophreniform disorder – most of the symptoms, but for less than six months;
- schizoaffective disorder – some of the symptoms, but due to a mood disorder;
- delusional disorder – non-bizarre delusions (plausible but still fantasy);
- shared psychotic disorder – folie à deux;
- brief psychotic disorder – the symptoms last less than one month.

Generally speaking, the positive and negative symptoms of schizophrenia are more or less the same as the positive and negative symptoms of most forms of psychosis. This is clearly a major source of diagnostic confusion ('Is this patient schizophrenic or is something else wrong?'). What usually happens (put in very crude terms) is that if the psychotic symptoms cannot be explained by one of the other mental disorders (severe depression, for example) and if there is no obvious physiological cause (organic disease; drug withdrawal, etc.), then schizophrenia is normally diagnosed.

THE POSITIVE SYMPTOMS OF SCHIZOPHRENIA

The positive symptoms of schizophrenia are so named because they are all active responses to whatever it is that triggers this disorder. In this case, 'positive' does not mean 'good'; it means 'overt', 'actual' or 'accentuated'. As far as the sufferers are concerned, all their experiences are real, their thinking is logical, and their feelings and actions are justified. In other words, cause is having effect – there is a result – something is actually happening.

The positive symptoms are usually clustered into groups. The following list is not exhaustive.

Thought content disturbance

This usually occurs in the form of delusions. Very often these delusions have a strong element of paranoia. For example, sufferers may 'know' that their thoughts are being controlled or are being sucked out and alien thoughts are being substituted. Sometimes thoughts become jumbled or subject to rapid shifts. This is sometimes called 'the flight of ideas'. *DSM IV* defines delusions as being erroneous beliefs that usually involve a misinterpretation of perceptions and experiences.

Perceptual abnormalities

These include visual and sensory hallucinations (false perceptions of reality). Many sufferers hear voices. Others see what is not really there. As far as the victim is concerned the hallucination is totally realistic. Therefore the sufferer is driven to respond to these apparently 'true' events. Schizophrenic patients do not *think* that they are seeing pink elephants; they *know* that they are seeing them; for them the pink elephants are really there.

Speech abnormalities

Sometimes this occurs in the form of neologisms, whereby the victim makes up words or uses old ones in new ways. Another speech abnormality is echolalia: the sufferer endlessly repeats words and phrases that he or she has just heard. Yet another speech abnormality is known as word salad, where the sufferer uses speech in a totally disorganised and jumbled up manner generating what is apparently total nonsense. There are a number of other such abnormalities.

Mood disturbances

These are defined in terms of inappropriate or disconnected emotional responses. For example, a schizophrenia sufferer might laugh at tragic news or be apparently emotionally unresponsive when hearing joyful news.

Psychomotor disturbances

These sorts of disturbances can result in immobility at one end of the scale and frenzied activity at the other. There might be peculiarities of movement, grimacing, posturing and so on. The victim might endlessly copy someone else's activities (echopraxia) or become unthinkingly obedient to commands or suggestions. Told to jump off something or to dash forward, the schizophrenic individual might well do so immediately, irrespective of the consequences. Unchecked, the results of some of these literally thoughtless actions might well endanger the sufferer or indeed anyone else in the vicinity.

THE NEGATIVE SYMPTOMS OF SCHIZOPHRENIA

Although not strictly speaking a symptom group, negativity is seen as a frequent accompaniment to schizophrenia. Negativity does not generate new or additional thoughts, emotions or behaviours. It obstructs, eliminates or flattens what is already there. It *negates* them. Negativity causes the psychotic individual to exhibit apathy, social withdrawal, lack of motivation, a general withdrawal from self and society, and many similar 'I just can't be bothered' attitudes and responses.

Of course, schizophrenia's negative symptoms may not necessarily be caused by the patient's mental disorder. For example, it is known that the anti-psychotic drugs are extremely powerful and can produce many unpleasant side effects (Healy, 2009). Perhaps the negative symptoms are just another byproduct of this class of medication. Another possibility might be that what seems to be schizophrenia-generated apathy is simply social disaffection (anomie). As we know, society has always had a tendency to isolate the apparently insane. So, if we shut them out, perhaps they shut us out.

THE SCHIZOPHRENIC'S WORLD

As we know, schizophrenia sufferers find themselves overwhelmed by thoughts, sensations and perceptions that seem highly irrational to the outsider. The experience has been likened to being in a waking dream in which the apparently fantastic seems very real and normal. To schizophrenics there is nothing abnormal about their worlds; it is the rest of us who just do not get it. They are not 'crazy' – we are.

The nineteenth-century belief that schizophrenia is a disorder normally found in younger people has been confirmed by modern surveys. It usually appears first in young adults (Bhugra, 2005). It rarely occurs before adolescence and tends to peak in males in their late twenties and in females in their early thirties (Rethink, 2006). Overall, there appears to be no gender difference in its occurrence, but this effect may be masked by either under-reporting or different cultural/social expectations. However, one apparently consistent gender effect is that females are more likely to recover, at least enough to return to, and maintain, a relatively normal lifestyle (Grossman et al., 2006).

It seems that schizophrenia affects between 1 per cent and 1.5 per cent of the population, (Goldner et al., 2002). According to Rethink (2006) about 25 per cent of its victims recover over a five-year period and another 60–65 per cent experience recurring symptoms over most of their lives. Only some 10–15 per cent experience severe, lifelong disruptions. Regrettably, about 30–40 per cent of schizophrenia sufferers attempt suicide, and about 1 in 10 of those succeed. Young men with chronic symptoms are the most vulnerable. The important fact to note is that with good management many schizophrenic patients can enjoy extensive periods of fulfilling life interspersed with occasional periods of difficulty.

Although schizophrenia is mainly considered to affect the sufferer's cognitions, it also affects many other areas of its victims' lives. Very often they are unemployed, live in poverty and can be homeless. Their life expectancy is reduced, substance abuse is common, and they are more likely to have general health problems (Brown, Barraclough and Inskip, 2000; Palmer, Pankratz and Bostwisck, 2005). Schizophrenia sufferers are also vulnerable to the major depressive and anxiety disorders (Sim et al., 2006).

SCHIZOPHRENIA AND VIOLENCE

Many mental health advocacy organisations (e.g. Rethink, SANE) argue that the mentally ill, including the schizophrenic, are actually much more likely to suffer from violence than to cause it. This belief is supported by a number of studies that indicate that when stable, the mentally disordered are no more likely to become violent than anybody else (Rueve and Welton, 2008).

It has been argued that the link between schizophrenia and criminality generally (including violence) is at best an indirect one (Schanda, 2006). For example, Fazel et al. (2009) carried out a meta-study into the risk that any particular grouping of individuals, schizophrenic or not, is likely to become violent. They found that both schizophrenic and non-schizophrenic groups were equally likely to become more violent than average if the group members were also substance abusers. Apparently the potential for violence is enhanced by the substance abuse and not by the psychotic disorder.

On the other hand, some studies have found a link between the schizophrenic disorders and increases in violent behaviour (Kooyman, Harvey and Walsh, 2007). The reported increases in actual risk are usually quite small (Walsh, Buchanan and Fahy, 2002) and usually do not exceed that found in the general population by more than 10 per cent (Taylor, 2008).

In sum, the overall trend of the evidence is that, generally speaking, the public's excessive fear of schizophrenia sufferers does not seem to be justified. However, none of this means that seriously aggressive or threatening psychotic people do not pose a risk. This is especially so if their illnesses have entered a severe phase (Schanda, 2006). Sadly, a number of well-publicised criminal trials tell us that a small minority of such acute schizophrenia sufferers might become extremely dangerous indeed.

THE PSYCHOSIS ISSUE

All the major classification systems (for example, Schneider, 1959; Feighner et al., 1972; *DSM IV*, 1994a) claim that psychotic hallucinations and delusions are essential symptoms in the diagnosis of schizophrenia. In the view of many theorists, the rule is 'no psychosis – no schizophrenia'. It is as simple as that. Of course, psychosis is also an important factor in a number of other mental disorders. It is therefore clearly important that counsellors and psychotherapists should know something about psychosis and its disconnections from reality.

Some authorities claim that any psychiatric condition that includes psychosis among its symptoms is one of the 'major mental disorders' (schizophrenia, bipolar disorder, severe depression, etc.). The clear implication is that if there are major mental disorders, then there must also be lesser psychological disturbances. Some theorists refer to these as being the neuroses or the 'minor mental disorders' (anxiety, mild depression, phobias, etc.). Whether or not there really is a clear distinction between the neurotic and the psychotic conditions is still a matter of debate (see Cutler and Marcus, 2010 for a review). Nevertheless, psychosis is often portrayed as being at one end of a disturbance continuum that has neurosis at its other end.

Neurosis

Neurosis is difficult to define. It was originally a term first used in 1769 by William Cullen to describe a general affliction of the nervous system. This term later became more popularly used by psychodynamic theorists to describe inner psychological conflicts (see the review by Kahn, 2002). The key to understanding neurosis is to appreciate that although neurosis might well impair normal daily activities, unlike psychosis it does not completely obstruct them. Indeed, some diagnosticians refer to the neurotic population as being part of the semi-functioning 'worried well' (see Pontius, 2002; Smith, 2002; and many others). However, no generally agreed, comprehensive, definition of neurosis seems to have been achieved (Oyebode, 2008). Today, the major classification systems such as *DSM IV* or *ICD 10* no longer recognise neurosis as a diagnosable mental disorder. It seems that the term 'neurosis' has fallen out of fashion. Nowadays it is rarely used, except when psychologists bicker about personality theory – and that is a very different story (reviewed in Claringbull, 2010).

Psychosis

Psychosis, on the other hand, is usually thought of as being a condition that affects a person's ability to connect with reality. In general, psychosis is considered to be a mental state in which the boundary between the real and the unreal has broken down. In other words, the psychotic client is delusional. Such patients 'hear' voices directing them to act in certain ways; they can 'feel' rays coming through the wall that warp their brains. They 'know' that the government is monitoring everything that they say or do, and so on. Unlike neurosis, psychosis does significantly interfere with normal daily activity. It can do much more than just interfere; it can totally disrupt or obstruct normal life, not just for sufferers but for everybody else around them too. However, psychosis is only a syndrome. It is an important factor in some of the mental disorders, but it is not a disorder in itself.

The causes of psychosis are far from being fully explained (see Bentall, 2004). It seems that psychosis can have both biological and psychological origins. Biologically, psychosis can result from brain tumours, biochemical imbalances, disease, substance misuse and many other causes. The sufferer is not insane – just temporarily deranged. If the biological cause can be successfully treated, then the psychosis usually goes away. The psychological explanations of psychosis are not so clear-cut.

Clearly psychosis is an integral part of certain mental disorders (schizophrenia, bipolar disorder, delusional disorder, and so on). This sort of explanation starts to get rather circular – certain mental disorders cause psychosis, which fuels certain mental disorders, and so on round and round. This is another reason why modern diagnosticians no longer recognise psychosis as a separate mental disorder. They see it as merely an indicator of other diagnosable conditions. In modern terminology we do not refer to psychosis as such. We refer instead to the 'psychotic episodes' that are considered to be integral factors in the major mental disorders.

WHO IS REALLY 'CRAZY'?

Many of the symptoms of the psychotic elements in schizophrenia could possibly be explained by cultural or social expectations. For example, believers in the supernatural already have a logical explanation for apparently unreal events – 'it's not psychosis but just another everyday manifestation of the paranormal'. Any such believers would not consider themselves to be deluded – to them, supernatural influences are part of normal, everyday life. Are we so sure that they are wrong? After all, if it is weird to try and appease evil spirits from the 'world beyond', why is it apparently quite normal to pray to a saint?

Why is one set of beliefs 'psychotic' and another set 'piety'? The answer probably depends on where people live or even on when they were alive.

Some might still believe that a witch's magic can really cure the sick; others are happy to believe that 'new age healing' actually works. Who is really 'crazy' and who is simply living differently? Suppose that a doctor's pills have not helped me, but a homeopath's remedies seem to have made me better. Am I cured, duped or hallucinating? The answer probably depends, at least in part, on my own belief systems.

So it seems that the dividing line between sanity and insanity might sometimes be rather thin. Our individual locations along the sanity/insanity continuum probably vary all the time. Sanity might not just be something that is in the mind of the sufferer but also, like physical beauty, something that is 'in the eye of the beholder'. Could the difference between psychosis and sanity be reduced to being just a matter of judgement? If it can, then where is the cut-off point? As the old saying goes, 'They're all right daft but me and thee, and I'm not so sure about thee.'

ACTIVITY 6.1

- Make a list of apparently delusional or psychotic behaviours. Explain them all rationally.
- Next make a list of acceptable behaviours. Think how you could explain each one as delusional or just plain 'crazy'.
- Think about an occasion when you unthinkingly called someone (or someone's behaviour) 'mad'. What was actually odd about it? What was irrational about it? How justified were you in thinking that the person you have in mind was at least temporarily insane? Did you ever check?

COMMENT

Referring to someone's behaviour as being psychotic means we are attaching a powerful label to that person. This is because it implies delusional, possibly uncontrolled thinking and unrestrained resultant actions. Psychosis can be dangerous, very probably much more so for the sufferers than for anybody else. Although all too many of us all too loosely use pejoratives such as 'crazy', perhaps as therapists we ought to be much more professionally precise in our use of language.

THEORETICAL EXPLANATIONS OF SCHIZOPHRENIA

Not all theorists accept that schizophrenia is a single or a unitary disease. They say that it is a range of different conditions (Tsuang, Stone and Faraone, 2000). In other words, there may be a number of separate, independent illnesses. For example, it has been argued that the current diagnostic emphasis on delusions is misleading as not all delusions are either fixed or totally false (Jones, 1999). In other words, it is difficult to find a cut-off point between normal perception and abnormal delusion. This might mean that the ill/well boundaries set by both *DSM IV* and *ICD 10* are arbitrary and lead to false diagnoses (Andreasen, 2000). Of course, if the schizophrenic 'cluster' is to be split up, then possibly different treatments might be needed for each apparently different illness. To date, these sorts of issues are far from being resolved. It is therefore unsurprising that there is considerable debate about both the causes of schizophrenia and the best way to treat its victims.

BIOLOGICAL EXPLANATIONS

There are a number of competing biological theories about the causes of schizophrenia. Genetic studies suggest that there may be an inherited predisposition to schizophrenia – that it sometimes 'breeds true' (see the review by Craddock, O'Donovan and Owen, 2006). As with so much in genetics, our knowledge is expanding exponentially. Other studies claim to have found that schizophrenia is associated with birth events (Clarke, Harley and Cannon, 2006). Factors such as hypoxia or slow foetal growth have all been investigated, but Craddock, O'Donovan and Owen (2006) suggest that the results are very mixed. Even connections between the season that people are born in and the likelihood that they will become schizophrenic have been considered (Davies et al., 2003). None of these studies has so far provided any useful information about the origins of schizophrenia. They certainly offer little advice about its likely treatment.

There appears to be growing evidence that substance misuse at least sometimes triggers schizophrenia (Arseneault et al., 2004). However, whether this is a cause of schizophrenia, a contributing factor, or merely the factor that activates an underlying schizophrenic predisposition is, as yet, far from clear (Swartz et al., 2006). A meta-analysis (Moore et al., 2007) has shown a statistical association between increased consumption of cannabis and an increased risk of psychotic disorder. However, it is also the case that most schizophrenics also use tobacco (De Leon and Diaz, 2005). Therefore it is clearly difficult to argue that one of those substances is involved with schizophrenia without implicating the other one, too.

Currently, the most popular biological explanations of schizophrenia have centred on brain function. Some investigators found faults in brain development and others found defects in the brain's hard wiring (see Flashman and Green (2004) for a review of these areas of investigation). This is a rapidly developing area of schizophrenia research, and new findings are being announced all the time. Other studies suggest that deficiencies in the brain's chemical neurotransmitters lie at the heart of the problem. Probably the most important findings to date in the biology of schizophrenia come from investigations into the way that the neurotransmitter dopamine acts in the brain.

THE DOPAMINE THEORY OF SCHIZOPHRENIA

The dopamine theory of schizophrenia was first suggested by Van Rossum (1967). Many later studies support his proposition that excessive dopamine production lies at the root of this condition (Seeman and Kapur, 2000; Martin, Travis and Murray, 2002; and many others). This theory is based on Van Rossum's observation that many, if not most, schizophrenics seemed to do best if they used one of the neuroleptic (antipsychotic) drugs. Neuroleptic means 'nerve seizing'. As the original, and still most popular class of these compounds (the phenothiazines – chlorpromazine, etc.) are known to act on the dopamine system, it seemed reasonable to suggest that defects in this chemical pathway in the brain cause schizophrenia.

Studies have indeed shown some alterations in the dopamine systems of schizophrenic patients (Meisenzahl et al., 2007; and many others). However, yet other studies suggest that these differences are so small that they might not have any clinical importance (Stone, Morrison and Pilowsky, 2006). There are two further problems with the dopamine theory of schizophrenia that so far seem to be unresolved. First, it is not certain that any observed alterations in the dopamine system actually cause patients to become schizophrenic. It is always possible that these changes are an effect of the original, *typical*, antipsychotic drugs that are used to treat sufferers. Second, a later generation of drugs, the *atypical* antipsychotics, seem to influence the serotonin system as well. Perhaps defects in the dopamine system are not the primary cause of schizophrenia. Could it be that schizophrenia results from defects in the serotonin system? In any event, unfortunately it appears to be the case that both the typical and the atypical antipsychotics help only to control or to relieve schizophrenia; regrettably, they do not 'cure' it.

SOCIAL/SOCIOLOGICAL EXPLANATIONS

Some sociologists claim to find an association between life events and schizophrenia. Living in an urban setting does seem to increase the risk (Van Os, 2004). Poverty, social disadvantage and unemployment seem to contribute (Selten, Cantor-Graae and Kahn, 2007). Family dysfunction and childhood abuse also seem to play some sort of a part in generating later-life schizophrenia (Schenkel et al., 2005). It therefore seems possible that there is a link between schizophrenia and unfavourable life events. Unfortunately, this is also true of the links between mental ill health and inequality generally (Pilgrim and Rogers, 2002). However, there is no evidence that schizophrenia sufferers have necessarily had more stressful pre-morbid lifestyles than the rest of the population. It may be that having an adverse social history tells us more about the likelihood that person will eventually recover than it does about the onset of the condition.

It is true that surveys show that schizophrenia is more prevalent in the lower social classes (Harrison et al., 2001). However, whether this is a *cause* of schizophrenia or a *result* of the disorder is open to debate. The social drift hypothesis argues that schizophrenia induces downward social mobility and that this results in a tendency for sufferers to relocate to the more deprived inner urban areas (Hurst, 2007). An alternative explanation is that it is the stresses of living under such unfortunate conditions that create the mental conditions for the disease to flourish (Fox, 1990) – chicken or egg?

ANTI-PSYCHIATRIC EXPLANATIONS

The arguments of the 'anti-psychiatry advocates' such as Theodore Lidz or Ronald Laing (see the review by Craddock and Owen, 2005) suggest that the very idea of schizophrenia is merely a form of attempted social control over people who hold unorthodox views (Cooper, 1969). Madness, they claim, is not an illness but an understandable reaction to adverse emotional and social conditions (Arieti, 1974). Schizophrenia is an indicator of psychological distress and, if treated properly, will be cathartic rather than harmful (Jaynes, 1976). In other words, schizophrenic patients (and the other so-called 'psychotics') need more social acceptance and less medication (Romme and Morris, 2007).

COGNITIVE AND PERCEPTUAL EXPLANATIONS

Psychologists have suggested that schizophrenia results from a deficit in attention. They have also suggested that it comes from an inability to process information or from a faulty conscious control process. None of these suggestions seems to have been robustly demonstrated as theoretical models, although some psychological treatments have sometimes proved to be of some help. Therapists interested in this sort of approach might find the cognitive analytical therapy model (Ryle, 1990) to be worth investigating.

PSYCHODYNAMIC EXPLANATIONS

The psychodynamic theories of schizophrenia traditionally rested on the proposition that the driving force behind human personality is libido. Freud originally suggested that when libido is so excessive as to be threatening, it is withdrawn into the inner self in order to prevent harm. This withdrawal, or disconnection, results in the outer world becoming meaningless. When, in due course, the sufferer attempts to reverse this withdrawal and to return to normality, then what is sometimes known as the 'noisy phase' of schizophrenia emerges – that is, when the psychotic symptoms became obvious to all.

As we know, Freud's structural model of the human psyche proposed that it is comprised of an instinct-driven Id, a rational Ego and a moral Superego (Jacobs, 2003 and 2005; and many others). More modern psychodynamic theorists believe that schizophrenia (and psychosis in general) is a result of conflicts or defects in the Ego. It is these conflicts that disrupt the sufferer's relationship with the external world (Berati, 2003). Psychodynamic theorists assume that such conflicts are caused by negative early-life experiences and early-years emotional deprivation.

The psychodynamic position on schizophrenia is a complex one and it cannot be done justice to in this chapter. However, Goldstein (1978) offers a useful overview of this topic. The psychoanalysts have generated a huge volume of literature on the subject of psychosis. It seems to endlessly fascinate them. However, as with the psychodynamic position in general, its theories on schizophrenia are difficult – impossible even – to test objectively. The fact of the matter is that there are not very many accounts of authenticated psychoanalytic 'cures' of schizophrenic patients, alleged or otherwise (Malmberg, Fenton and Rathbone, 2001). This deficiency makes it possible for other investigators to suggest that the psychodynamic theory of schizophrenia is just that – a theory and nothing more.

TREATING SCHIZOPHRENIA

As we know, treating schizophrenia is difficult. It is probably impossible to say that a patient will ever be permanently symptom-free. However, it is possible to help many schizophrenia sufferers to lead useful and fulfilling lives – to normalise their existences. Nevertheless, the treatment of schizophrenia is a difficult undertaking and one that might well be ongoing for all, or at least most, of many patients' lives.

The primary treatment model for schizophrenia is centred on the medical approach. NICE *Guideline 82* (2009) offers a comprehensive set of recommendations for medical practitioners. However, any emphasis on a medical basis for schizophrenia treatment does not mean that there is no role for counsellors and psychotherapists – far from it. In fact, *Guideline 82* emphasises the need to offer schizophrenic patients psychological and psychotherapeutic support and guidance. This is especially necessary when they are usually able to function well in the general community. It also recognises the need to offer various forms of psychotherapeutic help to the sufferers' relatives (or to anyone else with whom they have close relationships). Therefore it is clear that the talking therapies have much to contribute towards the treatment and management of schizophrenia. However, *Guideline 82* recommends that any such help should be provided as part of an overall care package, one that is offered by a care team that is supervised by a suitably experienced medical practitioner.

DRUG TREATMENTS (PSYCHOPHARMACOLOGY)

NICE unequivocally recommends drug therapy as the initial treatment of choice for schizophrenia. Drugs commonly in use include the phenothiazine-based (Generation 1) antipsychotics and the dibenzothiazepine-based (Generation 2) antipsychotics.

Generation 1

The 'typical' antipsychotic drugs (phenothiazines) are:

- chlorpromazine
- promazine
- thioridazine
- trifluoperazine
- flupentixol
- fluphenazine
- pimozide
- haloperidol
- zuclopenthixol

These drugs act on the *positive* symptoms of schizophrenia. All of these phenothiazine drugs are essentially similar, and no one really knows precisely how they work except that they all seem to have a major sedating effect (Healy, 2009). They also sometimes generate serious and sometimes irreversible side effects such as neuromuscular debilities, Parkinsonism and uncontrollable, involuntary body movements. This class of drugs is usually referred to as the 'typical antipsychotics'. This is because they seem to act on the typical, or the positive symptoms, of schizophrenia (hallucinations, delusions, disordered thinking, disordered behaviour, etc.).

Generation 2

More modern drug developments have now become commonly available. These are the dibenzothiazepine *'atypical antipsychotic'* medications. They are atypical because they appear to work on the negative symptoms of schizophrenia (affective flattening, de-socialisation, etc). NICE *Guideline 82* recommends that the atypical antipsychotics should routinely be prescribed for schizophrenic patients.

The 'atypical' antipsychotics (dibenzothiazepines) are:

- Zyprexa (olanzapine)
- Seroquel (quetiapine)
- Risperdal (risperidone)

- Clozaril (clozapine)
- Zeldox (ziprasidone)
- Solian (amisulpride)

These drugs act on the *negative* symptoms of schizophrenia. Clozaril (clozapine) is usually a 'last resort' drug – it is very effective but very expensive, and it can sometimes cause serious reductions in white blood cell count (agranulocytosis).

A major apparent advantage of the atypical antipsychotics is that they apparently have far fewer and far milder side effects. This in turn may encourage patient uptake. Failure to keep to a drug regime is an ever-present problem in schizophrenia treatment. Unsurprisingly, it is obviously difficult to persuade patients to take medication that might cause them more problems, even harm, in other ways. A major disadvantage of this newer class of drugs is that on average they are about ten times more expensive than the earlier typical antipsychotics. However, claims about their superior effectiveness have led Geddes et al. (2000) to argue that the new drugs might actually be cheaper in the long run. No doubt this is a debate that will rumble on.

It is important to note that neither the typical nor the atypical antipsychotics offer permanent 'cures'. Their primary purpose, and one that they often achieve very effectively, is to help sufferers to control their symptoms. In the opinion of the Royal College of Psychiatrists (RCPsych, 2010c) antipsychotic medication needs to be taken for a long time, very often for years. The RCPsych is also very blunt about what happens if patients stop their medication too soon. They say that the symptoms will return in three to six months.

PSYCHOLOGICAL TREATMENTS

This is the primary area where counsellors and psychotherapists can certainly play a useful role in the management of schizophrenic patients and in assisting their families.

Cognitive-behavioural

CBT interventions can sometimes help schizophrenic patients to manage some of their symptoms. At best they can help the patient become sufficiently in control to be able to lead a relatively normal life. However, this sort of work should ideally be carried out by very experienced therapists who are well supported and working as part of a properly supervised team.

Family therapy

Supportive work with families can be very helpful in the treatment of schizophrenia. Many studies indicate that a stable social structure is extremely beneficial in the remission/management of this most distressing mental disorder.

Counselling and supportive psychotherapy

The importance and the value of the supportive and containing effects of a beneficial psychotherapeutic relationship for a psychotic client cannot be overstressed. Just listening seriously to patients' accounts of their delusions can help to break the terrible feelings of isolation and difference that such mental health problems can bring about. The principle involved is one of acceptance rather than placating, of supporting rather than 'curing'.

Guided self-help

This is an area in which counsellors and psychotherapists can usefully employ their relationship-building skills to encourage patients to take as much responsibility as possible for their own care and treatment. Such self-help activities include:

- learning to recognise schizophrenic symptoms early on and so seek help in plenty of time;
- learning how to recognise, and then to avoid, stressful symptoms that make the disorder worse;
- learning to manage the symptoms by using relaxation techniques – one of the benefits claimed from the antipsychotics is their apparent sedative effect;
- finding 'behavioural tricks' that help control hallucinations such as hearing voices, etc. – this includes diversionary techniques such as keeping busy, spending time with other people, and so on;
- joining self-help groups or attending day centres;
- becoming as informed as possible about schizophrenia;
- keeping physically healthy – balanced diet, exercise, adequate sleep, etc.;
- taking medication regularly as prescribed – and if the side effects are unpleasant, not stopping or reducing the dosage without first consulting a doctor.

Technical assessment of schizophrenia

If you are interested in carrying out a technical assessment of schizophrenia, then this is how it works using *DSM IV*.

First, the following General Schizophrenic Criteria must be met:

A Characteristic symptoms: two or more of the following should each be present for a significant portion of time during a one-month period (less if successfully treated): i) delusions; ii) hallucinations; iii) disorganised speech, derailment/incoherence); iv) grossly disorganised or catatonic behaviour; v) negative symptoms (impoverished speech, etc.).

B Social/occupational dysfunction: one or more major areas of functioning (work, interpersonal relations, self-care, etc.) should be affected.

C The period of overall disturbance must have persisted for at last six months and include criterion A.

D There is no schizoaffective disorder (no severe depressive, manic or mixed mood episodes).

E The disturbance is not due to the effects of mind-altering substances or a general medical condition.

F There are no pervasive developmental disorders such as autism present.

Only one symptom from A is required if the delusions are sufficiently bizarre or the hallucinations include voices.

Once these criteria are met, *DSM IV* allows the following five subtype diagnoses to be carried out.

1 *Paranoid type*. Preoccupation with one or more delusions or frequent auditory hallucinations – the delusions are often threatening or persecutory but other delusions (jealousy, religiosity etc.) can occur. No prominent disorganised speech, catatonia or inappropriate effect.

2 *Disorganised type* (known as hebephrenia in *ICD 10*). All of the following are prominent: a) disorganised speech; b) disorganised behaviour; c) flat or inappropriate affect. The criteria for catatonic type schizophrenia are not met.

3 *Catatonic type*. At least two of the following: a) motor immobility (catalepsy, waxy flexibility or stupor); b) excessive (purposeless) motor activity; c) extreme negativism (motiveless resistance, or rigid posture, or mutism); d) peculiar voluntary movement (posturing/stereotyped, odd mannerisms, grimacing); e) echolalia (copying or repeating someone's else's speech) or echopraxia (copying another's movements).

continued overleaf

4 *Undifferentiated type.* When criterion A of the General Criteria is met but the criteria for paranoid, disorganised or catatonic are not met.
5 *Residual type.* No prominent delusions, hallucinations, disorganised speech, disorganised or catatonic behaviour; evidence of disturbance by any two of symptoms A i) – A iv) or symptom A v).

Note: *ICD 10* adds in two further subtypes:

6 *Post-schizophrenic depression.* Post schizophrenia depression, some residual schizophrenic symptoms.
7 *Simple schizophrenia.* Slow onset negative symptoms but no psychotic episodes.

As well as having the residual type diagnosis available, which is not dissimilar to the 'Not Otherwise Specified' option, *DSM IV* also includes 'schizophrenia-like' disorders. These allow the 'madness' symptoms in the General Criteria to be used more or less as seems appropriate at the time:

- *Schizophreniform disorder.* General Criteria A, D and E lasting one to six months.
- *Schizoaffective disorder.* General Criterion A for two weeks associated with a mood episode.
- *Delusional disorder.* Criterion A not met but non-bizarre delusions present. Subtypes to be specified (erotomania, grandiosity, persecutory, jealous, etc.).
- *Brief psychotic disorder.* Delusions, hallucinations disorganised speech/behaviour for between 1 and 30 days.
- *Shared psychotic disorder.* Two people share the same delusion (folie à deux).

And, just in case all of these are not enough, there is always NOS, our all-purpose get-out:

- *Psychotic disorder Not Otherwise Specified.* Prominent delusions/hallucinations only and not otherwise explained.

For a full explanation of all the above, see *DSM IV*, pp273–316.

Case study 6.1   How psychosis can take over its victims (and alarm their therapists)

Tom was a relationship therapist who worked for a well-known UK agency. He was meeting Bill and Mary for the first time. They had come along to see him 'to try and work out what's wrong with our marriage'. They seemed a pleasant enough couple at first sight.

Tom invited them to each take a turn at telling him about their problems as each saw them. Mary went first. She explained how she found it too difficult to keep up with Bill's demands of her. He wanted everything at once, and he was so intense about everything that he left her feeling frightened. Bill seemed to have great difficulty in waiting for his turn to speak. He kept on repeating what Mary was saying just under his breath, and he was clearly having a lot of difficulty in remaining in his chair. He even seemed to be repeating what Tom was saying. It was like having a very quiet echo in the room. Mary finished by saying that Bill had changed so much recently: 'We used to go out a lot with friends but now Bill won't see anybody – he just sits in his chair all day, he won't even speak to me, and it's got worse since he lost his job.'

Bill broke in, 'I keep telling you, all I need is for you to be on my side.' He started crying and laughing at the same time as he explained that they had got rid of him at work when 'they found out that I knew what they were secretly up to.' 'All I need is for people to push their positive thoughts into me and then I'll be OK; then I'll have the strength to fight back.' Bill's words and thoughts just kept pouring out of him. His ideas and words seemed like they were tripping over each other. The problem for Tom was that these thoughts and ideas were getting ever more contradictory. They didn't make sense. All Tom could make out was that Bill was being persecuted. He didn't know how, and he didn't know why, but he did know that 'they are all in it together; they are trying to get me'.

Tom wasn't sure about what to do. Both his instincts and his professional training were telling him that something was seriously wrong. Was Bill psychotic? He very much suspected that an urgent referral might be necessary. How could he go about persuading Bill and Mary to ask for the right sort of help? Was Mary in danger? Tom himself urgently needed advice – all this was too much for him alone.

REFLECTION POINT

- Think about Case study 6.1. On the surface, it seems that Bill might well be developing a serious mental disorder. However, are you quite sure about that? What if Bill really is being conspired against? Is Tom going to end up as one of his oppressors too? What might make Bill's story true? If it is true, what should Tom do about helping him?

- On the other hand, just suppose that Bill does need urgent psychological/medical treatment. What sort of help might be best for him? How can Tom go about persuading him to agree to access it? Think about where you live. Who could you contact on Bill's behalf if necessary?
- Finally what about Tom? What sort of help and support does Tom need when faced with cases like this one? What about you? Have you got something in place or, if not, how could you go about organising something?

COMMENT

Any counsellor or psychotherapist, at any time, might encounter someone who is possibly very seriously mentally disturbed. Therapists working alone or with the smaller agencies might not have ready access to sources of referral. Therefore, all practitioners would be well advised to set up a network of suitable professionals and organisations that can be contacted in case of need. At the very least, they might find it helpful to be familiar with their local GP practices, the local community mental health teams and the local drugs advisory agencies. No doubt you can think of many other contacts that might be useful. What about your practice? Have you got some suitable arrangements in place?

CHAPTER SUMMARY

Schizophrenia is a puzzling condition – we still do not really know what causes it. It is a contentious condition – argument rages about what it actually is and how to diagnose it. Schizophrenia is also a scary condition – it frightens its sufferers. It can also frighten anyone close to them, and it certainly frightens the public. However, this apparently widespread fear is far from being justified. Schizophrenia sufferers have fragmented personalities; their personalities are not uncontrollably split. All of us – patients, doctors, therapists and the public – can do a lot to help schizophrenia's victims. These unfortunates do not have to remain out in the psychological and social cold.

Current research trends are focusing on brain biochemistry in an attempt to get a better understanding of the origins of this disease. It may be that this is the route to devising better treatments. However, a core problem remains. The very scientific validity of schizophrenia is being questioned. Is it a single mental disorder that might have one cause and one cure? Is it a cluster of separate disorders, each with its own cause and each with its own cure? Does schizophrenia even exist? Is schizophrenia a psychiatric myth that is maintained just to serve the purposes of its diagnosticians? The

Campaigners for the Abolition of the Schizophrenia Label (see www.mental healthforum.net) claim that even just using the term 'schizophrenia' is a step backwards. In their view, schizophrenia would be better addressed if it were viewed as being a spectrum of conditions.

The simple fact is that there is yet much to learn about this mental disorder. In the meantime, those tasked with trying to help schizophrenia's sufferers have to get on with their work. Unfortunately, pills and humane care are mostly all that they currently have to offer. Could counsellors and psychotherapists offer a helping hand? What could you do?

SUGGESTED FURTHER READING

Haycock, D (2009) *The everything health guide to schizophrenia.* Avon MA: Adams Media.

It does as its title suggests. It's everything that victims, relatives, their therapists and other health care professionals need to know about schizophrenia. This book is set out in a very accessible, reader-friendly format. Therapists will find Chapter 6 'Warning Signs of Schizophrenia' valuable in their everyday practices.

Levine, J and Levine, I (2008) *Schizophrenia for dummies.* Indianapolis IN: Wiley.

A very easy read and an excellent beginners' guide to a complex topic – Part IV 'Living with Schizophrenia' offers some really helpful practical advice for sufferers and their families.

National Institute for Health and Clinical Excellence (2009) *Guideline 82, Schizophrenia: core interventions in the treatment and management of schizophrenia in adults in primary and secondary care,* www.nice.org.uk – type in schizophrenia.

Not a fun read but an essential one. It will tell you how NHS mental health care teams try to help their schizophrenic patients.

CHAPTER 7

Understanding bipolar disorder and the personality disorders

CORE KNOWLEDGE

- Bipolar disorder (manic depression) is classed as a mood disorder. Its sufferers' emotions vary between excessive elation and marked despair.
- Bipolar disorder is a long-term condition that is usually treated with the mood stabiliser class of drugs, psychotherapy and psycho-education.
- The personality disorders are located on Axis 2 of *DSM IV*. This means that many practitioners do not view them as personality faults but as inherent personal qualities. In other words, they are not disorders and so do not, by themselves, indicate mental ill health.
- There is intense debate about whether or not the personality disorders can be successfully treated.

BIPOLAR DISORDER

INTRODUCTION

Bipolar disorder (originally known as manic depression) is characterised by severe mood swings from the excessively elated to the exceedingly despairing. It seems to affect about 1 in every 100 adults (RCPsych, 2010e). There is evidence that bipolar disorder runs in families (Nurnberger and Foroud, 2000; Potash et al., 2007). It also seems possible that the bipolar disorders might be associated with certain abnormalities in the brain's physical structure (Kempton et al., 2008).

Psychological stresses and physical illnesses appear to be triggers for this disorder (Alloy et al., 2005). It has been claimed that each stressful episode lowers the threshold at which the next bipolar incident can be triggered. This concept underpins the 'kindling theory of bipolar disorder' (Hlastala et al., 2000). 'Kindling' refers to a process in which the latent bipolar disorder is likened to the glowing embers that become an active fire when some kindling wood (represented in this case by psychobiological stressors) is added.

The reality is, like so many of the mental disorders, the true causes of bipolar disorder are not yet properly understood. There is a lot more research and much more debate yet to come.

THE MOOD SPECTRUM

When we looked at depression in Chapter 4, we saw that it is classified in *DSM IV* as a 'mood disorder'. Actually, it might be more correct to say that depression lies at one end of a 'mood spectrum' (see Figure 7.1). People with depression remain at the depressive end of the mood spectrum until they recover. This is why depression is known as a *uni*polar disorder.

Mania lies at the other end of the mood spectrum. It is an overactive, overexcited, state of mind and behaviour. People who become manic often suffer from extreme and frequent mood swings. Therefore, they can easily change from being overly keyed-up, or excessively animated and excited, to being overly depressed. That is why this condition was formerly known as manic depression. Its sufferers can find themselves at either end of the mood spectrum. This is the reason why it is considered to be a *bi*polar disorder.

MOOD

DEPRESSION   NORMAL/BALANCED   MANIA

Figure 7.1: The mood spectrum

MANIA

Mania is described as being:

> *A distinct period of abnormality and persistently elevated, expansive, or irritable mood, lasting at least a week (or of any duration if hospitalisation is required).*

> (*DSM IV*, 1994a, p332)

Just as depression can range from severe to mild, so too can mania. Severe mania is very disruptive both for the victim and for everybody else. In its milder form, known as hypomania, the victims might appear to be able to function well and lead a more or less apparently normal life. However, those close to them will be familiar with the sufferers' bursts of abnormal emotional and behavioural 'highs' and then their inevitable 'lows'.

BIPOLAR SYMPTOMS

It would be wrong to think of bipolar disorder as being just another way of viewing the ups and downs of ordinary life. The mood swings are extreme and the effects can be serious. Normal life can be severely disrupted.

Sometimes bipolar sufferers have separate, but linked, *depressed episodes* and *manic episodes* (see Table 7.1).

A manic episode	A depressive episode
Mood Feeling 'high', overly happy Excessively outgoing Extremely irritated, agitated, 'wired' Grandiose	**Mood** Feeling down Feeling disconnected Feeling disinterested in life Lacking self-confidence
Behaviour Racing and erratic thinking and speech Easily distracted Restless/little sleep Over-ambitious, taking on lots of tasks Unrealistic beliefs about own abilities Impulsive; attracted to risky behaviour	**Behaviour** Diminished/lessened activities Social withdrawal Disturbed sleep/appetite Unable to concentrate Lack of self-care Self-harm
Note: when bipolar sufferers have both depressive and manic episodes all jumbled together for much of the time, they are said to be experiencing a 'mixed episode'.	

Table 7.1: The symptoms of depressive and manic episodes

BIPOLAR DISORDER TYPES

There are at least five subtypes of bipolar disorder (see Healy, 2009 for a review):

- Bipolar 1: manic or mixed episodes each of which has lasted for at least a week or mania at a level of severity that requires hospitalisation;
- Bipolar 2: shifts between hypomanic and depressed episodes;
- Cyclothymia: a mild form of bipolar with numerous periods of mild depression and mild hypomania that recur over a period of at least two years;
- Rapid cycling: more than four mood swings in a one-year period. This can happen in Bipolar 1 and Bipolar 2;

- Bipolar Not Otherwise Specified: the usual catch-all condition for symptoms that do not quite meet the main diagnostic criteria.

TREATMENT

Bipolar disorder is a condition that worsens if not treated (Goodwin and Jamieson, 2007). Sufferers who defer getting help usually find that their lives become increasingly disrupted (National Depressive and Manic-Depressive Association, 2001).

Like many of the mental disorders, there is no 'cure' as such for bipolar disorder. It tends to be a lifelong, recurrent condition that often requires management for much of a sufferer's life (Judd et al., 2005). The good news is that with proper treatment most people can gain sufficient control over their symptoms to be able to enjoy a reasonable quality of life (Huxley, Parikh and Baldessarini, 2000; Sachs and Thase, 2000).

The National Institute for Health and Clinical Excellence *Guideline 38, Bipolar disorder* (NICE, 2006), recommends long-term drug treatment programmes targeted at symptom reduction and relapse prevention. NICE also recommends augmenting medication regimes with counselling and psychotherapy targeted at promoting patient self-help and self-awareness. This includes teaching patients self-directed symptom management methods based on cognitive and behavioural techniques. The Royal College of Psychiatrists (RCPsych, 2010e) recommends that these combined treatment packages should be continued for at least two years after the symptoms have apparently remitted.

Medical

Bipolar sufferers' moods are unstable, and shift between the depressed, the normal and the manic. Therefore, so it would clearly benefit them if some sort of stability could be achieved. This is the hoped-for purpose of the class of drugs known as the *mood stabilisers*. They are mainly lithium compounds and certain anti-convulsants such as valproate, lamotrigine, or carbamazepine. Sometimes antipsychotic drugs such as olanzapine also seem to help.

Psychotherapy

Cognitive-behavioural therapy can be usefully employed to help sufferers gain control over their harmful or negative thought patterns and behaviours. CBT can also often be helpful in dealing with the depressive phases of bipolar disorder.

Family therapy

Bipolar disorder can cause great strains on relationships. It affects the sufferers' friends, families, and children. As with so many of the mental disorders, those close to the victims seem to suffer just as much as the afflicted do. Helping these 'para-patients' is clearly a 'good thing' just by itself. Benefiting them often benefits the bipolar victims, too.

Self-help and self-awareness

Encouraging patients to learn all that they can about their disorder, and how to manage it for themselves, can be very beneficial. This is because it puts the sufferers into the 'driving seat' and helps them regain control of their lives. If they can learn how to monitor their own moods, perhaps they might seek early treatment whenever a new episode emerges.

Electro-convulsive therapy (ECT)

There is some evidence that ECT can often be an effective 'last resort' in cases where the bipolar disorder is resistant to other forms of treatment (Vaida, Mahableshwarkar and Shaheel, 2003). It has been suggested that ECT helps the brain to generate new signalling pathways (Coyle and Duman, 2003). Such a proposition, if eventually confirmed, would certainly fit with the brain structure abnormalities theory of bipolar disorder mentioned in the introduction to this chapter.

ACTIVITY 7.1

- Undertake some research and find out what sorts of self-help groups, programmes, resources and so on are available in your area for bipolar disorder sufferers. Are they enough? What would you like to see added to what is on offer?
- Prepare a simple one-page information leaflet about this disorder that you could give to clients.

COMMENT

The ongoing treatment of bipolar disorder, which can be a long-term condition, is greatly helped if its victims can play an active part in managing their condition themselves. However, at first many sufferers are bewildered by their symptoms and fearful for their future. Practical guidance is often very useful in helping bipolar clients to regain a measure of stability in their lives.

Case study 7.1   Super-enthusiastic or super-needy?

Martin was a local youth worker attached to a project based in a particularly run-down housing estate. He was especially valued by the project's directors as he seemed to be tireless and worked all hours of the day and night. The young-sters with whom Martin worked admired him greatly, too; he was their 'special person'.

Martin led a team of dedicated volunteers. These people were the 'trouble'. That is why he had gone along to see Graham, the project's counsellor. It seemed that the volunteers were getting angry with Martin and didn't seem to appre-ciate all that he was doing for everybody. Martin was hoping that Graham could give him a few tips about leadership and how to properly defuse the situation.

Graham turned the conversion around a bit and got Martin to talk about himself. It seemed that Martin had had a serious addiction problem some years ago and that this had led him into all sorts of trouble. However, when he started his youth worker training, Martin had been able to get his life back on track. Martin said that he was OK now, apart from sometimes feeling a bit anxious and sometimes a bit low. He had been to see his GP about that. The doctor suggested that he might find Prozac helpful. That was great. Now Martin had even more energy and needed even less sleep.

As he was telling Graham all about this, Martin seemed to buzz with energy. He was clearly having difficulty in sitting still. Martin started talking about the great ideas that he was having about how to turn the estate into a showcase. 'If only my team will work with me there is nothing we can't achieve,' he almost shouted.

Then Martin seemed to catch hold of himself and he quickly 'sobered up'. 'Do I seem crazy to you?' he asked. 'Not crazy,' said Graham, 'but you do seem to have got yourself a bit worked up.' 'I suppose I have,' said Martin. 'That seems to happen a lot these days. Do you think that's what's upsetting my team? Perhaps I need help.' 'Perhaps you do,' replied Graham. 'Why not have another word with your GP?'

When they next met, Martin had been back to see his doctor, who had referred him to a psychiatrist. Graham was not surprised to hear that Martin had been prescribed lithium.

THE PERSONALITY DISORDERS

A CONTROVERSY

The personality disorders are often the focus of considerable public disquiet. Always a controversial issue, both politically and socially, these disorders have attracted intense argument about legislative intention and the likelihood of legislative effectiveness. Put crudely, could/should we detain anybody diagnosed as having an alleged dangerously defective personality? Within the caring professions, the identification and the treatment of these conditions is also the subject of considerable debate. From a psychiatric and a psychological point of view, there seem to be as many theories about the personality disorders as there are practitioners in this area (and probably a few more than that). The fact is that, at present, we neither really understand personality disorders nor do we really know how to respond to those who apparently suffer from them.

PERSONALITY

The very first problem lies with the use of the term 'personality'. In order to know if a personality is disordered we need to know a) what a personality is and b) how to define personality abnormalities. There are a number of theories of personality. For now, the 'Big Five' model (McCrae and Costa, 1997), seems to be the favourite for most psychologists.

The 'Big Five' model is based on the belief that personality can be measured along five specific dimensions. These are:

- neuroticism;
- extraversion;
- openness;
- agreeableness;
- conscientiousness.

Nevertheless, exactly how to define a 'normal' personality remains a contentious issue and one that is far from being resolved (for a review, see Claringbull, 2010). Therefore it is even more of a problem to define the adverse characteristics that will be found in those who supposedly have an 'abnormal' personality. However, although it is recognised that this is an area of considerable controversy it remains a fact that there are a number of disturbed individuals whose behaviour causes considerable disquiet, and in a minority of cases, a considerable danger, to themselves and to society generally.

THE CAUSES OF THE PERSONALITY DISORDERS

It should be noted that the personality disorders are grouped on Axis 2 of the *DSM* classification system. Remember that Axis 1 refers to clinical disorders such as depression or schizophrenia. It is assumed that the Axis 1 conditions are treatable, or will eventually become so. This is not the case with Axis 2 conditions. It is therefore arguable that the personality disorders, like the other Axis 2 disorders, are not actually mental abnormalities in the sense of being defects or illnesses. They are simply the results of how some people are made. If this is so, then a so-called 'disordered personality' is no more 'curable' than left-handedness or ginger hair.

However, some studies (Shea et al., 2002; Clark, 2007) have found that the assumed identifying characteristics of one or two of the personality disorders sometimes eventually diminish or even disappear. Therefore it might be the case that personality disorder is not quite such a fixed or inbuilt condition after all. There is also evidence that extremely adverse early-life experiences can at least exacerbate personality disorder (Miller and Lisak, 1999; Cohen, Brown and Smailes, 2001). Indeed, when using *DSM IV*, the diagnosis of a personality disorder depends on hindsight evidence that it first emerged in adolescence or soon after. It will be very interesting to see how *DSM V* classifies the personality disorders when it is published in a few years' time.

As ever, an alternative approach comes from the psychoanalysts, who view the external and overt expressions of disturbed behaviours and ideations as being indications of deeper, unconscious manifestations of disturbed inner personalities. For the psychoanalysts, the emphasis is on maladaptive psychological development rather than on maladaptive physiological development.

DIAGNOSIS

The diagnostician's first task is to find out if the patient really has an abnormal personality. Generally speaking, and bearing in mind the many counter-arguments, the following three features have traditionally been considered to be indicators of abnormal personality.

1   The individual has an inflexible attitude to life and life's circumstances. There is a lack of ability to learn or adapt.
2   The individual has maladaptive/provocative patterns of needs, perceptions and behaviours that set up 'vicious circles' of abnormality.
3   The individual overreacts to subjective stress and shows little resilience to pressures. There is a 'flight to disturbance'.

These sorts of descriptions tend to be circular. However, the underlying theme is an immovable resistance to making changes to behaviours, attitudes or responses. These rigidly maintained, dysfunctional attitudes are preserved despite the fact that they repeatedly result in unfavourable outcomes.

DSM IV, p630, defines a personality trait as being:

> *Enduring patterns of perceiving, relating to, and thinking about the environment and oneself that are exhibited in a wide range of social and personal contexts.*

It goes on to say that:

> *Only when personality traits are inflexible or maladaptive and cause significant functional impairment or subjective distress do they constitute Personality Disorders.*

> *The essential feature of a Personality Disorder is an enduring pattern of inner experience and behaviour that deviates markedly from the expectations of the individual's culture . . .*

On p632 *DSM IV* says:

> *The features of a Personality Disorder usually become recognisable during adolescence or early adult life.*

Note: 'recognisable' does not necessarily mean having been diagnosed at the time.

General diagnostic criteria for a personality disorder (*DSM IV*)

A An enduring pattern of inner experience and behaviour that deviates markedly from the expectations of the individual's culture. This pattern is manifested in two (or more) of the following areas:
1 Cognition (i.e. ways of perceiving and interpreting self, other people and events)
2 Affectivity (i.e. the range, intensity, lability, appropriateness of emotional response)
3 Interpersonal functioning
4 Impulse control
B The enduring pattern is inflexible and pervasive across a broad range of personal and social situations.
C The enduring pattern leads to clinically significant distress or impairment in social, occupational, or other important areas of functioning.

D The pattern is stable and of long duration and its onset can be traced back at least to adolescence or early adulthood.

E The enduring pattern is not better accounted for as a manifestation or consequence of another mental disorder.

F The enduring pattern is not due to the direct physiological effects of a substance (e.g. a drug of abuse, a medication) or a general medical condition (e.g. head trauma).

See *DSM IV*, pp629–33 for a full explanation.

TYPES OF PERSONALITY DISORDER

Once it has been established that an abnormal personality (in the clinical sense) is present, the second question is to ask just which sort of a personality disorder this particular patient actually has. *DSM IV* lists ten different personality disorders and groups them into three clusters as shown in the box.

Types of personality disorder

Cluster A
- Paranoid – irrational suspicions and mistrust of other people.
- Schizoid – disinterest in social relationships, unable to express emotions.
- Schizotypal – social and interpersonal deficits, uncomfortable in close relationships, distorted thoughts and perceptions, eccentric behaviour.

Cluster B
- Antisocial (psychopath; sociopath) – pervasive disregard for and violation of the rights of others.
- Borderline – instability in relationships and self-image, absolutist thinking, self-damaging behaviour.
- Histrionic – excessive emotionality and attention seeking, needs to be the centre of attention, dramatic attitude, provocative, seductive.
- Narcissistic – grandiosity, demands admiration, lacking empathy for others.

Cluster C
- Avoidant – social inhibition, feelings of inadequacy, hypersensitive to criticism.
- Dependent – excessive need to be taken care of that leads to submissive and clinging behaviour.

continued overleaf

- Obsessive compulsive – preoccupied with order, perfection and control of self and others, rigid conformity, inflexible and closed-off behaviour.

As usual, a 'catch-all' diagnosis is always available: personality disorder 'Not Otherwise Specified' – when none of the above disorders can really be said to be present but nevertheless, the general diagnostic criteria for a personality disorder have been met.

For a full explanation of all the above disorders, see *DSM IV*, pp634–73.

INTERVENTIONS

It should be noted that the term 'interventions' is being used here quite deliberately. This is because there is little evidence of there being any really successful medical or psychological treatments for the personality disorders. Indeed, research suggests that the benefits of psychotherapy are far from convincing (Bateman and Fonagy, 2000). There is no particular evidence that drugs are of much help either, except as a means of symptom control (National Institute of Mental Health, 2009).

A major problem for those charged with the management of personality disordered patients is that these disorders are often encountered in people who also have several other psychiatric conditions. This clearly causes serious difficulties in differential diagnosis and makes outcome research very problematical. What exactly is it that the researchers are measuring? Which outcome is being evaluated for which mental disorder? These are all very difficult variables to control.

The Royal College of Psychiatrists (RCPsych, 2009b) suggests that long-term psychodynamic and interpersonal therapies (including cognitive and cognitive-analytical treatments) appear to be of some help. That belief has not apparently been shared by the strategic health planners. They have cut the funding to the hospitals that were providing the necessary therapeutic communities. It has also been claimed that dialectical behavioural therapy is useful, particularly in the case of borderline personality disorder (Linehan and Dimeff, 2001). This is as yet unconfirmed, although the results of some studies have been encouraging (NICE, 2010a). However, many of the investigations into the alleged benefits of psychotherapy either do not seem to have effective control samples or use very small subject numbers. It would therefore be rash to try to draw too many inferences from them.

It is very unlikely that individual counsellors and psychotherapists have much to offer this client group. It is certainly true that short-term interventions appear to have very little, if any, beneficial effects. There is some limited evidence that highly skilled practitioners, who are able to offer some very long-term psychotherapy, might be of some eventual help (NICE, 2010b). Funding this sort of patient care is difficult. It is the sort of work that was carried out in specialist units such as the Henderson Hospital or the Cassel Hospital. They have both been closed. In any event, it is difficult to get patients with personality disorders to commit to, and to maintain, the necessary long-term relationships.

REFLECTION POINT

- Is there really a safe alternative to incarceration for the minority of personality disorder patients who are deemed to be dangerous? What risks should society take? What would you do?
- Given the current public climate of hostility towards the 'irresponsible' mental health professionals, should practitioners choose the all-round 'safest' intervention and recommend detention or some other form of containment?

COMMENT

People with personality disorders are often portrayed in the media as always being dangerous psychopaths. This has led previous governments to try to legislate for some form of permanent preventive detention. So far, in the UK at least, any such moves have been successfully resisted by the psychiatric profession. However, the downside of supporting patients' liberties becomes evident if a detained patient is released into the community and then subsequently does become dangerous. In these usually highly publicised cases, those involved in the offender's treatment are very likely to become publically vilified. It seems to be a 'lose–lose' situation.

CHAPTER SUMMARY

This chapter has been concerned with two difficult areas of mental health provision. It is certainly the case that the roles that individual counsellors and psychotherapists can play in such cases are limited. However, this does not mean that counsellors and psychotherapists have no roles to play – far from it. What it does mean is that they will probably be at their most productive if they are working in multi-disciplinary care teams rather than operating as lone practitioners. They will probably be personally safer too.

It seems that whereas bipolar disorder is a mood disorder located along a mood spectrum, personality disorder might not actually be located on any mental health spectrum at all. It might not even be a mental illness. However, both conditions are of concern to the medical profession. Bipolar disorder is often treatable with drugs, and personality disorder may sometimes need psychiatric attention if only to authorise detention.

In any event, it is clear when we examine both these conditions, and all the other conditions investigated in this book (depression, anxiety, schizophrenia), that medication plays a major part in all their treatments. This is why in the next chapter we will be looking further into the use of drugs in the management of mental health problems.

It is important that counsellors and psychotherapists have an understanding of the effects of the more commonly encountered mind-altering drugs (legal and illegal). We need to know about their effects, their side effects and their addictive potentials. That is what Chapter 8 explores.

SUGGESTED FURTHER READING

Elliott, C and Smith, L (2009) *Borderline personality disorder for dummies.* Hoboken NJ: Wiley.

A very useful and practical 'hands on' book – therapists will find that Part IV 'Treatments' is particularly helpful in their work with clients.

Jamison, K (1996) *Touched with fire: manic-depressive illness and the artistic temperament.* London: Simon & Schuster.

A fascinating account of how many of history's 'greats' overcame bipolar disorder and produced superb art, music and literature.

Owen, S and Saunders, A (2008) *Bipolar disorder: the ultimate guide.* Oxford: Oneworld Publications.

An excellent 'all you need to know' book for both lay readers and professionals, set out in a very readable 'Q&A' format.

Reiland, R (2004) *Get me out of here: my recovery from borderline personality disorder.* Center City MN: Hazelden Information and Educational Services.

A moving yet painful account of a real life sufferer and a heart warming account of her recovery.

CHAPTER 8

Prescription drugs, recreational drugs and addiction

CORE KNOWLEDGE

- Any substance (legal or illegal) that alters the mind or affects the mood is said to be 'psychotropic' or 'mind-altering'. Psychopharmacology is the study of the ways in which psychotropic substances affect the mind.
- Therapists usually find that the types of psychotropic drugs most likely being prescribed for their clients are:
  - antidepressants;
  - anxiolytics (anti-anxiety drugs);
  - antipsychotics;
  - mood stabilisers.
- Drug/substance dependency can usefully be split into three types:
  - Type 1: Rebound – temporary resumption of symptoms on withdrawal;
  - Type 2: Craving – a strong appetite for the substance in question;
  - Type 3: Therapeutic – permanent physiological changes.

INTRODUCTION

BACKGROUND

People have been using psychoactive drugs throughout the ages (Siegal, 2005). They still do; they probably always will. These 'mind-benders' have long been used for religious purposes, for cultural reasons, and just for plain old fun. Any substances, legal or illegal, that affect the mind are psychoactive drugs. These include the two that are the biggest killers – the ones that do the most harm worldwide, the 'daddies of them all' – alcohol and nicotine. By the way, technical words such as 'psychotropic', 'psychoactive' and 'psycho-affective' mean more or less the same thing – they alter your mood.

Of course, all drugs – psychoactive medications included – are poisons. They can harm us. To get round that unpleasant fact, we have to balance the expected toxic effects of a drug against its hoped-for beneficial effects. We then decide if we want to use it and how we want to use it. Sometimes we make the wrong choice. Sometimes that might be because we do not know any better. In far too many cases, researchers are still trying to find out exactly how particular drugs actually work, and these include the psychiatric drugs (Cottingham, 2009). However, as long as a pill seems to do us more good than harm, we will probably continue to use it, at least until something better comes along.

MYTHS

There are a number of myths around about drugs. One is that they all affect us all in the same way. They do not. I might get on well with Prozac; you might end up feeling much worse than before. You might get a buzz out of cannabis and I might find it does nothing for me. There are also some limited reports (see Healy, 2009) that for some people the mood-altering substances actually have reverse effects. Tranquillisers may wind some people up, antidepressants may make some people unhappier, and so on. In other words, for each patient there has to be a trial and error period. Doctors have to find out which pill and which dosage works best for which patient under what circumstances. That is why most doctors who are starting their patients on, say, an antidepressant will ask them to check back in again two or three weeks later. They need to 'fine-tune' their prescriptions. This is also the reason why patients who find that their prescribed medication is not helping – or even that it is making things worse – should immediately go back to their doctors.

Another commonly held myth is that pills are 'artificial chemicals' and that because they are apparently not 'natural' or 'organic' they are somehow unhealthy. Here is a newsflash: everything is made up of chemicals – and that includes your organic carrots and my supermarket tomatoes. So some people might prefer to use pharmacological chemicals manufactured under licensed and controlled laboratory conditions, while others might be happier to use herbal extracts prepared under more relaxed, more creative, conditions. The choice is yours. Both substance groups are still chemicals. Ultimately, both groups are still poisonous. However, at the end of the day whatever works, works.

It is also important not to fall into the trap of thinking that 'herbal' and 'natural' mean 'safe'. They do not. That is yet another myth. For example, St John's Wort is claimed to be nature's remedy for depression. Many people will swear that they have got better by using it. However, it is also a fact that St John's Wort is a dangerous chemical substance, and when misused or misapplied, it can cause some serious side effects. These include skin lesions, eye damage and adverse reactions with other medicines. Of course, experiencing side effects is not necessarily a reason to stop using any psychotropic drug (manufactured or natural). However, it is yet another reason why any drug's effects, good or bad, should be carefully and continually professionally monitored. Some side effects are bearable; others are not.

PSYCHOPHARMACOLOGY

Psychopharmacology is the study of the effects of mind-altering substances. Not only are the effects of prescription psychotropic drugs under investigation but so too are the effects of the other mind-benders. These include cannabinoids, alcohol, amphetamines, opiates, cocaine, nicotine, caffeine, anabolic steroids, the so-called 'designer drugs' and anything else that appears on the market.

It is widely thought that all the psychoactive drugs, legal or illegal, affect the brain's chemical pathways (Keltner, 2005; and many others). These include the neurotransmitters (the brain's chemical messengers). So, in theory at least, if you control these messengers, you control the message. The problem is, as we have already noted earlier, that these control mechanisms (the chemical pathways) are far from being properly understood. Therefore our ability to control the messages is as yet very crude and often ineffective. There is a further problem – in theory, anyway. Just suppose that we could fully master the activities of the neurotransmitters. Could/should we become 'cosmetic psychiatrists'? Could we create a world where we can chemically change our mood at whim? Even scarier, do we want to create a world where our moods are changed for us?

REFLECTION POINT

- Suppose you could use a drug to permanently alter a paedophile's mind so that sexual relations with children became abhorrent to him. Would you do it? Should you do it?
- Suppose you could add a drug to the public water supply that wiped out any form of fascist or discriminatory thinking. Would you do it?
- Now change that to 'controlling the birth rate'. What would be the arguments in favour of this sort of chemically powered 'social engineering'?

COMMENT

Drugs can be powerful weapons, not just for the doctors but for the state as well. Obviously, anything that has been invented for a good purpose can be diverted to a bad one. After all, motor cars transport both saints and sinners. It would be nice to think that with power comes responsibility. That is certainly what the medical profession would claim about the ways in which its practitioners use their various pills and potions. However, it is difficult for lay people to control the medics if they do not properly understand the implications of what they are up to. That is why all of us need to better understand just how powerful modern drugs can be and to what uses (good and bad) they can be put. As counsellors and psycho-therapists, we often find that our clients are on various medications. Do we always properly understand just what that might mean?

COUNSELLORS, PSYCHOTHERAPISTS AND DRUGS

Clearly, counsellors and psychotherapists need to know generally about the medicines that their clients are taking. More specifically, they need to know about psychotropic drugs and their effects. This is because all therapists are in some way working with their clients' thoughts, behaviours and emotions. The psychotropic drugs (legal or illegal) affect those thoughts, behaviours and emotions. Therapists who do not understand what such drugs do are unlikely to be able to properly understand their clients.

Twenty or so years ago, it used to be a counselling maxim that it was not possible to establish a true psychotherapeutic relationship with a client who was using any form of psychologically affective substance. This view is not so common today. Often the very reverse could be the case. For example, some clients might come along to see their therapists in such an extremely low mood that a helpful therapeutic bond just cannot be formed – there is just no way to set up a meaningful connection. Sometimes the timely use of an appropriate medication might help those clients regain enough emotional strength to be able to beneficially connect with their therapists.

Some clients might come along when they are seriously mentally incapaci-tated by an unfortunate reaction to a prescribed drug. They might not even be aware of the fact. For example, amiodarone (a drug used to regulate heart rhythm) can affect the thyroid gland. This can sometimes cause extremely disruptive levels of anxiety. When a client is in such a seriously chaotic state, then establishing a productive client/counsellor relationship is probably unachievable. Indeed, some practitioners might consider that psycho-therapy is impossible until the client's medication has been reviewed. In any event, before psychotherapy can begin, a referral back to the doctor is essential.

In sum, it is obvious that the 'when', 'how' and 'why' of a client's use (or misuse) of psychoactive substances, whether prescribed or not, all poten-tially impact on the therapeutic relationship. Whether or not that impact is helpful, unhelpful or even irrelevant will vary from case to case. That is why counsellors and psychotherapists need to find out all they can about mind-altering chemicals.

PRESCRIPTION DRUGS

FINDING OUT ABOUT MEDICATION

Counsellors and psychotherapists are rarely medically trained. They are also unlikely to have been schooled in pharmacy. Nevertheless, they still need to be able to make rough assessments about the likely impact of their clients' drug regimes on the therapeutic process. Actually, finding out enough about medicines to decide if they are likely to be relevant to the counselling is easy enough. You do not have to learn a lot of pharmacology – you just have to know how to look things up. There's no need to panic – no great scientific know-how is required. The standard reference sources might look a bit technical at first glance, but do not let that put you off. All you do need to know is what the medicines are for, what they are supposed to do and what the possible side effects are.

Always remember: if in doubt, ask. Most doctors and pharmacists are pretty approachable. You also need to remember that no matter what qualifications you do or do not have, your client already has a doctor, and it is not you. You do need a little knowledge about psychopharmacology, but if you are ever tempted to misapply it or to over-value it, then never forget that a little knowledge can be a dangerous thing. Never give clients any medical advice about their drugs. Doing so would be unethical and potentially dangerous.

There are three very easy ways to find out about medicines.

1   Type the drug's name into Google. It's all there – all you will ever need to know and much, much more. If you are not sure about the name, then type in 'medicines for . . .' or 'drugs used in . . .', or something similar.
2   Get a copy of the *Monthly Index of Medical Specialities* (MIMS). Your local GP's surgery, or perhaps a local pharmacist, will probably give you an old one. If not, visit www.mims.co.uk. It is free. Each drug is grouped in its relevant section or sub-section. For example, Gaviscon is listed under 'gastrointestinal – acid peptic disorders'. There is a set of prescribing notes at the start of each section. Always read these first and make sure that you understand all the abbreviations and symbols.
3   Get a copy of the *British National Formulary* (BNF). Again, you could scrounge one as above or visit http://bnf.org. You will need to register. Again, make sure that you read the 'up front' stuff in each section.

By the way, when you look up a drug, it is worth remembering that they all have two types of name, generic and proprietary. No matter what the name, they are chemically identical. Let us take a common analgesic as an example. Like all the other drugs it has two name types. They are:

- Generic name: paracetamol
- UK trade names: Panadol, Solpadol, etc.

Drugs also have different trade names in different parts of the world. For example, paracetamol (with a little caffeine added) is often marketed as Tylenol in the United States.

PSYCHOTROPIC DRUGS TODAY

Nowadays, probably the most commonly prescribed mood-altering medications are antidepressants, anxiolytics, antipsychotics and mood stabilisers. Therefore, these four classes of psychoactive drugs are probably of the most interest to counsellors and psychotherapists. Obviously, doctors working with psychiatrically disturbed patients have many other medications at their disposal, too. By the way, it is important to note that a number of psychiatric drugs are also used in non-psychiatric medicine. For example, the antidepressant amitriptyline is sometimes used in certain forms of pain management.

There are two other types of psychotropic drugs that are of interest to counsellors and psychotherapists. These are the recreational drugs: the popular and legal 'mind-benders' such as caffeine, nicotine and alcohol, and the equally popular but illegal 'mind-benders' such as marijuana or cocaine.

Of all of these drugs, legal and illegal, alcohol is without doubt the most mentally and physically harmful, and this is certainly the case in the UK today (Nutt, King and Phillips 2010). Unfortunately, because of alcohol's widespread availability, its social acceptability and its extensive consumption, its misuse seems all too often to go unnoticed. Wise counsellors and psychotherapists will be aware of the need to check out the drinking habits of *all* their clients (see Chapter 3 of this book on 'Assessment').

THE ANTIDEPRESSANTS

Developmental history

As with so many psychoactive drugs, modern antidepressants were discovered by accident. In the 1950s, some drugs that were actually being developed to combat tuberculosis were also found to have what was then called a 'psycho-energising' effect. Those drugs, now known as the monoamine oxidase inhibitors (MAOIs), were the first of a new kind of anti-melancholia drug (remember that 'melancholia' was the original name for depression). They were also the first drugs to be marketed as 'anti-depressants'.

Again in the 1950s, at more or less the same time as the MAOIs were being developed, another accidental discovery was being made. A different drug, one that was being tested for its properties to reduce post-surgery shock, was also found to have an anti-melancholic effect. This led to the development of the tricyclic antidepressants, so called because their chemical base is arranged in three rings.

The initial appeal of these two new classes of antidepressant was that they did not appear to be as dangerous or as addictive as the drugs that they replaced. Those much earlier anti-melancholia remedies were the amphetamine-based stimulants such as Benzedrine and Dexedrine, which supposedly gave depressed patients some chemically inspired 'get up and go'.

A major study in 1965 appeared to demonstrate that the tricyclics were more effective than the MAOIs. Actually, it did not. A closer investigation of the results suggests that the real 'best treatment' was probably electro-convulsive therapy (see Healy, 2009). Nevertheless, partly as a result of that study and partly because they react badly with certain foods (the 'cheese effect'), the MAOIs fell out of fashion.

It was believed that the tricyclics acted mainly on the brain's serotonin system. This eventually led to the development of another class of anti-depressant, one that prevented the reduction (inhibited the reuptake) of that particular neurotransmitter. These drugs are known as the selective serotonin reuptake inhibitors (SSRIs). The first SSRI to be marketed was the very well-known drug Prozac. The SSRIs were allegedly non-addictive and supposedly had fewer side effects than the tricyclics or the MAOIs. One advantage that the SSRIs certainly do have is that they are easy to administer. The usual requirement is only one capsule daily.

Later investigations indicated that lowered levels of another neurotransmitter, noradrenaline, also seemed to be involved in depression. As a result the serotonin–noradrenaline reuptake inhibitors (SNRIs) have been made available. Again, see Healy (2009) for a full review of this research.

In addition to the MAOIs, the tricyclics, the SSRIs and the SNRIs, even newer types of drugs are emerging all the time. The range of drugs available for the treatment of depression is becoming ever wider – see Table 8.1 overleaf.

	Generic name	UK trade name
Tricyclics	amitriptyline dosulepin desipramine imipramine lofepramine doxepin clomipramine nortriptyline trimipramine	Tryptophan Prothiaden Pertofrane Tofranil Gamanil Sinepin Anafranil Allegron Surmontil
Monoamine oxidase inhibitors (MAOIs)	phenelzine isocarboxazid tranylcypromine selegiline	Nardil Marplan Parnate Eldepryl
Selective serotonin reuptake inhibitors (SSRIs)	fluoxetine escitalopram citalopram paroxetine sertraline fluvoxamine	Prozac Cipralex Cipramil Seroxat Lustral Faverin
Serotonin–noradrenaline reuptake inhibitors (SNRIs)	venlafaxine duloxetine	Effexor Cymbalta
Noradrenergic and specific serotonergic antidepressants (NASSAs)	mirtazapine mianserin	Zispin Tolvon
Noradrenaline reuptake inhibitors (NDRIs)	reboxetine viloxazine	Edronax Vivalan
Augmenter drugs (used in combination with other antidepressants)	buspirone trazodone	Buspar Molipaxin

Notes:
1 For a full and up-to-date list consult the latest *British National Formulary*.
2 Other antidepressant classes (not all available in the UK) include: noradrenaline–dopamine reuptake inhibitors; noradrenaline–dopamine disinhibitors; selective serotonin reuptake enhancers; serotonin antagonist and reuptake inhibitors.
3 This list is for information only and it is not to be used for treatment purposes.

Table 8.1: Commonly used antidepressant drugs

A major issue

The core question to be asked is, 'Do modern drug treatments for depression actually work?' Up until 2003 the answer to this question was a resounding 'Yes'. The then published studies suggested that there was a 95 per cent recovery rate (see comments by Meyers, 2000; Turner et al., 2008). There were a few doubters but they were ignored.

However, in 2004, an important meta-study, one that called this astonishing success rate into serious doubt, was made public. This study was different because it included both the published data (mostly positive) *and* the unpublished data (mostly negative). When all the data was taken into account, the true success rate was more like 50 per cent than 95 per cent (Moncrieff, Wessely and Hardy, 2004). This finding appears to have been confirmed by later studies (Pigott et al., 2010). As about 50 per cent of depressed patients taking placebos also seem to improve, it might be argued that actually antidepressants do not really work.

However, the situation might not be quite so clear-cut. For instance, what if depression is a common outcome – but one that actually arises from a variety of diverse chemical imbalances in the brain? In such a case, different antidepressants might work differently for different people. Are all the various outcomes studies really comparing like with like?

The fact is that many randomised control studies have apparently demonstrated that antidepressants do have a positive effect. So does anecdotal clinical experience. Indeed the Royal College of Psychiatrists (RCPsych, 2010d) claim that antidepressants actually appear to be about twice as effective as placebos. What does seem to be the case is that when antidepressants do work, they do so fairly quickly (RCPsych, 2010d). That fact alone might justify their use, even if their total cure rate, over, say, a 12-month period, does not exceed that obtained from natural recovery. Put simply, with antidepressants it might be the case that although people get better with or without them, patients get better much quicker with them.

So perhaps the real question is, 'Are we really ready to abandon antidepressant drug treatment for depression?' Doing so would be a very bold, and doubtlessly very contentious, step. Even if we are ready to give up our antidepressants, the inevitable next question is, 'What will we replace them with?' Modern antidepressants might eventually go away; depression will not.

Taking antidepressants

Modern antidepressant medications do have their drawbacks. Some patients experience some unpleasant side effects when they first start using them.

These side effects can include palpitations, insomnia, dry mouth, tremors, headaches, and so on. Normally these effects are mild and dissipate over the first five to ten days. However, in some cases the side effects can be quite severe, and they can even cause major psychiatric and physical symptoms. Some people can just stop taking their antidepressants without any bother while others experience some withdrawal symptoms. As always, patients should consult their doctors about any such problems.

It is usual to keep taking antidepressants for at least six months. Unfortunately a number of patients are deceived into thinking that because after three to four weeks they are feeling better, the underlying condition has remitted. They might unilaterally decide to stop their medication, only to quickly relapse. Of course, modern therapeutic practice is to combine medication with psychotherapy. However, it is interesting to note that for patients with severe, treatment-resistant depression, sometimes electro-convulsive therapy (ECT) turns out to be the best, even the only, effective treatment method.

REFLECTION POINT

- How do you feel about the idea of one of your clients having ECT?
- Suppose you are seeing a severely depressed, extremely distressed, client who has not responded at all to any type of therapy, including medication. Are you prepared to suggest ECT as a 'last resort'?
- Do you routinely consider ECT for any of your severely depressed clients? If not, why not?

COMMENT

Many therapists, especially those who have seen the film *One Flew Over the Cuckoo's Nest*, are very wary of ECT. To them it is very much a dangerous 'sledgehammer to crack a walnut'. Are they trying to save their clients from the alleged 'horrors' of the psychiatrists or are they letting their personal biases getting in the way of effective treatment for their clients?

THE ANXIOLYTICS (ANTI-ANXIETY DRUGS)

What they do

The anxiolytics are drugs that are used to combat anxiety disorders. The first commonly used anti-anxiety agents were the highly addictive and highly dangerous barbiturates. Those original drugs have a powerful 'turning off' effect and are known as sedatives. Today they have largely been replaced by the benzodiazepines (diazepam, lorazepam, etc.). The drugs in this class are often referred to as the 'minor tranquillisers'.

Other drugs, usually not in themselves specifically viewed as tranquillisers, are also sometimes used to combat anxiety. These include some of the antipsychotics, some of the SSRIs, some of the beta-blockers, and even some of the psycho-stimulants.

It should be noted that many of the anti-anxiety drugs have other important medical uses. For example, diazepam can be used as a pre-surgery muscle relaxant and beta-blockers are primarily used to regulate cardiac rhythms.

Types of anxiolytic

Although using the minor tranquillisers is the most common way of medically treating anxiety, other drugs can also have a calming effect – as we have already noted – and they, too, are sometimes used as anxiolytics. Roughly speaking, the anti-anxiety drugs can be divided into six groups. These are:

- benzodiazepines
- beta-blockers
- antidepressants
- antipsychotics
- drugs that act on the serotonin system – buspirone, mirtazapine, etc.
- psycho-stimulants – Dexedrine, Ritalin, etc.

The benzodiazepines

Probably the most widely known class of anxiety-combating drugs currently in use are the benzodiazepines. When they were first developed, they were seen to have a calming, rather than a sedating effect, and that is why they were called 'tranquillisers'. Initially, the benzodiazepines were thought to be a 'wonder drug' and to be the cure for most of society's emotional ill health (Tone, 2008). Their fall from grace, once their addictive nature was realised, has been spectacular. Now this class of drug is used only for very short-term anxiety interventions. However, it has been argued by some that the addictive properties of the benzodiazepines have been greatly exaggerated and that, if used carefully, they can actually be very beneficial, even for long-term treatments (see the review in Healy, 2009).

It is believed that the benzodiazepines act on a neurotransmitter called gamma-aminobutyric acid (GABA). Their effect is neither to block nor to enhance the functioning of this particular chemical messenger but rather to turn its effects down a bit (see the review in Tozer and Rowland, 2006).

The result is that anxiety levels are reduced, and the sufferers become calmer or more *tranquil*.

Beta-blockers

Another, and allegedly addiction-free, group of anxiolytics that is gaining in popularity is the class of drugs known as beta-blockers (propranolol, atenolol, etc.). The argument for their use is that as increased heart rate is one of the signs associated with anxiety, turning down this symptom is likely to reduce anxiety levels. It seems that psychopharmacology is starting to catch up with some of the biofeedback techniques (relaxation therapy, etc.) that counsellors and psychotherapists have long been using with their anxious clients.

Commonly used anxiolytic drugs are set out in Table 8.2 opposite.

THE ANTIPSYCHOTICS

Developmental history

As we know from Chapter 6, currently there are two major classes of antipsychotic drugs. These are the *typical* and the *atypical* antipsychotic medications. Remember, they are so named because the first group allegedly works on the so-called *typical* symptoms of psychosis (delusions, speech abnormalities, etc.) and the second group supposedly works on the *atypical* symptoms (flattened mood, loss of motivation, etc.).

In 1952, the first typical antipsychotic drug, chlorpromazine, was discovered by Henri Laborit (Healy, 2004). As usual it was discovered by accident – he was actually looking for a new antihistamine. However, because this drug was believed to work across the entire mental illness spectrum (and to work with certain other general medical conditions as well), it was considered to have a wide-ranging or a 'large' action. Hence the trade name Largactil. Other drugs in this class rapidly followed.

Unfortunately, it was also soon noticed that the typical antipsychotics that were the most effective for schizophrenia often produced Parkinsonian-type side effects such as muscle stiffness/freezing, and abnormal movements and tremors. It was believed that these very unpleasant reactions were caused by the effects that this first generation of antipsychotics had on the nervous system. They appeared to 'grip' the nervous system and so obstruct its operation. This is why they are also known as the neuroleptics (nerve-seizers).

From the 1950s to the 1980s, researchers tried to find an antipsychotic drug that did not have such alarming side effects. The first of these to be

Class	Generic name	UK trade name
Benzodiazepines	diazepam	Valium
	lorazepam	Ativan
	oxazepam	Serenid
	bromazepam	Lexotanil
	alprazolam	Xanax
	clobazam	Frisium
	medazepam	Nobrium
	clorazepate	Tranxene
	chlordiazepoxide	Librium
Beta-blockers	propranolol	Inderal
	atenolol	Tenormin
	bisoprolol	Emcor
Psycho-stimulants	methylphenidate	Ritalin
	modafinil	Provigil
	atomoxetine	Strattera
	dexamphetamine	Dexedrine
Azapirones	buspirone	Buspar
	gepirone	Ariza
	tandospirone	Sediel
SSRIs	See Table 8.1	
Antipsychotics	See Table 8.3	
Barbiturates (rarely used today)	phenobarbital	Luminal
	barbital	Veronal

Notes:
1 For a full and up-to-date list consult the latest *British National Formulary.*
2 This list is for information only and is not to be used for treatment purposes.

Table 8.2: Commonly used anxiolytic drugs

discovered, or more accurately rediscovered, was clozapine. This second-generation antipsychotic drug and the others in its class (the atypical antipsychotics) were thought to have far fewer side effects than the Generation 1 'typicals' (see the review by Ellenbroek and Cools, 2000).

How they work

It is widely believed that the antipsychotics mainly work on the dopamine system. This idea is the basis of the dopamine theory of schizophrenia (see Chapter 6). However, it is also known that they work on many of the other neurotransmitters as well, particularly the serotonin, noradrenaline and acetylcholine systems (see Torrey, 2006). Because it is not yet possible to separate out all the effects of the antipsychotics, it is also not yet possible to really say how they work. It seems that this class of drugs may act more like a shotgun than a sniper's rifle – that is, they hit everything in sight just to make sure. This means that the dopamine theory of schizophrenia is just that, a theory and not a fact – at least, not yet.

Class	Generic name	UK trade name
Typical antipsychotics (Generation 1)	chlorpromazine	Largactil
	zuclopenthixol	Clopixol
	flupentixol	Fluanxol/Depixol
	perphenazine	Fentazin
	trifluoperazine	Stelazine
	pericyazine	Neulactil
	promazine	Sparine
	tetrabenazine	Xenazine
	sulpiride	Sulpital/Dolmatil/Sulpor
	molindone	Moban (US)
	haloperidol	Serenace/Haldol/Dozic
Atypical antipsychotics (Generation 2)	clozapine	Clozaril
	amisulpride	Solian
	risperidone	Risperdal
	olanzapine	Zyprexa
	quetiapine	Seroquel
	paliperidone	Invega
	aripiprazole	Abilify
	ziprasidone	Geodon (US)
	zotepine	Zoleptil

Notes:
1 For a full and up-to-date list consult the latest *British National Formulary*.
2 This list is for information only and it is not to be used for treatment purposes.

Table 8.3: Commonly used antipsychotic drugs

A major problem

Managing patients who take antipsychotics is particularly difficult for their doctors (and their psychotherapists). The antipsychotics are long-term drugs, often taken for many years. This class of drugs, even including the atypicals, produces many serious side effects (Saltz et al., 2000; Gardner and Teehan, 2010) and so their users are understandably reluctant to take them. This means that counsellors and psychotherapists who are working with psychotic patients will need to continually assess their clients' reactions to their actual use – their real-life use – of psychotropic medication. It may be unrealistic to assume that these patients will always follow 'doctor's orders' – perhaps even unreasonable. Why should people remain compliant if their pills cause them harm? Commonly used antipsychotic drugs are set out in Table 8.3 opposite.

THE MOOD STABILISERS

A number of drug types are used in the treatment of bipolar disorder. These include lithium compounds, some of the antipsychotics and certain benzo-diazepines. Occasionally, ECT is found to be effective. Sometimes a number of approaches are needed in the management of bipolar disorder. If the manic episodes are sufficiently disruptive, then inducing a period of calm might be necessary. This might involve the use of both the major and the minor tranquillisers. Hospitalisation might even be required. It is important to try to prevent further recurrences of the disorder, so drugs that also have prophylactic (preventative) effects (the mood stabilisers) are used.

There are five preventative drugs, or mood stabilisers, that are commonly used to ward off bipolar disorder. All of them can have unpleasant side effects. They are:

- lithium;
- carbamazepine;
- valproate;
- lamotrigine;
- gabapentin.

There is also some evidence that the antipsychotic drug clozapine, already commonly used to deal with the manic phase of bipolar disorder, might, when taken in low doses, also act as a mood stabiliser (Fehr, Ozcan and Suppes, 2007).

ACTIVITY 8.1

- Access the Royal College of Psychiatrists website – www.rcpsych.ac.uk – and click on 'Mental Health Info'. Now think of a recent client who might have had one of the conditions shown on the drop down menu – preferably a condition that you do not know too much about. Read up what the RCPsych has to say on that topic.
- Next, review your case notes and consider how you could have/might have managed that client differently in the light of your new knowledge. Would employing a psychotropic drug have been beneficial?

RECREATIONAL DRUGS

The term 'recreational drugs' is used here to refer to self-administered, or self-selected, psychoactive substances, legal or illegal. Presumably, the original intention of the user is to attain pleasure from the hoped-for mood-enhancing effects that these substances appear to provide. However, in the case of people who have become dependent on their daily 'fix', their need is often not so much to gain pleasure but to ward off the unpleasant effects of not using – the *withdrawal symptoms*. It should be noted that in most parts of the world, many of the recreational drugs are illegal. Which ones are illegal and under what circumstances varies from place to place. For example, in Dubai, even many over-the-counter UK drugs (codeine etc.) are illegal.

However, the paradox is that the two drugs that are by far the biggest sources of harm worldwide (alcohol and nicotine) are generally legal or, if not legal, easily attainable. They are usually socially acceptable as well (even in Dubai). It is also often forgotten that caffeine too is a psychoactive drug and that it can be addictive. In addition, other legal drugs that are routinely prescribed for perfectly proper reasons – for example, morphine-based painkillers – can be obtained illegally and subsequently misused. It would be impossible in an introductory text such as this one to list all the available recreational drugs or to tell you all their latest street names. In any event, the recreational drugs 'menu' is ever expanding and fashions among their users are ever-changing (Shapiro, 2004 has a good review). You will very easily find all the up-to-date information on the internet.

COMMONLY USED RECREATIONAL DRUGS

These are the most commonly used recreational drugs:

- *alcohol*: ethanol diluted with water; highly toxic, especially when undiluted; damages virtually every part of your body; initially acts as a relaxant and produces apparent euphoria; actually a depressant, particularly if used to excess;
- *tobacco*: contains nicotine and beta-carboline alkaloids – both a stimulant and a relaxant; causes cancers, cardiovascular disease, etc; nicotine is highly poisonous in its pure form;
- *caffeine*: found in tea, coffee, some soft drinks – a mild stimulant; addictive;
- *amphetamines*: powerful stimulants – very addictive and very dangerous;
- *cannabis* (marijuana, hemp, etc.): contains tetrahydrocannabinol (THC) – a relaxant;
- *cocaine*: a stimulant derived from the coca plant – highly addictive;
- MDMA: 3,4-Methylenedioxymethamphetamine, commonly known as ecstasy; produces euphoria, diminished anxiety and depression; creates a sense of intimacy with others;
- *opium*: a sedative drug obtained from certain poppy plants; generates euphoria;
- *morphine*: an alkaloid derived from opium; sedative and euphoric;
- *heroin*: an opioid drug synthesised from morphine; another powerful euphoric;
- *hallucinogenics*: LSD, 'acid', 'magic mushrooms' (Psilocybin), designer drugs – often known as 'trippers';
- *amyl and butyl nitrate*: known as 'poppers' – produce a 'party rush' and also used to enhance climatic sexual activity;
- *ketamine*: actually a veterinary anaesthetic – produces 'out-of-body' experiences;
- *aromatic solvents and volatile chemicals*: 'glue sniffing' – very cheap and easily available, and so popular with young people.

Indirectly recreational are:

- *anabolic steroids*: used by some athletes to gain body mass – not psychoactive as such but prolonged use can generate high levels of aggression.

ADDICTION

PHYSICAL DRUG DEPENDENCY AND WITHDRAWAL

In some psychotherapeutic situations, especially those where the client is seriously misusing psychotropic substances, abstinence will be a desirable, if not an essential, goal. Sometimes it might even be a prerequisite for the whole counselling process. Of course, throughout the world as a whole, there are many, many, people who are harming themselves by improperly using all sorts of mood-altering chemicals. They too would greatly benefit if they could stop doing so. In many cases they would literally be saving their own lives. Clearly, if any individual can stop the misuse (the abuse even) of psychoactive drugs, then that is a 'good thing' – the problem is, how?

Actually, anyone can stop using an addictive substance. That is easy. It is 'staying stopped' that is hard. That is why the 'dry them out and chuck them out' treatment policies of the 1970s and 1980s failed alcohol-dependent patients so badly. Staying dry in the detox unit was doable. Staying that way in the outside world was a very different matter. The fact is that helping someone to successfully and permanently stop using their own particular type of 'chemical friend' is incredibly difficult, and experience tells us that it is a form of client work that is dogged by failure.

There are doubtlessly many reasons why helping addicts to change their self-harming behaviour is so hard. One of them could be that counsellors and psychotherapists might not always properly understand how chemical dependency works. After all, you have to know your enemies in order to be able to beat them. Healy (2009) offers us some very useful ideas about how psychotropic substance dependency might actually work. He argues that chemical dependency can be broken down into three distinct types.

Type 1 dependency

This is also known as *rebound symptomology* or *withdrawal reaction*. As we know, psychotropic drugs regulate the ability of the brain to take up certain neurotransmitters. Some patients, and some habitual drug users, become reliant on their drugs blocking any neurotransmitters that might trouble them. As a result, they seem to have become hypersensitive to the presence of any particularly upsetting 'chemical messengers'. Therefore when the blocking drugs are withdrawn, the resultant 'flood' of previously blocked neurotransmitters can cause extreme reactions. In other words, from a chemical point of view the drug misuser's body has got wildly out of balance. The process of regaining balance (homeostasis) can be likened to a swinging pendulum that oscillates back and forth before achieving equilibrium (Rinomhota and Marshal, 2000, offer a useful discussion of this topic).

All this means that a rebound effect can cause the patient to re-experience the original symptoms (or worse). So, for example, withdrawing beta-blockers might cause palpitations, withdrawing alcohol might cause fits or hallucinations and benzodiazepine withdrawal might cause extreme anxiety. In most cases, including the much feared opiate withdrawal, the rebound effect dissipates over three or four days and is rarely, if ever, fatal. However, because alcohol withdrawal can be occasionally physically dangerous for the patient it might sometimes need medical supervision.

Type 2 dependency

This is the *craving* type of chemical dependency. It has long been known that some of the 'pleasure spots' in the brain can be stimulated by the influx of certain drugs or chemicals (Olds and Milner, 1954; Bozarth, 1994). Stimulating these pleasure centres causes dopamine and other opioides to be produced, and this generates a 'feel good factor' in the user. Stop the drug and you stop the pleasure. This is the reason that many drug users who have apparently successfully withdrawn from their drug will frequently slide back into using it again. Without their dopamine-stimulating drugs, life just seems dull and pointless. However, their cravings are more than just a psychological need for pleasure. There are also physical needs (appetites) for the pleasure-generating biochemicals. The actual mechanism is complex (see Volkow et al., 2004, for an example). Complex or not, the resultant appetite is a sort of physical 'hunger' (a craving) that the dependent person feels driven to satisfying. This craving is very difficult to resist.

These pleasure-generating biochemicals can also be produced by activities that generate adrenaline, such as physical exercise, or by risk-taking behaviour, such as gambling, so it is as possible for some people to be as addicted to excessive or extreme behaviours as it is for others to be addicted to specific substances. These sorts of clients need extensive help, support and encouragement. Clearly, working with clients who are trying to overcome the behavioural, psychological, and physical components of any form of drug dependency is very much the role of counsellors and psycho-therapists.

Type 3 dependency

This is also known as *therapeutic dependency*. It occurs when someone who has been exposed to a drug or other addictive substance for a sufficiently long time undergoes a permanent change in his or her metabolism. The change is probably irreversible, and if the drug is withdrawn, the effects will be insupportable or even crippling. Therapeutically dependent people might well need that drug for the rest their lives in order to function at a reasonable level. If a regular supply of the substance in question can be secured, then the addict may well be able to live a normal existence. However, social prejudices, some professional practice beliefs, and political expediency usually prevent this. For example, GPs are reluctant to prescribe a permanent benzodiazepine regime for fear of being sued for medical negligence. Government policy still obstructs the therapeutic provision of cocaine, even for registered addicts. The public are 'against drugs'.

A DILEMMA

Counsellors and psychotherapists working with substance using/misusing clients can sometimes find themselves in a quandary. It is this: can counselling take place when the client is very much under the influence of a mood-affecting substance or obviously intoxicated? Put plainly, could you work successfully with a drunk? Would this intoxication mask the real person? Indeed, some therapists insist that their clients are free of all mind-altering drugs, even if prescribed by a doctor. Is this sensible psychotherapy or is it therapeutic cruelty? What do you think?

Case study 8.1   Pills versus talk for Percy

Percy wasn't feeling too good about himself. He felt generally dispirited, close to tears all the time, and he often thought about doing away with himself. 'I'd be better off dead,' he told himself. Percy was lonely, sad, and going downhill fast.

Eventually, he got so fed up with himself that he went to see his GP. The consultation took only two minutes. 'It's depression,' pronounced the doctor. 'Just take these pills.' Percy came away feeling very much dehumanised. He felt like he was just another medical statistic.

Percy took his pills. They didn't work, and anyway they made him feel sick, so he just stopped taking them. There didn't seem to be any point in going back to the GP. By now Percy was feeling even worse about himself and his life. It was 'last resort time', so Percy was even prepared to give counselling a go.

Percy went to see a counsellor. He didn't expect much and he definitely didn't get much. The counsellor didn't seem to say anything very much – she certainly didn't do anything. She seemed to be well meaning enough in a vague sort of way, but Percy just didn't 'get' her. She wasn't making him feel any better. They did make another appointment to meet, but Percy just couldn't see the point so he didn't turn up. The counsellor noted that 'this client is obviously not psychologically ready to engage with the therapeutic process', and she closed the file.

Just another DNA – the counsellor felt quite pleased with herself even if Percy wasn't feeling quite so chuffed.

The funny thing is that both the GP and the counsellor belong to the same mental health forum. They know each other quite well. However, as they both always agree, 'It isn't right to talk about cases.' As they always said, 'Doctors only look after bodies; it's the counsellor's job to look after minds.'

Poor old Percy; it's just as well that he seems a bit better these days. However, he is still very worried that his depression might come back again one day. That's scary because if it does, he has no idea where to go for help.

CHAPTER SUMMARY

The mind–body dilemma underpins much of the debate over the psychological explanations of the mental disorders. Are these disorders caused by psychological dysfunctions in the psyche (the mind) or by physical dysfunctions in the body? Traditionally, doctors have concentrated on the body, whereas counsellors and psychotherapists have concerned themselves with the mind. Equally traditionally, these two groups of professions, up until now at least, have tended to work in isolation from each other. It is time for a change.

Clearly, the use of psychoactive drugs is, at least on the surface, a commitment to the biological explanation of mental disorders. Taking this approach tends to support the idea that mental disorders are actually physical illnesses or biological 'errors'. It certainly seems reasonable – superficially so anyway – to argue that pharmacological treatments are very different from counselling and psychotherapeutic treatments. Put crudely, 'pills actually treat ills; talk is only talk'. This alleged philosophical and scientific split might well lie at the very heart of the old-fashioned medicine versus psychotherapy rivalries. Fortunately, these rivalries are rapidly disappearing.

Modern research is narrowing the apparent gap between the mind's cognition patterns and the body's functions. We can clearly see that psychotropic drugs affect the psychological mind, and we are increasingly finding that psychological treatments impact on the body. As we know, the power of the placebo in medical treatments is well established. The ability of the mind to cause changes in physical functioning has long been known. This leads us to wonder if the mind–body split has any meaning today. Has it become an artificial and outdated debate?

It is even arguable that the mind–body split has already been passed over by the doctors. After all, most of the psychotropic medications are dispensed with the advice that patients will normally benefit more if the drugs are accompanied by counselling and psychotherapy. The modern rule is very much 'pills *and* talk'. Indeed, very few doctors today will gainsay the importance of the psychological therapies. Perhaps it is now time for counsellors and psychotherapists to be equally generous in their attitudes to their medical colleagues. How many talking therapists routinely advise their clients of the potential benefits that they might gain if they got some help from their doctors? What about you? What do you do?

In sum, it can be strongly argued that counsellors and psychotherapists will be better able to properly help their clients if they better understand what is going on between those clients and their doctors. Part of achieving this improved understanding is to gain a better appreciation of the dos and don'ts of psychoactive medication and other mind-altering substances.

SUGGESTED FURTHER READING

Beddoe, R (2007) *Dying for a cure: a memoir of antidepressants, misdiagnosis and madness.* Sydney: Random House.

A very moving, very personal account of a journey through 'madness'.

Healy, D (2009) *Psychiatric drugs explained* – 5th edition. London: Churchill Livingstone Elsevier.

Essential reading – get it and read it right through. This is one of the few textbooks that you will need to read from cover to cover. Section 11, 'The marketing of tranquillity', is an eye-opener about modern medication use and misuse.

Moncrieff, J (2009) *A straight talking introduction to psychiatric drugs.* Ross-on-Wye: PCCS Books.

An alternative view on psychotropic drugs that challenges conventional wisdom – puts the consumer in the driving seat. Chapter 10, 'Withdrawing from psychiatric drugs', is essential reading.

Shapiro, H (2004) *Recreational drugs – a directory.* London: Collins and Brown.

CHAPTER 9

Legal and ethical issues

CORE KNOWLEDGE

- The 1983 Mental Health Act provides for 'the reception, care and treatment of the mentally disabled'.
- Section 1 of the 1983 Act defines mental disorder as 'mental illness, arrested or incomplete development of mind, psychopathic disorder and any other disorder or disability of mind'. There are four subcategories: severe mental impairment, mental impairment, psychopathic disorder, mental illness.
- Sections 2, 3 and 4 of the Act permit the compulsory detention and treatment of the mentally disordered under certain clinically necessary circumstances. This process is commonly known as 'sectioning'.
- The 2007 Mental Health Act amends the 1983 Act as follows:
  - gives only one definition of a mental disorder: 'any disorder or disability of mind';
  - applies only if the disorder is currently treatable.
- The 2005 Mental Capacity Act sets out the right that adults have to make their own decisions. This includes making decisions about their mental health treatment. The Act is based on five key principles:
  - everyone is assumed capable of making decisions, unless proved otherwise;
  - individuals must be given the support necessary in order to make decisions;
  - individuals may make eccentric or unwise decisions;
  - anything done for mentally incapable people must be in their best interests;
  - any intervention made on behalf of mentally incapable people should be the least restrictive of their basic rights and freedoms.

INTRODUCTION

The law and the talking therapies are uncomfortable bedfellows. The law is about specific rules. Therapy is about general guidelines. However, these two professions do inevitably interact from time to time. One key area where they certainly impact on each other is in the application of mental health law. These laws are not just about the state's rights over those suspected of mental incompetence; they are also about the rights of the mentally troubled to fair treatment and respect. This includes their right to be safe.

It is important for counsellors and psychotherapists to realise that they have no exemptions from the law. If their professional values and the law clash, then if therapists refuse to conform, they must pay the price. As the British Association for Counselling and Psychotherapy states in its ethical framework:

> *Practitioners should be aware of and understand any legal requirements concerning their work, consider these consciously and be legally accountable for their practice.*
>
> (BACP, 2002, p6)

In other words, 'it's up to you'.

To outsiders (including counsellors and psychotherapists) the law appears to be generally authoritarian and inflexible – 'rules are rules'. However, it is not consistent – what is apparently unlawful in one set of circumstances might be perfectly lawful in another set of circumstances. The courts will ask, 'How is the public interest best served?' (see Jenkins, 2007, Chapter 5). Is public interest better served by acting in one way or by acting in another way? For example, generally speaking professional confidences are protected by law. Clearly, this is usually in the public interest. However, confidentiality can be broken if doing so best serves a more important public need. This happened in the well-known case of *W* v *Egdell* (1990). W, who was a mental health patient, lost his action for breach of trust. He tried to sue a psychiatrist who broke confidence and told the authorities about W's apparently genuine intention to harm others with firearms and explosives. In other cases, the courts might conclude that the public interest is best served by maintaining confidentiality. Take the case of *D* v *NSPCC* (1978). A mother who was falsely accused of mistreating her child attempted to force the NSPCC to divulge the identity of her accuser. The court held that the public interest was best served by supporting the NSPCC's confidential links with the public.

Apart from those working in certain specialist settings, it is unlikely that very many counsellors and psychotherapists will have any direct dealings with mental health law. Most of their clients who have had psychiatric treatment or hospitalisation will have done so voluntarily. Nevertheless, some clients will have been (or might become) compulsorily detained or treated in hospital. Clearly, it would be useful if counsellors and psychotherapists better understood under what legal powers this might come about.

CURRENT MENTAL HEALTH LAW

In this chapter we are mainly concerned with the law as applied to England and Wales. Scotland has its own system, in particular the Mental Health (Care and Treatment) (Scotland) Act 2003 (www.scotland.gov.uk). However, as far as detention and treatment are concerned, there appear to be far more similarities than differences in the ways in which both legislatures have addressed the needs of the mentally disordered.

Until September 2007, the main UK mental health legislation was contained in the Mental Health Act 1983 and the Mental Capacity Act 2005. These Acts have now been amended by the Mental Health Act 2007. It should be noted that the 2007 Act is new legislation and has only recently started to come into force (November 2008 onwards). It is only now that it is starting to be tested in practice and it has not yet been properly tested in the courts. Almost certainly, there will be a raft of case law decisions yet to come, all of which will doubtlessly be complicated by the yet to be made decisions of the European courts.

Both the 2007 Mental Health Act and the 2005 Mental Incapacity Act are very much couched in terms of how they impact on the original 1983 Act. Therefore it is essential to first find out some of the key ways in which the 1983 Mental Health Act works.

THE MENTAL HEALTH ACT 1983

The stated purpose of the Mental Health Act 1983 is to provide for 'the reception, care and treatment of mentally disordered patients, the management of their property and other related matters' (Department of Health, 1983). This Act is divided into ten parts and 189 sections. The powers set out in the first four parts are of particular interest to counsellors and psychotherapists.

Part 1

In Part 1 the Act tells us how the law defines a mental disorder. According to the 1983 Act, 'mental disorder' means 'mental illness, arrested or incomplete development of mind, psychopathic disorder and any other disorder or disability of mind'.

There are four sub-categories of mental disorder:

i   *severe mental impairment*: a state of arrested or incomplete development of mind that includes severe impairment of intelligence and social functioning and is associated with abnormally aggressive or seriously irresponsible conduct on the part of the person concerned;

ii *mental impairment*: a state of arrested or incomplete development of mind (not amounting to severe mental impairment) that includes significant impairment of intelligence and social functioning and is associated with abnormally aggressive or seriously irresponsible conduct on the part of the person concerned;

iii *psychopathic disorder*: a persistent disorder or disability of mind (whether or not including significant impairment of intelligence) that results in abnormally aggressive or seriously irresponsible conduct on the part of the person concerned;

iv *mental illness*: a sub-category that is not defined. [This is a curious omission, especially as this sub-type of mental disorder is the one most commonly referred to in legal proceedings.]

Remember – these are *legal* definitions of what a mental disorder is. Classifying the actual disorder (depression, schizophrenia, etc.) depends on *clinical definitions*.

It is also important to remember what the legal definition of mental disorder is not. The 1983 Act states very clearly that people must not be deemed to have a form of mental disorder 'by reason only of promiscuity or other immoral conduct, sexual deviancy or dependence on alcohol or drugs'. Given that in the recent past people have been detained in mental hospitals because, for example, they have had illegitimate children or because they have engaged in certain sexual practices, this statement is an important safeguard.

Part 2

This is where the Act confers powers to detain someone in a hospital. When these powers have been applied, the patient is said to have been 'sectioned'. The compulsory detention and treatment procedures are as follows.

Section 2 Admission for assessment
This section permits detention for up to 28 days. An application to detain must be made by the patient's nearest relative or an Approved Mental Health Practitioner (formerly an Approved Social Worker). The application must also be approved by two doctors.

Section 3 Admission for treatment

This section permits detention for up to six months. It can be extended for an additional six months and then for one year at a time. Applications should be from relatives or Approved Mental Health Practitioners and must be confirmed medically.

Section 4 Emergency admission

Only one doctor is needed to confirm a Section 4 admission. The patient can be detained for up to 72 hours. However, after that an extended detention under other sections of the Act is always a possibility.

Part 3

This is the part of the 1983 Act that permits the courts to remand accused or convicted people to hospital for assessment and treatment.

Part 4

This is the part of the Act that permits compulsory treatment of patients. Compulsory treatment can include being referred to psychological therapists.

REFLECTION POINT

- What would you do if you had a client referred to you by a court for compulsory assessment? Can you argue a case for? What is the case against?
- Are you sure that all your current clients have really and truly come to see you on a voluntary basis? Do any of them feel that they have no choice? Are any of them, in effect, being 'sent' along? Does any of this really matter? Does it affect your work? How does it affect your work?

COMMENT

It has long been a professional mantra that therapists should only see clients who have come along voluntarily. However, that somewhat idealistic intention may not always match reality. It is always possible that some clients may feel compelled – if only indirectly – to see a counsellor or psychotherapist in order to escape some sort of penalty. For example, some clients may be trying to save their jobs and other clients may be trying to save their marriages.

As we know, before the client and the therapist first meet, there are usually quite a lot of fantasy expectations around. So it is possible that the 'Did they jump or were they pushed?' question does not really matter. Perhaps the real question is 'How can the therapist ensure that the client really wants to come back next time?'

MENTAL CAPACITY ACT 2005

This Act was brought into being as a result of the European Court of Human Rights (2004) decision in the so-called 'Bournewood case'. The Court found that HL, a 49-year old autistic man, had been unlawfully detained when he was compulsorily admitted to Bournewood Psychiatric Hospital due to supposed mental incapacity. Although HL was apparently content with his 'friendly, but involuntary' detention, the European Court found that the initial assumption of HL's incapacity was insupportable because his capabilities had not been formally assessed.

The Mental Capacity Act states that 'a person who lacks capacity' means:

> *a person who lacks the capacity to make a particular decision or take a particular action for themselves at the time that the decision or action needs to be taken.*
>
> (Mental Capacity Act, 2005, Code of Practice)

The Act is designed to protect an individual's best interests. The problem lies in deciding just what someone's best interests really are. The Act requires practitioners to ask themselves: 'Is the person in question really incapable of acting on their own behalf?' Any assumption that someone lacks the ability to make meaningful decisions is tested by the following questions.

1 Is there an impairment or disturbance in the functioning of the person's mind or brain?
2 Is the impairment or disturbance sufficient that the person lacks the capacity to make a particular decision?

The whole of the 2005 Act is underpinned by a set of five key principles.

- *A presumption of capacity* – every adult has the right to make their own decisions and must be assumed to have capacity to do so unless it is proved otherwise.
- *Support in decision making* – individuals must be given all appropriate assistance before anyone concludes that they cannot make their own decisions.
- *Unwise decisions* – individuals must retain the right to make what might be seen as eccentric or unwise decisions.

- *Best interests* – anything done for or on behalf of people without capacity must be in their best interests.
- *Least restrictive intervention* – anything done for or on behalf of people without capacity should be the least restrictive of their basic rights and freedoms.

The assessment of incapacity is *task specific*. A demonstration of incapacity in one area of someone's life does not automatically demonstrate incapacity in another area. For example, a person may have the capacity to undertake sheltered employment but not be capable of managing money. Furthermore, if the incapacity is likely to be temporary (for example, drug-induced dementia), then unless obviously urgent decisions are necessary, all other decisions about that person's life should be deferred until the temporary loss of function is over and the capacity to make decisions has been regained.

THE MENTAL HEALTH ACT 2007

The main purpose of the 2007 Act is to amend the 1983 Act. It is also being used to introduce Deprivation of Liberty Safeguards (DOLS) by amending the Mental Capacity Act 2005.

As we now know, the 1983 Act is largely concerned with the circumstances in which a person with a mental disorder can be forcibly detained for treatment. It also sets out the safeguards for patients, together with the processes that must be followed, in order to ensure that they are not being inappropriately detained or treated. The main purpose of this legislation is to ensure that people with serious mental disorders that threaten their well-being or safety, or the safety of the public, can be treated irrespective of their consent where it is necessary to prevent them from harming themselves or others.

These are the main changes and amendments to the 1983 Mental Health Act made by the 2007 Act:

- contains only one definition of a mental disorder, which is 'any disorder or disability of mind';
- applies only if the disorder is currently treatable;
- might not apply to personality disorders;
- introduces Supervised Community Treatment – a sort of 'release under licence' provided the patient keeps up with any planned treatments; failure to comply can result in recall to hospital;
- allows patients the right to access advocacy services;
- offers patients more scope to refuse electro-convulsive therapy;
- allows the role of 'nearest relative' to be challenged; civil partners are recognised;

- widens the range of practitioners who can assume professional roles in patient care and treatment;
- improves patients' access to mental health review tribunals;
- requires age-appropriate mental health services to be provided for young people.

ETHICAL ISSUES AND MENTAL HEALTH

It is likely that most counsellors and psychotherapists are more focused on their profession's ethical values than they are on what the law requires of them. However, these two forms of professional control are not necessarily in competition. For example, the ethical codes published by most of psychotherapy's professional organisations emphasise the importance of 'beneficence'. This ethical value is not dissimilar to the principle of 'duty of care' that the law demands of any service provider in any field of activity.

Parsons (2000) suggests that most ethical codes share common features that usually include firm moral dimensions. It therefore seems reasonable to assume that the British Association for Counselling and Psychotherapy's Ethical Framework (www.bacp.co.uk/ethical_framework/) is typical of the ethical codes usually found in the caring professions. Anyway, it seems that many counsellors and counselling organisations, whether members or not of the BACP, claim to comply with this particular ethical code. Let us now look at how the BACP framework interacts with the law's demands in the case of counsellors and psychotherapists who work with the mentally disturbed or the psychiatrically disordered.

Fidelity

Ethical Framework: *Practitioners should be trustworthy and regard confidentiality as a professional obligation.*

The law: *Practitioners are duty bound to maintain confidences and to act in a faithful (fiduciary) manner.*

For instance, suppose a client who is known to have a diagnosable mental disorder reveals that they are behaving in a way that is causing severe psychological harm to another person. Perhaps this client is aggressively stalking someone. Does that belief, which may be based on factual evidence, permit the therapist to consider breaking that trust to seek some help for the victim? Ethical constraints might advise against so doing. On the other hand, the law does sometimes permit a breach of confidentiality – after all, stalking someone is a highly illegal criminal activity. It is a long-established legal principle that 'there is no confidence in iniquity' (*Gartside v Outram*, 1856). In other words, if you confess to someone that you have committed a crime and that you intend to carry on doing so, then you forfeit your right to confidentiality.

Autonomy

Ethical Framework: *Practitioners should respect the client's right to be self-governing and should not manipulate clients against their will, even for beneficial social ends.*

The law: *Practitioners must have clear contracts with their clients that are freely entered into on a basis of informed consent. In mental health law, the capacity to consent (or not) to treatment is always assumed unless incapacity can be demonstrated.*

For instance, suppose a counsellor encounters a seriously disturbed client. The counsellor might well decide to persuade, or even to pressure, that client into consulting a psychiatrist. In some circumstances this might result in the client being detained in a secure mental unit and even forced to undergo treatment. Perhaps the client is dangerously demented. Compulsory detention might be necessary in order to prevent harm to others.

On the other hand, such a constraining course of action might mean that a high-quality creative talent, albeit one that was being expressed in unorthodox ways, is being stifled. With the benefit of hindsight, it might have been a 'good thing' to have imprisoned Fred West or Peter Sutcliffe 'in advance'. However, what about 'crazies' such as van Gogh or William Blake? Should they too have been incarcerated and their 'mad' activities curtailed?

Beneficence

Ethical Framework: *Practitioners should act in the best interests of their clients and work within their own individual limits of competence.*

The law: *Practitioners have a duty of care towards their clients.*

Take the case of a therapist who has been working for some time with a client and has reason to believe that some useful progress is being made. For example, perhaps the client's depression appears to be lifting a bit. Now suppose that the therapist subsequently discovers that this client is drinking at health-threatening levels and has been doing so for some time. Should the therapist specifically advise the client about the personal and physical dangers of misusing alcohol? Should the answer to that question, or even the degree of responsibility for providing professional advice, depend on just how expert the therapist is in alcohol abuse issues?

Non-maleficence

Ethical Framework: *Practitioners should have a commitment to avoiding harm to the client. This includes not acting incompetently or inappropriately and having a responsibility to challenge incompetence or malpractice in others.*

The law: *Practitioners must work in accordance with professional standards.*

It seems likely that therapists can claim to be working to accepted professional standards if they can show that any actions taken (or not taken) are in accordance with the practices of a significant number (not a majority) of responsible professional colleagues. This is the so-called 'Bolam' defence (*Bolam* v *Friern Hospital*, 1957). Of course, whether or not counsellors and psychotherapists are likely to find support from their colleagues for their individual methodological idiosyncrasies remains to be seen.

Justice

Ethical Framework: *Practitioners should attempt to treat all their clients fairly and without discrimination and be aware of any potential conflicts between ethical intentions and legal obligations.*

The law: *Everyone, without exception, must comply with anti-discriminatory, equal access, and human rights legislation.*

Both legally and ethically, these are universally accepted principles – at least in theory. Their practice, however, is not always quite so straightforward. For example, it might be acceptable to insist that all psychotherapists working in women's refuges must be female. However, would it be equally acceptable for a counselling agency to accept only black clients or for a private practitioner to prefer to work with elderly white clients?

Self-respect

Ethical Framework: *Practitioners should be responsible for their own self-care and for maintaining their capability to remain competent therapists. A high degree of self-awareness is essential.*

The law: *Practitioners must be able to take all reasonable care and exhibit all reasonable skills when applying their trade. Consumer protection law applies, and appropriate insurance policies should be kept in force.*

Clearly therapists must be sufficiently personally healthy, both emotionally and physically, to be able to offer their clients their best attentions and services. In other words, they need to apply all of the ethical principles listed above to themselves as well. Suppose a counsellor is working with a couple who are going through a bad patch in their relationship – perhaps they have both been bereaved recently. Also suppose that after, say, five fairly productive sessions, the counsellor learns that one of his own close relatives has just received a terminal diagnosis. Should that counsellor stop work, and if so, how should this be managed in respect of the troubled couple or, indeed, for any other current clients? Alternatively, can it be argued that it might be better for all concerned if the counsellor stays at work and tries to carry on leading as normal a life as possible?

Case study 9.1   Client care, client harm, or just plain old-fashioned exploitation?

Olaf was a devotee of the encounter group movement; he was a 'groupie's groupie'. Carl Rogers and Fritz Perls were his idols. Olaf absolutely loved being in the encounter groups. He especially valued those where nudity was encouraged. That's where he felt that everyone was being totally 'genuine'.

In his work as a person-centred counsellor, Olaf was insistent that absolutely nothing should come between him and his clients. This, he eventually decided, included clothes. He managed to persuade some of his clients that they and he should strip off in order to be 'more open with each other'. One of them, an early-twenties female patient, although initially compliant, was eventually sufficiently disturbed by Olaf's methods to make a complaint to his professional association.

At the subsequent enquiry Olaf argued that although nude counselling was unusual, he was actually working to acceptable professional standards (the 'Bolam' defence). He is still working on an explanation of why his admittedly curious professional practices seem to have been applied only to his more attractive female clients.

CHAPTER SUMMARY

Some counsellors and psychotherapists might feel that what they do is so special that it deserves privileged protection. The law does not agree – everybody in our society is equally subject to the rule of law, and there are no special provisions for therapists. If, for example, like psychotherapist Anne Hayman (see Hayman, 1965), you choose to take what you might think is a principled stand against the law's demands, then, like her, you must be prepared for the consequences. Anne Hayman refused to breach client confidentiality and she got away with it. You might not be so lucky.

Clearly, all counsellors and psychotherapists need to work both within the law generally and within mental health law in particular. Getting you up to speed on mental health law is what this chapter has been all about.

Therapists will do well to always remember the well-known legal maxim, 'ignorance of the law is no excuse'. So do have a look at the suggested further reading list for this chapter. One day you might be very glad you did so.

SUGGESTED FURTHER READING

Barber, P, Brown, R and Martin, D (2008) *Mental health law in England and Wales.* Exeter: Learning Matters.

Excellent chapters on the very latest legislation. Contains the full text of the main body of the Mental Health Act (as amended) as well as the relevant rules and regulations.

Bond, T (2009) *Standards and ethics for counselling in action,* 3rd Edition. London: Sage.

It's the classic guide for all counsellors – buy it, read all of it, keep it handy.

Brown, R, Adshead, G and Pollard, A (2009) *The approved mental health professional's guide to psychiatry and medication.* Exeter: Learning Matters.

A very good 'jargon-busting' book that provides a handy quick-reference guide to many mental health issues. An excellent explanation of the work of the mental health professionals.

Jenkins, P (2007) *Counselling, psychotherapy and the law.* London: Sage.

Essential reading – all of it. Very well set out and easy to work through. It is all you need to know.

Jenkins, P (ed.) (2002) *Legal issues in counselling and psychotherapy.* London: Sage.

A well-presented, very well-written anthology that contains lots of very interesting and instructional tales about therapy and the law. This is a particularly informative book as it is written by practising therapists and lawyers.

CHAPTER 10

New ideas about mental health

CORE KNOWLEDGE

- Our understanding of mental health as a function of brain activity is rapidly expanding as our knowledge of the brain's biological processes and physiological structures also advances. The current areas of active investigation include:
  - the neurological functioning of the brain and what that will tell us about personality and everyday behaviours;
  - the biochemical functioning of the brain and what that will tell us about the mental disorders;
  - the genetic development of the brain and what that will tell us about our inherent personal qualities and developmental potentials.
- Research-led progress in medical science is currently unlikely to eliminate the need for counselling and psychotherapy. It might instead provide a solid evidential basis for future practices in the talking therapies. Such advances might help therapists to identify their clients' problems more precisely. They might help therapists to more accurately tailor their psychotherapeutic responses to client need. Perhaps yet to be gained knowledge will help therapists to become better at properly measuring the successes or failures of their therapeutic activities.
- Counsellors and psychotherapists will find it profitable to keep up with the coming advances in the scientific understanding of mental health.

INTRODUCTION

Clearly, medical science in all it guises (genetic, biochemical, physiological, psychological, and so on) will have much to say about future trends in mental health as they emerge over the coming years. Obviously, counsellors and psychotherapists who are scientifically minded will be comfortable about keeping up with all that is going on. However, maintaining a detailed – or a highly technical and academic – watch over the research is not essential for everybody. Of course, this does not mean that therapists should not carry out their own enquiries if they so wish. What it does mean is that therapists need only be 'intelligent users' of the research findings; they are not necessarily obliged to be researchers themselves. Counsellors and psychotherapists only really need to have a broad-brush understanding of all that is likely to be going on generally in mental health research. However, maintaining and updating such a general awareness and appreciation of what is emerging in professions beyond their own is a truly vital task for the modern talking therapist.

The key question for all counsellors and psychotherapists is to ask what the future might hold for them as professional practitioners. What new ideas might emerge that will have an impact on their work with their clients? For the everyday practitioner, new ideas about, say, the biochemistry of the neurotransmitters are of no immediate relevance if they cannot be applied in the 'here and now' of today's therapy room. However, this does not mean that any such new ideas are unimportant; it just means that they might not be important right now.

As well as evolving in a scientific and a theoretical sense, counselling and psychotherapy will also be evolving in a practice-delivery sense. What sorts of changes in the practice of psychotherapy are happening today that are likely to affect the ways that we approach the mental health issues of tomorrow?

So where are all the new ideas in mental health currently coming from? Where are they likely to be found? How might they affect the everyday practice of counselling and psychotherapy? It might be helpful if we now take a brief look at what the future might hold.

NEUROPSYCHOLOGY

There are huge developments going on in our ability to map the brain. Powerful electronic scanners are allowing investigators to learn more and more about how the brain works. Modern technology allows us to observe the electrical activity in the brain as various psychological events unfold (Rapp, 2001; Cabeza, 2006; and many others). Some claim that these, and similar neuropsychological techniques, allow researchers to 'see' depression as it evolves or to 'watch' anxiety in action as it appears in someone's physical brain (Posner et al., 2009). It is even possible that we might eventually be able to observe all of someone's psychological emotions and interactions as they physiologically unfold in the brain (Frith and Frith, 2003). From a therapy point of view, such a sophisticated level of understanding brain activity could have a number of uses.

For example, perhaps understanding brain activity properly could help us to check out our theoretical bases and biases. After all, much of our client work depends on our assumption that our clients' minds work in certain ways. According to our therapeutic backgrounds, we think that we can explain how our clients get anxious, why they are concerned about relationships, what makes them become depressed, and so on. Brain imaging might be able to test if these beliefs have any substance. For instance, if the neurophysiology does not eventually support Freud's ideas about how our minds are supposed to have a typology that includes an Id, an Ego and a Superego, then psycho-dynamic practitioners will have an awful lot of rethinking to do.

In another example, perhaps it might turn out that monitoring the brain's electrical activity could help therapists to check up on the progress of their work with their clients or even to evaluate their own professional abilities. For instance, suppose that a cognitive-behavioural practitioner is attempting to help a client with depression. Further suppose that neuroimaging could 'see' that client's depression. What if that imaging was showing no reduction in the patient's depression levels despite the cognitive-behavioural practitioner's best efforts? Could this mean that the CBT theorists might have been wrong all along, or might it simply be that this particular practitioner is incompetent? Perhaps CBT is the wrong treatment for this particular patient?

BIOCHEMISTRY

From a biochemical point of view there is much that is yet to be discovered. All we actually know is that it is very likely that the neurotransmitters are intimately connected with mental function (Healy, 2009; and many others). However, it could be argued that we only really know about how this might work from a backwards point of view. The research pattern seems to be that we find (or rediscover) the drug first and only then find (or invent) a disease that fits it. Then we hypothesise about how this new medication does its job. By the way, it is worth remembering that 'hypothesise' is only a posh word for 'making a guess'.

It works like this. A new drug might be developed or an old one might be reassessed. By chance it is discovered that this drug offers some relief for a certain mental disorder. We also come to believe that this drug affects a certain neurotransmitter in some way or other. Therefore, this neurotransmitter is alleged to be at the root of that particular 'mental abnormality'. However, time and time again we find that this apparently obvious cause-and-effect link is not as clear-cut as we first thought (Moncrieff, 2007; Tone, 2008). For example, as we saw in Chapter 6, the links between schizophrenia and dopamine are nothing like as simple as was first thought (Seeman et al., 2005).

It seems that none of psychiatry's so-called new 'miracle drugs' has ever been quite as miraculous as was first hoped (Kirsch, 2009). In every case, the biochemical mechanism has turned out to be much more complex than we first thought it would be (Lake, 2006). It seems that we are still a long way away from developing specific drug therapies for the mental disorders (Fonagy, 2004) – if, indeed, we can ever do so. This does not mean that trying to use drug therapy to help the mentally disordered is wasted effort. Medication does help many people, or at least it gives them a measure of relief. Drugs often enable mentally disordered people to lead fulfilling and functioning lives. Realistically, no cure in medical science generally works for everybody, and no remedy can guarantee permanent freedom from the original disease. Why should we expect anything more from the psycho-active medications?

GENETICS

Again, there is much yet to be learned. However, as far as we can tell at the moment, it seems unlikely that we will discover a specific gene for each mental disorder (see the review by Leigh, 2010). For now, the general trend is towards thinking that we might find that a particular combination of genes can create a socio-biological vulnerability to certain mental disorders (Plomin and McGuffin, 2003). If that were to be the case, then we could think about developing some new types of treatment to help our patients/clients overcome this vulnerability. For example, it might become possible to provide some sort of yet to be discovered preventative medication. In another example, we might become able to provide some psychological 'reinforcement therapy' targeted at beefing up the client's coping mechanisms. Perhaps therapists might develop new ways of helping clients strengthen their emotional functioning in order to prevent the predicted disorders ever emerging.

There is increasing evidence to suggest that the mental disorders are the result of complex interactions between genetic vulnerability and personal environmental deficits (Goldberg and Goodyer, 2008). As these environmental deficits include psychosocial problems, there may well be a place for counselling and psychotherapy either in the prevention (or the resolution) of any personal problems that might eventually arise from these supposed genetic vulnerabilities.

REFLECTION POINT

Many current practitioners in the various talking therapies initially found themselves attracted to these sorts of disciplines because they seem to be based on creative and informal principles. However, the general drift of the latest theoretical research and modern practice development seems to go against such a free-ranging philosophical approach. Possibly a move towards a much more formal, much more science-based professional structure is emerging. Would any such changes result in a more firmly rooted therapeutic discipline or might something essential be lost along the way?

- What about you? Are you, or do you want to be, a researcher-practitioner perhaps with a solid scientific underpinning, or would you prefer a looser calling and practice as an innovative and creative humanistic therapist?
- Practitioner-science or practitioner-licence? Where do you stand?

COMMENT

This last question seems to be a never-ending debate in the talking therapies. Put crudely, is psychotherapy an art or a science? These sorts of issues are further complicated by the possibility that counselling and psychotherapy might become a statutorily regulated profession. If this does come about, then it will almost certainly put a rules-bound straitjacket around what has traditionally been seen as being a rules-free profession.

However, it might be that the art versus science debate is something that we can relegate to history. After all, perhaps one day neuroimaging will show us all the electrical workings of an artist's brain and identify the 'creative circuits' in action. If we can do that, then we might well have at long last merged art and science. Perhaps we will have finally demonstrated that they are both simply different aspects of a unitary and fundamental way of 'knowing'. Of course, some people already take such a view of learning and being – it did not need any advanced research to get them there either.

NEW IDEAS AND NEW PSYCHOTHERAPY

Research-based

The problem with psychotherapeutic research to date is that it seems to have left us with far more questions than answers. For example, we do not know very much about which people benefit – or, indeed, how they benefit – from which types of counselling and psychotherapy (Lambert, 2004). We know that generally the talking therapies do work, but we do not really know why they work (Wampold, 2001; Farmer et al., 2002). This is just not good enough. Why should counsellors and psychotherapists insist on a respected place in society if they cannot show why they deserve such a privilege?

Is it possible that counselling and psychotherapy might be better able to justify itself if new research in the psychological therapies could be more firmly linked with new developments in psychopathology? Perhaps if we could observe how neurophysiological and biochemical mechanisms cause mental disorders, we might also be able to monitor the actual effects of the various psychotherapies on those disorders. Suppose that we could say, 'Yes, my therapy works for depression and here is a brain scan to prove it.' If we could eventually obtain such solid evidence in support of psychotherapy, just think how confident its future practitioners could be about their work. After all, today's psychotherapies are mainly based on ideas that assume human personalities work 'as if' ('as if' they are influenced by a transference-like process; 'as if' people need to self-actualise, and so on). Perhaps the therapies of the future could be designed in the light of a more informed knowledge base, one that replaces 'as if' with 'it is'.

If we could monitor the progress of our work in ways that inspire scientific confidence, then we might be able to discard the therapies that do not really work, or do not work efficiently enough. We could also fine-tune the ones that do work. We might even be able to use newly derived psychopatho-logical principles to create new therapies. In other words, the psycho-therapies of the future could be purpose-designed. For example, suppose a genetic predisposition to developing anxiety under certain social conditions were to be discovered. Therapists might then be able to help their clients to avoid those situations in the first place. Alternatively they might be able to help clients to gather the inner psychological resources necessary to overcome any adverse circumstances before a need to use them ever arises. Perhaps we might find ourselves developing some radically new forms of counselling and psychotherapy to meet those anticipated needs? One day, might there be a truly 'preventative' form of counselling and psychotherapy, perhaps a form of psychological 'vaccination'?

Practice-based

It is not just science that is propelling forward new ideas about mental health. Money is having a major effect, too. As we know, the general trend of the research (Roth and Fonagy, 2005; and many others) seems to show that the drug-based treatments and the talking therapies are, when taken in the round, about equally useful in cases of mental health need. That seems clear enough. Apparently it does not really seem to matter very much what sorts of treatments we choose to provide.

However, when expressed in financial terms, one form of treatment stands out. CBT (as currently envisaged by the National Health Service) is easily the least expensive to provide. This is because it is routinely delivered in six sessions or less by some very cheap-to-train technicians, and that is why the government is investing so heavily in its 'Improving Access to Psychological Therapies' programme (Department of Health, 2008a). The government's intention is quite clear. It is actively promoting an ongoing huge expansion in the availability of CBT throughout the NHS and a similarly huge expansion in the number of CBT 'para-therapists' who are being trained to carry out this work. This is not a wishy-washy NHS 'mission statement' – it is actually happening right now.

The overwhelming majority of these extra health workers will be those classed as 'psychological wellbeing practitioners'. The NHS is recruiting trainee wellbeing practitioners who 'will not necessarily possess previous clinical or professional expertise in mental health' (Department of Health, 2008b). Initially coming from minimally qualified backgrounds, each of this new breed of psychological para-therapists is given 45 days' training and then let loose on an unsuspecting public. Recruiting and training these practitioners is simple and certainly very inexpensive. They do not need to be paid very much either (around £20k full-time) – a management 'dream'. The first of these new-style mental health care workers entered service in 2010.

Clearly these new mental health technicians will eventually replace many of the more expensive to run – and much more expensive to train – professional counsellors and psychotherapists who currently work in the NHS and elsewhere. These new developments are having a knock-on effect outside the NHS, too. For example, anecdotal evidence suggests that therapists currently working in the Employee Assistance Programmes are increasingly being required to hold a CBT qualification. It looks like there are going to be some major changes in mental health services and provision in the UK, irrespective of any possible research-led changes in counselling and psychotherapy innovation.

CONCLUSION

Counselling and psychotherapy seem to be on the brink of fundamental change. The profession is likely to become statutorily regulated and therefore more controlled, and expansions in the NHS are likely to increase the demand for psychological therapists. As society becomes ever more pressured, the need for demonstrably effective psychological relief is likely to become even more essential. All this will very probably mean that counsellors and psycho-therapists will not only have to operate to nationally approved standards but that they will also have to prove that they do, and counsellors and psychotherapists will find themselves increasingly being measured against other 'traders' in the supply of mental health services. Therefore, therapists will inevitably need to know what the other caring professions are up to. The talking therapies will no longer be able to exist in majestic isolation.

Counselling and psychotherapy is likely to remain an integral part (but only a part) of the overall world of mental health patient care. In particular, responding properly to the demands of the future will mean that counsellors and psychotherapists must gain a much better understanding of the medical approaches to mental health. However, as they do this, there is a core message that counsellors and psychotherapists need to take on board: medics are not their rivals but their co-workers in an area of health care practice where the doctors have as much to learn from the psychological therapists as the psychological therapists have to learn from them.

It would be fascinating to be able to peek, say, twenty years into the future, to see just what books like this one will be saying then. Perhaps the current methodological divisions in psychotherapy will have disappeared. Possibly therapy might have become more of a science than an art. On the other hand, it might well still remain the case that the totality of the person (what makes someone 'tick') is simply too complicated to be reducible to scientific rules and manipulation. Maybe, as far as humans are concerned, the whole really is more than the sum of the parts.

In any event, counsellors and psychotherapists need not fear the future if they are prepared to embrace all that it might hold. The evidence to date is that the probable advances in our understanding of how the mind actually works are unlikely to diminish the need for, or the status of, the therapist's task. After all, the role of the psychological therapist has so far been an expanding one and health care providers seem to be ever increasing their provision of the psychological therapies. For now, it is not very likely that counsellors and psychotherapists will find themselves reduced to mere psychological 'technicians' whose mundane job it is to devise ways of lessening or eliminating the effects of predictable, even preventable, mental crises.

The key to making counselling and psychotherapy a respected and innovative profession, one that provides the highest standards of service to its clients, is learning: learning about ourselves, learning about our profession, and learning about what our colleagues can offer. By increasing our professional knowledge we will gain professional confidence. If we increase our cross-disciplinary learning we become equipped to no longer fear our colleagues in the parallel professions but, instead, can respect them from a position of professional parity.

Of course, in terms of workaday counselling and psychotherapeutic practice none of this speculation about the future really matters, at least not for now. What does matter is just what you are going to say to the real-life clients who you will be seeing today. The core message of this book is that, irrespective of how good you are at working with your clients (or how good you think you are), other people can help them too, and this includes the medical profession. This book has been all about telling you how to take advantage of what the medical profession can offer both you and your clients. It has also been about suggesting ways in which doctors could usefully take advantage of your skills in return. I hope you have found it helpful.

SUGGESTED FURTHER READING

At this stage of your learning you really need to be keeping up with the latest developments in mental health concerns as they are emerging. You will probably best do this if you monitor the online publications including the suggested websites listed below. You should also look out for any new texts by checking the book reviews in the various professional journals such as *Therapy Today* or *The Psychotherapist*. It is a good idea to keep an eye on the forthcoming books listed on the Learning Matters website, too.

Online resources:

- the Royal College of Psychiatrists: go to www.rcpsych.ac.uk and click on 'Mental Health Info';
- National Institute for Health and Clinical Excellence: go to www.nice.org.uk and click on 'Find guidance'; type the name of the topic (e.g. 'depression', 'bipolar') into the search box;
- *DSM V*: go to www.dsm5.org and keep up with how the production of the forthcoming next edition of this vital reference text is progressing;
- Improving Access to Psychological Therapies (IAPT): go to www.iapt.nhs.uk and check out all the developments as they happen.

References

Abbott, R (2009) Religious fundamentalism and mental illness: a group analytic exploration. *Group Analysis*, 42 (1), 47–61.

Abreu, P and Santos, C (2008) Behavioural models of depression: a critique of the emphasis on positive reinforcement. *International Journal of Behavioural Consultation and Therapy*, 4 (2), 130–45.

Acarturk C, Cuijpers P, van Straten A and de Graaf, R (2009) Psychological treatment of social anxiety disorder: a meta-analysis. *Psychological Medicine*, 39 (2), 241–54.

Adshead, G and Jacob, C (2007) *Personality disorder: the definitive reader*. London: Jessica Kingsley.

Aldwin, C (2007) *Stress, coping and development: an integrative perspective*. New York: Guilford Press.

Alloy, L, Abramson, L, Urosevic, S, Walshaw, P, Nusslock, R and Nareen, A (2005) The psychosocial context of bipolar disorder: environmental, cognitive, and developmental risk factors. *Clinical Psychology Review*, 25 (8), 1043–75.

Andreasen, N (2000) Schizophrenia: the fundamental questions. *Brain Research*, 31 (2–3), 106–12.

Arieti, S (1974) *Interpretation of schizophrenia*, republished 1994. Lanham MD: Jason Aronson.

Arseneault, L, Cannon, M, Witton, J and Murray, R (2004) Causal association between cannabis and psychosis: an examination of the evidence. *British Journal of Psychiatry*, 184, 110–17.

BACP (British Association for Counselling and Psychotherapy) (2002) *Ethical framework for good practice in counselling and psychotherapy*. Leicester: BACP. Online at www.bacp.co.uk/ethical_framework/.

Bager-Charleson, S and van Rijn, B (2011) *Understanding assessment in counselling and psychotherapy*. Exeter: Learning Matters.

Bandura, A (1977) *Social learning theory*, Englewood Cliffs NJ: Prentice-Hall.

Barber, P, Brown, R and Martin, D (2008) *Mental health law in England and Wales: a guide for approved mental health professionals*. Exeter: Learning Matters.

Barker, P and Buchanan-Barker, P (2010) No excuses: the reality cure of Thomas Szasz. *The Journal of Critical Psychology, Counselling and Psychotherapy*, 10 (2).

Barry, A-M and Yuill, C (2008) *Understanding the sociology of health: an introduction*. London: Sage.

Bateman, A and Fonagy, P (2000) Effectiveness of psychotherapeutic treatment of personality disorder. *The British Journal of Psychiatry*, 177, 138–43.

Beck, A (1967) *Depression: causes and treatment*. Philadelphia PA: University of Pennsylvania Press.

Beck, A (1991) *Cognitive therapy and the emotional disorders*. London: Penguin.

Beck, A and Alford, B (2009) *Depression: causes and treatment*, 2nd edition. Philadelphia PA: University of Pennsylvania Press.

Beck, A, Emerey, G and Greenberg, R (1985) *Anxiety disorders and phobias: a cognitive perspective*, republished 2005. New York: Basic Books.

Beck, J S (1995) *Cognitive therapy: basics and beyond*. New York: Guilford Press.

Beck, U (1992) *Risk society: towards a new modernity*. London: Sage.

Beddoe, R (2007) *Dying for a cure: a memoir of anti-depressants, misdiagnosis and madness.* Sydney: Random House.

Bentall, R (2004) *Madness explained: psychosis and human nature.* London: Penguin.

Berati, S (2003) Psychoanalytic psychotherapy of psychosis. *Annals of General Hospital Psychiatry*, 2 (Suppl 1): s52.

Bhugra, D (2005) The global prevalence of schizophrenia. *Public Library of Science Medicine*, 2 (5), 151–71.

Bicchieri, C (2005) *The grammar of society: the nature and dynamics of social norms.* Cambridge: Cambridge University Press.

Boardman, J, Currie, A, Killaspy, H and Mezey, G (eds) (2010) *Social inclusion and mental health.* London: RCPS Publications.

Bond, T (2009) *Standards and ethics for counselling in action*, 3rd edition. London: Sage.

Bowlby, J (1991) *Attachment and loss: sadness and depression.* London: Penguin.

Bozarth, M (1994) Pleasure systems in the brain, in Warburton, D (ed.) *Pleasure: the politics and the reality.* New York: Wiley.

Bracke, P, Colman, E, Symoens, S and Van Praag, L (2010) Divorce, divorce rates, and professional care seeking for mental health problems in Europe: a cross-sectional population-based study. *BioMed Central Public Health*, 10, 224.

Brampton, S (2009) *Shoot the damn dog: a memoir of depression.* London: Bloomsbury Publishing.

Brown, A (2008) *Has there been a decline in values in British society?* Joseph Rowntree Foundation. Online at www.jrf.org.uk/publications/has-there-been-decline-values-british-society.

Brown, G and Harris, T (1978) *The social origins of depression.* London: Tavistock Publishing.

Brown, R, Adshead, G and Pollard, A (2009) *The approved mental health professionals' guide to mental health law*, 2nd edition. Exeter: Learning Matters.

Brown, S, Barraclough, B and Inskip, H (2000) The causes of excess mortality of schizophrenia. *British Journal of Psychiatry*, 177, 212–17.

Bush, F, Redden, M and Shapiro, T (2004) *Psychodynamic treatment of depression.* Arlington VA: American Psychiatric Publishing.

Butler, A, Chapman, J, Forman, E and Beck, A (2006) The empirical status of cognitive-behavioural therapy: a review of a meta-analysis. *Clinical Psychology Review*, 26 (1), 17–31.

Butler, G, Fennel, M and Hackman, A (2008) *Cognitive-behavioural therapy for anxiety disorders* (Guides to Individualised Evidence-based Treatment). New York: Guilford Press.

Bynum, W, Porter, R and Shepherd, M (1984) *The anatomy of madness, Vol 1.* London: Tavistock Press.

Cabeza, R (2006) *Handbook of functional neuroimaging of cognition.* Cambridge MA: MIT Press.

Canino, G and Allegria, M, (2008) Psychiatric diagnosis: is it universal or relative to culture? *Journal of Child Psychology and Psychiatry*, 49 (3), 237–50.

Churchill, S (2011) *The troubled mind: a handbook of therapeutic approaches to psychological distress.* Basingstoke: Palgrave Macmillan.

Claringbull, N (2010) *What is counselling and psychotherapy?* Exeter: Learning Matters.

Clark, D, Beck, A and Alford, B (1999) *Scientific foundations and therapy of depression.* Chichester: Wiley.

Clark, L (2007) Assessment and diagnosis of personality disorder: perennial issues and an emerging reconceptualisation. *Annual Review of Psychology*, 58, 227–57.

Clarke, M, Harley, M and Cannon, M (2006) The role of obstetric events in schizophrenia. *Schizophrenia Bulletin*, 32 (1), 3–8.

Cohen, P, Brown, J and Smailes, E (2001) Child abuse and neglect and the development of mental disorders in the general population. *Development and Psychopathology*, 13 (4), 981–99.

Cooper, D (1969) *The dialectics of liberation.* London: Penguin.

Cottingham, K (2009) How do psychotropic drugs work? *Journal of Proteome Research*, 8 (4), 1618.

Coyle, J and Duman, R (2003) Finding the intracellular signalling pathways affected by the mood disorder treatments. *Neuron*, 38, 157–60.

Craddock, N and Owen, M (2005) The beginning of the end for the Kraepelinian dichotomy. *British Journal of Psychiatry*, 186, 364–66.

Craddock, N, O'Donovan, M and Owen, M (2006) Genes for schizophrenia and bipolar disorder? Implications for psychiatric nosology. *Schizophrenia Bulletin*, 32 (1), 9–16.

Cutler, J and Marcus, L (2010) *Psychiatry.* New York: Oxford University Press.

Daines, B, Gask, L and Howe, A (2007) *Medical and psychiatric issues for counsellors.* London: Sage.

Davies, G, Welham, J, Chant, D, Torrey, E and McGrath, J (2003) A systematic review and meta-analysis of Northern Hemisphere season of birth studies in schizophrenia. *Schizophrenia Bulletin*, 2 (3), 587–93.

De Leon, J and Diaz, F (2005) A meta-analysis of worldwide studies demonstrates an association between schizophrenia and tobacco smoking behaviors. *Schizophrenia Research*, 76 (2–3), 135–57.

Den Boer, J (2006) Looking beyond the monoamine hypothesis. *European Neurological Disease*, 1–9.

Department of Health (1983) *Mental Health Act 1983.* London: DH Publications.

Department of Health (2001a) *Treatment choice in psychological therapies and counselling.* Crown Copyright. London: DH Publications.

Department of Health (2001b), *Choosing talking therapies.* Crown Copyright. London: DH Publications.

Department of Health (2005) Mental Capacity Act 2005. London: DH Publications.

Department of Health (2007) Mental Health Act 2007. London: DH Publications.

Department of Health (2008a) *Implementing access to psychological therapies implementation plan: national guidelines for regional delivery.* Crown Copyright. London: DH Publications.

Department of Health (2008b) *Implementing access to psychological therapies implementation plan: curriculum for low-intensity therapy workers.* Crown Copyright. London: DH Publications.

Digman, J (1990) Personality structure: emergence of the five-factor model. *Annual Review of Psychology*, 41, 417–40.

Double, D (2006) *Critical psychiatry: the limits of madness.* Basingstoke: Palgrave Macmillan.

Dryden, W (2005) *Rational emotive behaviour therapy in a nutshell (counselling in a nutshell).* London: Sage.

Dryden, W and Feltham, C (1992) *Psychotherapy and its discontents.* Buckingham: Open University Press.

DSM IV (1994a) *Diagnostic and Statistical Manual of Mental Disorders, 4th edition (DSM IV)* Washington DC: APA Publishing.

DSM IV (1994b) *Quick Reference to the Diagnostic Criteria from DSM IV.* Washington DC: APA Publishing.

Eghigian, G (2010) *From madness to mental health: psychiatric disorder and its treatment in western civilisation.* Piscataway NJ: Rutgers University Press.

Elbogen, E and Johnson, S (2009) The intricate link between violence and mental disorder: results from the National Epidemiologic Survey on Alcohol and Related Conditions. *Archives of General Psychiatry,* 66 (2), 152–61.

Ellenbroek, B and Cools, A (2000) *Atypical antipsychotics (milestones in drug therapy).* Berlin: Birkhauser Basel.

Elliott, C and Smith, L (2009) *Borderline personality disorder for dummies.* Hoboken NJ: Wiley.

Ellis, A (1962) *Reason and emotion in psychotherapy.* Secaucus NJ: Lyle Stuart.

Ellis, A (2001) *Overcoming destructive beliefs, feelings and behaviors: new directions for rational emotive behaviour therapy.* New York: Prometheus Books.

Ellison, G (1994) Stimulant-induced psychosis, the dopamine theory of schizophrenia, and the habenula. *Brain Research Reviews,* 19 (2), 223–39.

Engel, G (1980) The clinical application of the biopsychosocial model. *American Journal of Psychiatry,* 137, 535–44.

Eysenck, H (1952) The effects of psychotherapy: an evaluation. *Journal of Consulting Psychology,* 16, 319–24.

Eysenck, M (1992) *Anxiety: the cognitive aspect.* London: Psychology Press.

Falloon, I and Fadden, G (1993) *Integrated mental health care.* Cambridge: Cambridge University Press.

Farmer, E, Compton, S, Burns, B and Robertson, E (2002) Review of the evidence base for treatment of childhood psychopathology: externalising disorders. *Journal of Consulting and Clinical Psychology,* 70, 1267–302.

Fazel, S, Gulati, G, Linsell, L, Geddes, J and Grann, M (2009) Schizophrenia and violence: systematic review and meta-analysis. *Public Library of Science Medicine,* 6 (8).

Fehr, B, Ozcan, M and Suppes, T (2007) Low doses of clozapine may stabilise treatment-resistant bipolar patients. *European Archives of Psychiatry and Clinical Neuroscience,* 255 (1), 10–14.

Feighner, J, Robins, E, Guze, S, Woodruff, R, Winokur, G and Munoz, R (1972) Diagnostic criteria for use in psychiatric research. *Archives of General Psychiatry,* 26, 57–63.

Feltham, C and Horton, I (2006) *The Sage handbook of counselling and psychotherapy,* 2nd edition. London: Sage.

Finn, S (2007) *In our clients' shoes: theory and techniques of therapeutic assessment.* New York: Routledge.

Flashman, L and Green, M (2004) Review of cognition and brain structure in schizophrenia: profiles, longitudinal course, and effects of treatment. *Psychiatric Clinics of North America,* 27 (1), 1–18.

Fonagy, P, (2004) Psychotherapy meets neuroscience: a more focused future for psychotherapy research. *Psychiatric Bulletin,* 28, 357–59.

Forty, L, Smith, D, Jones, L, Jones, I, Caesar, S, Cooper, C, Fraser, C, Gordon-Smith, K, Hyde, S, Farmer, A, McGuffin, P and Craddock, N (2008) Clinical differences between bipolar and unipolar depression. *British Journal of Psychiatry,* 192, 388–89.

Fournier, J, DeRubeis, R, Hollon, S, Dimidjian, S, Amsterdam, J, Shelton, R and Fawcett, J (2010) Antidepressant drug effects and depression severity. *The Journal of the American Medical Association,* 303 (1), 47–53.

Fox, J (1990) Social class, mental illness, and social mobility: the social selection-drift hypothesis for serious mental illness. *Journal of Health and Social Behaviour,* 31 (4), 344–53.

Freidman, R (2006) Violence and mental illness: how strong is the link? *New England Journal of Medicine,* 355, 2064–66.

Freud, S (1926) *Inhibitions, symptoms and anxiety (The standard edition)* (Complete psychological works of Sigmund Freud – reissued 1990). New York: Norton.

Frith, U and Frith, C (2003) Development and neurophysiology of mentalising. *Philosophical Transactions of the Royal Society of London Biological Sciences*, 358, 459–73.

Gardner, D and Teehan, M (2010) *Antipsychotics and their side effects*. Cambridge: Cambridge University Press.

Garfield, S, and Eysenck, H (1992) The outcome problem in psychotherapy, in Dryden, W and Feltham, C (eds) *Psychotherapy and its discontents*. Buckingham: Open University Press.

Gask, L (2004) *A short introduction to psychiatry*. London: Sage.

Geddes, J, Price, J and McKnight, R (2011) *Psychiatry*, 4th edition. Oxford: Oxford University Press.

Geddes, J, Freemantle, N, Harrison, P and Bebbington, P (2000) Atypical antipsychotics in the treatment of schizophrenia: systematic overview and meta-regression analysis. *British Medical Journal*, 321 (1731).

Ghaemi, Nassir (2009) The rise and fall of the biopsychosocial model. *British Journal of Psychiatry*, 195, 3–4.

Gilbert, P (2002) Understanding the biopsychosocial approach: conceptualisation. *Clinical Psychology*, 14, 13–17.

Gilbert, P (2004) Depression: a biopsychosocial approach, in Power, M, (ed.) *Mood disorders: a handbook of science and practice*. Chichester: Wiley.

Gilbert, P (2007) *Psychotherapy and counselling for depression*, 3rd edition. London: Sage.

Gilbert, P (2009) *Overcoming depression: a guide to recovery with a self-help programme*. London: Robinson.

Goldberg, D and Huxley, P (1992) *Common mental disorders*. London: Routledge.

Goldberg, D and Goodyer, I (2008) *The origins and course of common mental disorders*. London: Routledge.

Goldner, E, Hsu, L, Waraich, P and Somers, J (2002) Prevalence and incidence studies of schizophrenic disorders: a systematic review of the literature. *Canadian Journal of Psychiatry*, 47 (9), 833–43.

Goldstein, W (1978) Toward an integrated theory of schizophrenia. *Schizophrenia Bulletin*, 4 (3), 426–35.

Golightly, M (2008) *Social work and mental health,* 3rd edition. Exeter: Learning Matters.

Goodwin, F and Jamieson, K (2007) *Manic depressive illness: bipolar disorders and recurrent depression*, 2nd edition. Oxford: Oxford University Press.

Gould, N (2009) *Mental health social work in context*. Exeter: Learning Matters.

Grant, A, Townend, M, Mills, J and Cockx, A (2008) *Assessment and case formulation in cognitive behavioural therapy*. London: Sage.

Grossman, L, Harrow, M, Rosen, C and Faull, B (2006) Sex differences in outcome and recovery for schizophrenia and other psychotic and nonpsychotic disorders. *Psychiatric Services*, 57, 844–50.

Guthrie, E (2008) Medically unexplained symptoms in primary care. *Advances in Psychiatric Treatment*, 14, 432–40.

Hales, E, Yudofsky, S and Gabbard, G (2010) *Essentials of Psychiatry,* 3rd edition. London: Jessica Kingsley.

Hardy, L, and Fazey, J (1987) *The inverted-U hypothesis: catastrophe for sport psychology*. British Association of Sports Sciences Monograph No. 1. Leeds: The National Coaching Foundation.

Harrison, G, Gunnell, D, Glazebrook, C, Page, K and Kwiecinski, R (2001) Association between schizophrenia and social inequality at birth. *British Journal of Psychiatry*, 179 (4), 346–50.

Haslam, N, Ban, L and Kaufmann, L (2007) Lay conceptions of mental disorder: The folk psychiatry model. *Australian Psychologist*, 42, 2, 129–37.

Haycock, D (2009) The everything health guide to schizophrenia. Avon MA: Adams Media.

Hayman, A (1965) Psychoanalyst subpoenaed. *The Lancet*, 321, 785–86.

Healy, D (1998) *The antidepressant era*. Cambridge MA: Harvard University Press.

Healy, D (2002) *The creation of psychopharmacology*. Cambridge MA: Harvard University Press.

Healy, D (2004) *The creation of psychopharmacology*. Boston MA: Harvard University Press.

Healy, D (2009) *Psychiatric Drugs Explained*, 5th edition. London: Churchill Livingstone Elsevier.

Heinrichs, R (2003) Historical origins of schizophrenia: two early madmen and their illness. *Journal of the History of Behavioral Sciences*, 39 (4), 349–63.

Hlastala, S, Frank, E, Kowalski, J, Sherrill, J, Tu, X, Anderson, B and Kupfer, D (2000) Stressful life events, bipolar disorder, and the 'kindling model'. *Journal of Abnormal Psychology*, 10, 9 (4), 777–86.

Holmes, J (2002) *Depression (ideas in psychoanalysis)*. London: Icon Books.

Hood, R, Hill, P and Williamson P (2005) *The psychology of religious fundamentalism*. New York: Guilford Press.

Hunter, R and McAlpine, I. (1963), *Three hundred years of psychiatry*, Hartsdale NY: Carlisle Publishing.

Hurst, C E (2007) *Social inequality: forms, causes, and consequences*. Boston MA: Pearson Education.

Huxley, N, Parikh, S and Baldessarini, R (2000) Effectiveness of psychosocial treatments in bipolar disorder: state of the evidence. *Harvard Review of Psychiatry*, 8 (3), 126–40.

Huxley, P and Thornicroft, G (2003) Social inclusion, social quality and mental illness. *The British Journal of Psychiatry*, 182, 289–90.

ICD 10 (2000) *The WHO guide to mental health in primary care*. London: RSM Press.

Jacobs, M (2003) *Sigmund Freud*, 2nd edition. London: Sage.

Jacobs, M (2005) *The presenting past*, 3rd edition. Buckingham: Open University Press.

Jamison, K (1996) *Touched with fire: manic-depressive illness and the artistic temperament*. London: Simon & Schuster.

Jaynes, J (1976) *The origin of consciousness in the breakdown of the bicameral mind*. Boston MA: Houghton Mifflin.

Jenkins, P (ed.) (2002) *Legal issues in counselling and psychotherapy*. London: Sage.

Jenkins, P (2007) *Counselling, psychotherapy and the law*. London: Sage.

Jones, E (1999) The phenomenology of abnormal belief: a philosophical and psychiatric inquiry. *Philosophy, Psychiatry and Psychology*, 6 (1), 1–16.

Jones, R (2009) *Mental Health Act manual*. Andover: Sweet and Maxwell.

Jordison, T (2005) *The joy of sects: an A–Z of cults, cranks and religious eccentrics*. London: Robson Books.

Judd, L, Akiskal, H, Schettler, P J, Endicott, J, Leon, A C, Solomon, D A, Coryell, W, Maser, J D and Keller, M B (2005) Psychosocial disability in the course of Bipolar I and II disorders: a prospective, comparative, longitudinal study. *Archives of General Psychiatry*, 62 (12), 1322–30.

Kahn, M (2002) *Basic Freud*. New York: Basic Books.

Kelly, G (1955) *The psychology of personal constructs*, Vols 1 and 2. New York: Norton.

Keltner, N (2005) *Psychotropic drugs*. St Louis MO: Mosby (Elsevier).

Kempton, M, Geddes, J, Ettinger, U, Williams, S and Grasby, P (2008) Meta-analysis, database, and meta-regression of 98 structural imaging studies in bipolar disorder. *Archives of General Psychiatry*, 65, 1017–32.

Kendal, R and Jablensky, M (2003) Distinguishing between the validity and the utility of psychiatric diagnoses. *American Journal of Psychiatry*, 160, 4–12.

Khan, A, Redding, N and Brown, W (2007) The persistence of the placebo response in antidepressant clinical trials. *Journal of Psychiatric Research*, 42 (10), 791–96.

Khan, A, Leventhal, R, Khan, S, and Brown, W (2002) Severity of depression and response to antidepressants and placebo: an analysis of the Food and Drug Administration database. *Journal of Clinical Psychopharmacology*, 22, 40–45.

Kirsch, I (2009) *The emperor's new drugs: exploding the anti-depressant myth*. London: The Bodley Head.

Kleinplatz, P and Moser, C (2007) Is SM pathological?, in Barker, L (ed.) *Safe, sane and consensual: contemporary perspectives on sadomasochism*. Basingstoke: Palgrave Macmillan.

Kooyman, I, Harvey, S and Walsh E (2007) Outcomes of public concern in schizophrenia. *British Journal of Psychiatry Supplement*, 29–36.

Lake, J (2006) *Textbook of integrative mental health*. New York: Thieme Publications.

Lalich, J (2004) *Bounded choice: true believers and charismatic cults*. Berkeley CA: University of California Press.

Lambert, M (2004) *Bergin and Garfield's handbook of psychotherapy and behaviour change*, 5th edition. New York: Wiley.

LaPlanche, J and Pontalis, J (1998) *The language of psychoanalysis*. London: Karnac.

Lazarus, R (1966) *Psychological stress and the coping process*. New York: McGraw-Hill.

Leader, D (2009) *The new black*. London: Penguin.

Leahy, R (2003) *Cognitive therapy techniques: a practitioner's guide*. New York: Guilford Press.

Lee, S (2001) From diversity to unity: the classification of mental disorders in 21st-century China. *Psychiatric Clinics North America*. 24 (3), 421–31.

Leigh, H (2010) *Culture and mental illness*. New York: Springer.

Levine, J and Levine, I (2008) *Schizophrenia for dummies*. Indianapolis IN: Wiley.

Linehan, M and Dimeff, L (2001) Dialectical behavioural therapy in a nutshell. *The California Psychologist*, 34, 10–13.

Livesley, W (2003) *Practical management of personality disorders*. New York: Guilford Press.

Lorenz, S, Wickrama, K, Conger, R and Elder, G (2006) The short-term and decade-long effects of divorce on women's mid-life health. *Journal of Health and Social Behaviour*, 47, 111–25.

Luborsky, L (2001) The only clinical *and* quantitative study since Freud of the preconditions for recurrent symptoms during psychotherapy and psychoanalysis. *International Journal of Psychoanalysis*, 82, 1133–54.

Malmberg, L, Fenton, M and Rathbone, J (2001) Individual psychodynamic psychotherapy and psychoanalysis for schizophrenia and severe mental illness. Cochrane Database of Systematic Reviews, Issue 3. Art. No CD001360. DOI: 10. 1002/14651858. CD001360.

Marquis, A (2007) *The integral intake: a guide to comprehensive idiographic assessment in integral psychotherapy*. New York: Routledge.

Martens, R, Burton, D, Vealey, R, Bump, L and Smith, D (1990) The development of the competitive state anxiety inventory-2 (CSAI-2), in Martens, R, Vealey, S and Burton, D (eds) *Competitive anxiety in sport*. Champaign IL: Human Kinetics.

Martin, S, Travis, M and Murray, R (2002) *An atlas of schizophrenia*. London: Parthenon.

Martin-Merino, E, Ruigomez, A, Wallander, M, Johansson, S and Garcia-Rodriguez, A (2010) Prevalence, incidence, morbidity and treatment patterns in a cohort of patients diagnosed with anxiety in UK primary care. *Family Practice*, 2 (1), 9–16.

Masson, J (1992) *Against therapy*. London: HarperCollins.

McCrae, R, and Costa, P (1997) Personality trait structure as a human universal. *American Psychologist*, 52, 509–16.

McLeod, J (2009a) *An introduction to counselling,* 4th edition. Maidenhead: Open University Press.

McLeod, J (2009b) Counselling: a radical vision for the future. *Therapy Today,* 20 (6), July.

McManus, S, Meltzer, H, Brughas, T, Bebbington, P and Jenkins, R (2007) *Adult psychiatric morbidity in England.* London: NHS Information Centre.

McNally, R (1999) Theoretical approaches to the fear of anxiety, in Taylor, S (ed.) *Anxiety sensitivity: theory, research and treatment.* Hillsdale NJ: Lawrence Erlbaum.

Meisenzahl, E, Schmitt, G, Scheuerecker, J and Moller, H (2007) The role of dopamine for the pathophysiology of schizophrenia. *International Review of Psychiatry*, 1, 9 (4), 337–45.

Metzl, J (2003) *Prescribing gender in the era of wonder drugs.* Durham NC: Duke University Press.

Meyer, A (1952) *The collected papers of Adolf Meyer.* Baltimore MD: Johns Hopkins University Press.

Meyers, S (2000) Use of neurotransmitter precursors for treatment of depression. *Alternative Medicine Review*, 5 (1), 64–71.

Miller, P and Lisak, D (1999) Associations between childhood abuse and personality disorder symptoms in college males. *Journal of Interpersonal Violence*, 14 (6), 642–56.

Milner, J and O'Byrne, P (2003) *Assessment in counselling: theory, practice and decision-making.* Basingstoke: Palgrave Macmillan.

Minkel, J (2009) Putting madness in its place. *Scientific American*, 301, 16–19.

Moncrieff, J (2007) *The myth of the chemical sure: a critique of psychoactive drug treatments.* Basingstoke: Palgrave Macmillan.

Moncrieff, J (2009) *A straight talking introduction to psychiatric drugs.* Ross-on-Wye: PCCS Books.

Moncrieff, J, Wessely, S and Hardy, R (2004) Active placebos versus antidepressants for depression. *Cochrane Systematic Review*, (1): CD003012.

Mooney, C (2009) *Theories of attachment: an introduction to Bowlby, Ainsworth, Gerber, Brazelton, Kennell and Klause.* St Paul MN: Redleaf Press.

Moore, T, Zammit, S, Lingford-Hughes, A, Barnes, T, Jones, P, Burke, M and Lewis, G (2007) Cannabis use and risk of psychotic or affective mental health outcomes: a systematic review. *Lancet*, 370 (9584), 319–28.

Munk-Jorgensen, P, Allgulander, C, Dahl, A, Foldager, L, Holm, M, Rasmussen, I, Virta, A, Huuhtanen, M and Wittchen, H (2006) Prevalence of generalized anxiety disorder in general practice in Denmark, Finland, Norway and Sweden. *Psychiatric Services*, 57, 1738–44.

Nasser, M (1995) The rise and fall of anti-psychiatry. *Psychiatric Bulletin*, 19, 743–46.

National Depressive and Manic Depressive Association (2001) *Constituency survey: living with bipolar disorder; how far have we really come?* NIH Publication 08-3679. Washington DC: Department of Health and Human Services, National Institutes of Health.

National Health Service Information Centre (2007) *Adult psychiatric morbidity in England, 2007: results of a household survey.* Leicester: National Centre for Social Research and the Department of Health Sciences, University of Leicester. UK Data Archive Study Number 6379 – Adult Psychiatric Morbidity Survey.

National Institute of Mental Health (2009) *Bipolar disorder.* Washington DC: US Department of Health and Human Services.

NICE (National Institute for Health and Clinical Excellence) (2004) *Guideline 23, Depression: management of depression in primary and secondary care.* Leicester: British Psychological Society.

NICE (2006) *Guideline 38, Bipolar disorder*. Leicester: British Psychological Society.

NICE (2007) *Guideline 22, Anxiety*. Leicester: British Psychological Society.

NICE (2009) *Guideline 82, Schizophrenia: core interventions in the treatment and management of schizophrenia in adults in primary and secondary care*. Leicester: British Psychological Society.

NICE (2010a) *Guideline 78, Borderline personality disorder*. Leicester: British Psychological Society.

NICE (2010b) *Guideline 77, Anti-social personality disorder*. Leicester: British Psychological Society.

Nurnberger J and Foroud T (2000) Genetic effects of bipolar affective disorder. *Current Psychiatry Reports*, 2 (2), 145–57.

Nutt, D, King, L and Phillips, L (2010), Drug harms in the UK: a multicriteria decision analysis, *The Lancet*, 376 (9752), 1558–65.

O'Driscoll, P (2010) *What are counselling and psychotherapy?* BACP Information Sheet C2. Leicester: BACP Publications.

Olds, J, and Milner, P (1954) Positive reinforcement produced by electrical stimulation of septal area and other regions of rat brain. *Journal of Comparative and Physiological Psychology*, 47, 419–27.

Owen, S and Saunders, A (2008) *Bipolar disorder: the ultimate guide*. Oxford: Oneworld Publications.

Oyebode, F (2008) *Sims' symptoms in the mind: an introduction to descriptive psychopathology*. New York: Saunders (Elsevier).

Palmer, B, Pankratz, V and Bostwisck, J (2005) The lifetime risk of suicide in schizophrenia: a reexamination. *Archives of General Psychiatry*, 62 (3), 247–53.

Palmer, S (2002) Dialectical behaviour therapy for borderline personality disorder. *Advances, Psychiatric Treatment*, 8, 10–16.

Parker, G (2000) Classifying depression: should paradigms lost be regained? *American Journal of Psychiatry*, 157, 1195–203.

Parsons, R (2000) *The ethics of professional practice*. Boston MA: Allyn and Bacon.

Pigott, H, Leventhal, A, Alter, G and Bora, J (2010) Efficacy as effectiveness of antidepressants: current status of research. *Psychotherapy and Psychosomatics*, 79, 267–79.

Pilgrim, D (2002) The biopsychosocial model in Anglo-American psychiatry: past, present and future? *Journal of Mental Health*, 11, 6, 585–94.

Pilgrim, D (2009) *Key Concepts in mental health*. London: Sage.

Plomin, R and McGuffin, P (2003) Psychopathology in the postgenomic era. *Annual Review of Psychology*, 54, 205–28.

Pontius J (2002) Understanding the 'worried well'. *Journal of Family Practice*, January.

Porter, R (2003) *Madness: a brief history*. Oxford: Oxford University Press.

Porter, R and Berrios, G (1995) *A history of clinical psychiatry: the origin and history of psychiatric disorders*. London: Athlone Press.

Posner, J, Russell, J, Gerber, A, Gorman, D, Colibazzi, T, Yu, S, Wang, Z, Kangarlu, A, Zhu, H and Peterson, B (2009) The neurophysiological bases of emotion: an fMRI study of the affective circumplex using emotion-denoting words. *Journal of Human Brain Mapping* 30 (3), 883–95.

Potash, J, Toolan, J, Steele, J, Miller, E B, Pearl, J, Zandi, P P, Schulze, T G, Kassem, L, Simpson, S G, and Lopez, V (2007) The bipolar disorder phenome database: a resource for genetic studies. *American Journal of Psychiatry*, 164 (8), 1229–37.

Power, M, (ed.) (2004) *Mood disorders: a handbook of science and practice*. Chichester: Wiley.

Rapp, B (2001) *The handbook of cognitive neuropsychology*. Hove: Psychology Press.

RCPsych (Royal College of Psychiatrists) (2008a) *Depression*. London: RCPsych Public Education Board.

RCPsych (2008b) *Electroconvulsive therapy (ECT)*. London: RCPsych Public Education Board.

RCPsych (2009a) *Mental health and social inclusion: making psychiatry and mental health services fit for the 21st century*. London: Central Policy Coordination Committee, RCPsych Publications.

RCPsych (2009b) *Personality disorders: key facts*. London: RCPsych Public Education Editorial Board.

RCPsych (2010a) *Antidepressants*. London: RCPsych Public Education Editorial Board.

RCPsych (2010b) *Anxiety and phobias*. London: RCPsych Public Education Editorial Board.

RCPsych (2010c) *Schizophrenia*. London: RCPsych Public Education Editorial Board.

RCPsych (2010d), *Antidepressants*, London, RCPsych Public Education Editorial Board.

RCPsych (2010e) *Bipolar disorder (manic depression)*. London: RCPsych Public Education Editorial Board.

Read, J and Saunders, P (2010) A straight talking guide to the causes of mental health problems. Ross-on-Wye: PCCS Books.

Read, R, Mosher, L and Rentall, R (2004) *Models of madness: psychological, sociological and biological approaches to schizophrenia*. Hove: Brunner-Routledge.

Reiland, R (2004) *Get me out of here: my recovery from borderline personality disorder*. Center City MN: Hazelden Information and Educational Services.

Reiss, R and McNally, R (1985) Anxiety sensitivity, in Taylor, S (ed.) (1999) *Anxiety sensitivity: theory, research, and treatment of the fear of anxiety* (Personality and clinical psychology). Hillsdale, NJ: Lawrence Erlbaum.

Rethink (2006) *Schizophrenia fact sheet*. London: Schizophrenia Fellowship.

Richard, F, Quill, T and McDaniel, S (2009) *The biopsychosocial approach: past, present and future*. New York: Boydell and Brewer.

Richards, M, Hardy, R and Wadsworth, M (1997) The effects of divorce and separation on mental health in a national UK birth cohort. *Psychological Medicine*, 27, 1121–28.

Rinomhota, A and Marshal, P (2000) *Biological aspects of mental health nursing*. London: Churchill Livingstone.

Romme, M and Morris, M (2007) The harmful concept of schizophrenia. *Mental Health Nursing*, 7–11 March.

Rosenhan, D (1973) On being sane in insane places. *Science*, 179 (70), 250–58.

Roth, A and Fonagy, P (2005) *What works for whom? A critical review of psychotherapy research*, 2nd edition. New York: Guilford.

Rottenberg, J and Gotlib, I (2004) Socio-emotional functioning in depression, in Power, M (ed.) *Mood disorders: a handbook of science and practice*. Chichester: Wiley.

Roy-Byrne, P, Craske, M, Sullivan, G, Rose, R, Edlund, M, Lang, A, Bystritsky, A, Chavira, D, Golinelli, D, Campbell-Sills, L and Sherbourne, C (2010) Delivery of evidence-based treatment for multiple anxiety disorders in primary care: a randomised controlled trial. *Journal of American Medical Association*, 303 (19), 1921–28.

Rueve, M and Welton, R (2008) Violence and mental illness. *Psychiatry*, 5 (5), 35–48.

Ryle, A (1990) *Cognitive-analytic therapy: active participation in change: a new integration of brief psychotherapy*. Chichester: Wiley.

Sachs, G and Thase, M (2000) Bipolar disorder therapeutics: maintenance treatment. *Biological Psychiatry*, 48 (6), 573–81.

Saltz, B, Woerner, M, Robinson, D and Kane, J (2000) Side effects of antipsychotic drugs. *Postgraduate Medicine*, 107 (2), 2000.

Schanda, H (2006) Investigating the association between psychosis and violence. *Fortschritte der Neurologie-Psychiatrie*, 74 (2), 85–100.

Schenkel, L, Spaulding, W, Dilillo, D and Silverstein, S (2005) Histories of childhood maltreatment in schizophrenia: relationships with premorbid functioning, symptomatology, and cognitive defects. *Schizophrenia Research*, 76 (2–3), 273–86.

Schneider, K (1959), *Clinical psychopathology*, 5th edition. New York: Grune and Stratton.

Scioli, A and Biller, H (2009) *Hope in the age of anxiety*. Oxford: Oxford University Press.

Seeman, P and Kapur, S (2000) Schizophrenia: more dopamine, more D2 receptors. *Proceedings of the National Academy of Science of the United States of America*, 5, 97 (14), 7673–75.

Seeman, P, Weinshenker, D, Quirion, R et al. (2005) Dopamine supersensitivity correlates with D2 states implying many paths to psychosis. *Proceedings of the National Academy of Sciences*, 102 (9), 3513–18.

Seligman, M, Walker, E and Rosenhan, D (2001), *Abnormal psychology*, 4th edition. New York: Norton.

Selten, J, Cantor-Graae, E and Kahn, R (2007) Migration and schizophrenia. *Current Opinion in Psychiatry*, 20 (2), 111–15.

Shapiro, H (2004) *Recreational drugs – a directory*. London: Collins and Brown.

Shea, M, Stout, R, Gunderson, J, Morey, L C, Grilo, C M, McGlashan, T, Skodol, A E, Dolan-Sewell, R, Dyck, I, Zanarini, M C and Keller, M B (2002) Short term diagnostic stability of schizotypal, borderline, avoidant and obsessive-compulsive personality disorders. *American Journal of Psychiatry*, 159, 2036–41.

Shepherd, B (2000) *A war of nerves: soldiers and psychiatrists 1914–1994*. London: Cape.

Siegal, R (2005) Intoxication: the universal drive for mind-altering substances. Rochester VT: Park Street Press.

Silagy, C, Jones, R, Britten, N, Gass, D, Mant, D, Grol, R and Culpepper, L (2005) *The Oxford textbook of primary medical care*. Oxford: Oxford University Press.

Sim, K, Chua, T, Mahendran, R and Chong, S (2006) Psychiatric comorbidity in first episode schizophrenia: a 2 year longitudinal outcome study. *Journal of Psychiatric Research*, 40 (2), 653–63.

Sims, A (2000) *Symptoms in the mind*. New York: Saunders.

Sims, A and Snaith, P (1998) *Anxiety in clinical practice*. Chichester: Wiley.

Skinner, B (1953) *Science and human behaviour*. New York: Macmillan.

Smail, S (2005) *Power, interest and psychology: elements of a social materialist understanding of distress*. Ross-on-Wye: PCCS Books.

Smith, R (2002) Minor acute illness: a preliminary research report on the 'worried well'. *Journal of Family Practice*, January.

Sommers-Flanagan, J and Sommers-Flanagan, R (2004) *Counselling and psychotherapy theories in context and practice*. Hoboken NJ: Wiley.

Spitzer, R, Endicott, J and Robins, E (1975) *Research diagnostic criteria for a selected group of functional disorders*. New York: New York Biometrics Research Division, New York State Institute, available at www.garfield.library.upenn.edu/classics 1989/A1989U309700001.pdf.

Stein, G and Wilkinson, G (2007) *Seminars in general adult psychiatry*, College Seminars Series. London: RCPsych Publications.

Stone, J, Morrison, P and Pilowsky, L (2006) Review: Glutamate and dopamine dysregulation in schizophrenia – a synthesis and selective review. *Journal of Psychopharmacology*, 21 (4), 440.

Swartz, M, Swanson, J, Hiday, V, Borum, R, Wagner, H and Burns, J (2006) Substance use in persons with schizophrenia: baseline prevalence and correlates from the NIMH CATIE study. *Journal of Nervous Mental* Disease, 194 (3), 164–72.

Szasz, T (1984) *The myth of mental illness.* London: Harper Perennial.

Szasz, T (1991) Diagnoses are not diseases. *The Lancet,* 338, 1574–76.

Szasz, T (2010) *The myth of mental illness: revised edition.* London: HarperCollins.

Taylor, P (2008) Psychosis and violence: stories, fears and reality, *Canadian Journal of Psychiatry,* 53 (10), 647–59.

Taylor, S (1999) Anxiety sensitivity: theory, research, and treatment of the fear of anxiety (personality and clinical psychology). Hillsdale NJ: Lawrence Erlbaum.

Tew, J (2005) *Social perspectives in mental health: developing social models to understand and work with mental distress.* London: Jessica Kingsley.

Tone, A (2008) *The age of anxiety: a history of America's turbulent affair with tranquillisers.* New York: Basic Books.

Torrey, E (2006) *Surviving schizophrenia: a manual for patients, families and providers,* 5th edition. New York: Harper.

Tozer, T and Rowland, M (2006) Introduction to pharmacokinetics and pharmacodynamics: the quantitative basic of drug therapy. Philadelphia PA: Lippincott Williams and Wilkins.

Tsuang, M, Stone, W and Faraone, S (2000) Toward reforming the diagnosis of schizophrenia. *American Journal of Psychiatry,* 157 (7), 1041–50.

Turner, E, Matthews, A, Linardatos, E, Tell, R and Rosenthal, R (2008) Selective publication of antidepressant trials and its influence on apparent efficacy. *New England Journal of Medicine,* 358 (3).

Twenge, J (2000) The age of anxiety? Birth cohort change in anxiety and neuroticism, 1952–1993. *Journal of Personality and Social Psychology,* 79 (6).

UK ECT Review Group (2003) Efficacy and safety of electroconvulsive therapy in depressive disorders: a systematic review and meta-analysis. *The Lancet,* 361 (9360), 799–808.

US Department of Health and Human Services (2009) *Child Maltreatment 2008.* Online at www.acf.hhs.gov/programs/cb/pubs/cm08/cm08.pdf.

US National Survey on Drug Use and Health (2005) *Depression among adults,* Washington DC: US Dept of Health. Online at www.oas.samhsa.gov.

Vaida, N, Mahableshwarkar, A, and Shaheel, S (2003) Continuation and maintenance ECT in treatment-resistant bipolar disorder. *Journal of ECT,* 19 (1), 10–16.

Vaknin, S (2009) *Malignant Self Love: Narcissism Revisited.* Czech Republic: Narcissus Publications.

Van Os, J (2004) Does the urban environment cause psychosis? *British Journal of Psychiatry,* 184 (4), 287–88.

Van Rossum, J (1967) The significance of dopamine-receptor blockade for the action of neuroleptic drugs. Neuropsychopharmacology, Proceedings Fifth Collegium Internationale Neuropsychopharmacologicum, Amsterdam, Excerpta Medica Foundation, 321–29.

Van Schaik, D, van Marwijk, H, van der Windt, D, Beekman, A, de Haan, M and van Dyck, R (2002) Effectiveness of psychotherapy for depressive disorder in primary care. *Journal of Dutch Psychiatry,* 44 (9), 609–19.

Veale, D (2008) Psychotherapy in dissent. *Therapy Today,* February.

Viner, R (1999) Putting stress in life: Hans Selye and the making of stress theory. *Social Sciences,* 239, 3, 391–410.

Volkow, N, Fowler, J, Wang, G and Swanson, J (2004) Dopamine in drug abuse and addiction: results from imaging studies and treatment implications. *Molecular Psychiatry,* 9, 557–69.

Walsh, E, Buchanan, A and Fahy, T (2002) Violence and schizophrenia: examining the evidence. *British Journal of Psychiatry*, 180, 490–95.

Wampold, B (2001) *The great psychotherapy debate: models, methods and findings.* London: Routledge.

Warme, G (2006) *Daggers in the mind: the myth of mental disease.* Vancouver: House of Anansi Press.

Webb, T (2010) Medically unexplained symptoms. *Therapy Today*, 21 (3), 10–14.

Westbrook, D, Kennerly, H and Kirk, J (2007) *An introduction to cognitive behaviour therapy.* London: Sage.

Wills, F (2008) *Skills in cognitive behaviour counselling and psychotherapy.* London: Sage.

Willson R and Branch, R (2006) *Cognitive behavioural therapy for dummies.* Chichester: Wiley.

Withers, M (2007) Assessment, in Hemming, A and Field, R (eds) *Counselling and psychotherapy in contemporary private practice.* London: Routledge.

Wolpert, L (1999) *A malignant sadness: the anatomy of depression.* London: Simon & Schuster.

Woolfe, R, Strawbridge, S, Douglas, B and Dryden, W (eds) (2010) *Handbook of counselling psychology*, 3rd edition. London: Sage.

Yerkes, R and Dodson, J (1908) The relation of strength of stimulus to rapidity of habit-formation. *Journal of Comparative Neurology and Psychology*, 18, 459–82. Online at http://psychclassics.yorku.ca/Yerkes/Law.

Zahradnik, M, Stewart, S, Marshall, G, Schell, T and Jaycox, L (2009) Anxiety sensitivity and aspects of alexithymia are independently and uniquely associated with posttraumatic distress, *Journal of Trauma Stress*, 22, 2, 131–38.

Index